Esther Higgins

SIERRA SOUTH

100 Back-country trips in California's Sierra

by Thomas Winnett and Karl Schwenke

Wilderness Press
BERKELEY

First printing May 1968
Second printing January 1969
Third printing March 1970
Fourth printing January 1971
Fifth printing June 1971
Sixth printing March 1973
Seventh printing April 1974
SECOND EDITION March 1975

Front-cover photo by Louise Weamer
Back-cover photo by Howard Weamer
Map by Jeff Schaffer

Library of Congress card number 74-27688
ISBN: 911824-41-3
Manufactured in the United States

Published by Wilderness Press
2440 Bancroft Way, Berkeley CA 94704

FOREWORD

In The Beginning

there is nothing quite so humbling as a long set of switchbacks or the start of a new book. One's conditioning and capacities make themselves known as the going becomes rocky, the way convoluted, and the grade steep. The End, consequently, takes on the aspect of a goal, and all too often we arrive only to find that we've forgotten what it was we saw and felt enroute. And so, at this inception, we pledge ourselves to enjoy the doing—not

The End.

K.S.
T.W.

FOREWARD TO THE SECOND EDITION

Although the mountains change hardly at all in a man's lifetime, trails change every year. A guidebook, to be useful, must be up to date. Therefore, the job of revising *Sierra South* began the day the first edition went to the printers. And so it will be with this new edition. Meanwhile, this new edition not only contains the latest information I have been able to gather, but it also contains 21 new trips.

Something else has changed since *Sierra South* first came out: there is much more awareness of the problem of preserving the wilderness. That is why this new edition contains a chapter on The Care and Enjoyment of the Mountains. I invite you to enjoy them, and I urge you to care for them.

T. W.

ACKNOWLEDGEMENTS

A guidebook like this requires a lot of input, and I have been fortunate enough to meet many gracious and generous Sierra lovers who have helped me bring the old trail descriptions up to date and to present the descriptions of the new trips: Jeff Schaffer, John W. Robinson, Ed Roberts, J. C. Jenkins, Ron Felzer, Bob and Margaret Pierce, Don Denison, Karl Schwenke, David Poast, Thomas Dum, Jim Watters, David Pesonen, E. P. Pister, Cecelia Hurwich, Norman Jensen, Sam Stephens, Michael Stephens, Grant Barnes, Galen Rowell, Andy Smatko, Gordon Peterson, Edwin Rockwell, Genny Schumacher Smith, John Allen Ryan, Gordon Boyd, Stephen Stocking and Jason Winnett.

The chapter on The Care and Enjoyment of the Mountains was adapted from an article by Michael Loughman.

T.W.

Other books by Thomas Winnett

Backpacking for Fun
Sierra North (with Karl Schwenke)
The Tahoe-Yosemite Trail (with Don Denison)
The Comstock Guide to California Backpacking
The Comstock Guide to Pacific Northwest Backpacking
Backpacking in the Wilderness Rockies
The Pacific Crest Trail, Vol. 1
Tuolumne Meadows
Matterhorn Peak
Mono Craters
Mt. Whitney
Mt. Abbot

Table of Contents

Introduction

Whether on foot or on horseback, the backcountry traveler knows the exhilaration of the out-of-doors in a rich, personal way that is beyond the ken of the ordinary car camper. Far from the crowds that infest the roadside campgrounds, he comes to realize the value of solitude, and he learns the calmness of spirit that derives from a fundamental relationship with the mountains. He comes to know the simple satisfactions of deep breaths, hardened muscles and a sound sleep under brilliant stars. But, above all, in renewing his bond with the wilderness he rekindles that cherished spark of childlike innocence that is so easily extinguished by the pressures of city life. It is these pressures that account for the dramatic increase in the demand for wilderness experiences. The Sierra, offering some of the finest and most spectacular wilderness in the United States, has drawn more than its share of the demand, and its backcountry sees thousands of new faces each year.

Together with the companion volume *Sierra North,* this book is a discriminating effort to meet the demands of both the newcomer and the "old hand." Taking up where *Sierra North* left off, this book describes backcountry trails between Mono Creek and the southern end of Sequoia National Park. Here are trips ranging in length from overnighters to two-week expeditions; trips that will sate the appetite of the most avid angler, naturalist or camera bug.

These trips were chosen after considerable screening that entailed interviews with rangers, packers and mountaineers, and substantial research. Finally, they were walked—almost all by one of the authors, the rest under their direction in the field. After this screening, the final selections were made on the basis of (1) scenic attraction, (2) wilderness character (remoteness, primitive condition) and (3) recreational potential (fishing, swimming, etc.). After walking the trip, the author decided how long it should take if done at a leisurely pace, how long at a moderate pace, and how long at a strenuous pace. In deciding, he considered not only distance but also elevation change, heat, exposure, terrain, availability of water, appropriate campsites and finally, his subjective feeling about the trip. For each trip, then, we suggest how many days you should take to do it at the pace ("Leisurely," "Moderate" or "Strenuous") you prefer. Some trips simply don't lend them-

Left: Hitchcock Lakes from the Mt. Whitney Trail *Thomas Winnett*

selves to a leisurely pace—maybe not even a moderate pace—and some are never strenuous unless you do the whole thing in one day. Such trips have a blank in the number-of-days spot for the corresponding pace at the beginning of the trip.

The last decision about pace was the decision of which pace to use in describing the trip, day by day. Since this book is written for the average backpacker, we chose to describe most trips on either a leisurely or moderate basis, depending on where the best overnight camping places were along the route. The exceptions were the trips that involve an initial climb of more than 3000 feet—as much as 6000 feet—to get from the east side over the Sierra crest or from Mineral King into Sequoia Park. We deemed all such trips strenuous.

The author's subjective consideration also carries over to the evaluation of campsites. Campsites are labeled "poor," "fair," "good" or "excellent." The criteria for assigning these labels were amount of use, immediate surroundings, general scenery, presence of vandalization, availability of water, kind of ground cover and recreational potential—angling, side trips, swimming, etc.

Angling, for many, is a prime consideration when planning a trip. The recommendations in this book are the result of (1) research into the California DF&G's fresh-water fish-stocking program, (2) study of DF&G-sponsored surveys ("Anglers' Guides"), (3) on-the-trail sampling and feed evaluations and (4) interviews with commercial packers. When a conflict arose between paper research and trail sampling, the latter was given precedence. Like the campsites, fishing was labeled "poor," "fair," "good" or "excellent." It should be noted that these labels refer to the quantity of fish in the stream or lake, not the fishes' inclination to take the hook. Experienced anglers know that the size of their catch relates not only to quantity, type and general size of the fishery, which are given, but also to water temperature, feed, angling skill, and that indefinable something known as "fisherman's luck." Generally speaking, the old "early and late" adage holds: fishing is better early and late in the day, and early and late in the season.

Deciding when in the year is the best time for a particular trip is a difficult task because of altitude and latitude variations. Low early-season temperatures and mountain shadows often keep some of the higher passes closed until well into August. Early snows have been known to whiten alpine country in late July and August. Some of the trips described here are low-country ones, designed specifically for the itchy hiker who, stiff from a winter's inactivity, is searching for a "warm-up" excursion. These trips are labeled "early season," a period that extends roughly from late

May to early July. "Midseason" is here considered to be from early July to early September, and "late season" from then to early October.

Most of the trails described here are well maintained (the exceptions are noted), and are properly signed. If the trail becomes indistinct, look for blazes (peeled bark at eye level on the trees) or "ducks" (two or more rocks piled one atop the other). Two other significant trail conditions have also been described in the text: (1) degree of openness (type and degree of forest cover, if any, or else "meadow," "brush" or whatever); and (2) underfooting (talus, granite, pumice, sand, "duff"—deep humus ground cover of rotting vegetation—or other material).

Two other designations used in the descriptive text warrant definition. "Packer" campsite is used to indicate a semipermanent camp (usually constructed by packers for the "comfort of their clients") characterized by a nailed-plank table or a large, "stand-up" rock fireplace or both. "Improved" campsite is a U.S. Forest Service designation for places where simple toilets have been installed.

Blest silent groves!

O may you be
    Forever mirth's best nursery!

My pure contents
    Forever pitch their tents

Upon these downs, these meads, these rocks,
    these mountains,

And peace still slumber by these purling
    fountains:

Which we may every year

Meet when we come a-fishing here.*

*Venator's toast quote from Sir Henry Wotton in *The Compleat Angler*

The Care and Enjoyment of the Mountains

The mountains are in danger, particularly the High Sierra. More than 400,000 people camped in the Sierra wilderness in 1970, almost double the use level of the previous year. Unless restrictions are imposed the figure could reach one million by 1975. Backpacking is something everybody knows about and almost everybody is going to want to try. With California's population edging toward 25 million, the wilderness is threatened with destruction, particularly the High Sierra.

Litter is not the problem! Increasingly, wilderness campsites, even when free of litter, have that "beat out" look of overcrowded roadside campgrounds. The fragile high country sod is being ground down under the pressure of too many feet. Lovely trees and snags are being stripped, scarred, and removed altogether for firewood. Dust, charcoal, blackened stones and dirty fireplaces are accumulating. These conditions are spreading rapidly, and in a few years *every* High Sierra lakeshore and streamside may be severely damaged.

The national park service and the forest service are faced with the necessity for reservation systems, designated campgrounds, restrictions on fire building, increased ranger patrols, and perhaps even rationing of wilderness recreation. Not only the terrain but the wilderness experience is being eroded. Soon conditions may be little different from those we wanted to leave behind at the roadhead.

The solution to the problem depends on each of us. We must change our habits so as to have as little effect on the terrain as possible. We must try to leave no traces of our passing. This was the rule in the wilderness when Indians and trappers traveled through other people's territory. It is still a good rule today. It does take a little trouble. In an earlier day that extra trouble was the price of saving one's scalp or load of beaver pelts. Today it is the price of saving the wilderness. A few basic principles of wilderness preservation—particularly aimed at High Sierra conditions but applicable elsewhere too—are offered below.

Learn to go light. This is largely a matter of acquiring wilderness skills, of learning to be at home in the wilderness rather than in an elaborate camp. The "free spirits" of the mountains are those experts who appear to go anywhere under any conditions with neither encumbrances nor effort but always with complete enjoyment. John Muir, traveling along the crest of the Sierra in the 1870's with little more than his overcoat and pockets full of biscuits, was the archetype.

Modern lightweight equipment and food are a convenienience and a joy. The ever-practical Muir would have taken them had they been available in his day. But a lot of the stuff that goes into the mountains is burdensome, harmful to the wilderness, or just plain annoying to other people seeking peace and solitude. Anything that is obtrusive or that can be used to modify the terrain should be left at the roadhead: gigantic tents, gas lanterns, radios, saws, hatchets, firearms (except in the hunting season), etc.

Pick "hard" campsites, sandy places that can stand the use. The fragile sod of meadows, lakeshores and streamsides is rapidly disappearing from the High Sierra. It simply cannot take the wear and tear of campers. Its development depends on very special conditions. Once destroyed, it does not ordinarily grow back.

Be easy with the trees! In the timberline country wood is being burned up faster than it is being produced. The big campfires of the past must give way to small fires or to no fires at all. Wood is a precious resource; use it sparingly. Where it is scarce use a gas stove, not a saw or hatchet. Trees, both live and dead, are part of the scenery. They should never be *cut.* The exquisite golden trunks left standing after lightning strikes should be left completely alone. Sadly, in some popular areas they have already been destroyed for firewood, and you would never know they *were* there.

In established, regularly used campsites a single, small, substantial fireplace should serve for both cooking and warming. If kept scrupulously clean it should last for many years. Unfortunately, fireplaces (and campsites) tend to become increasingly dirty and to multiply. There are now, by actual survey, a hundred times as many fireplaces as are needed in the High Sierra. The countless dirty fireplaces should be eradicated. Many campsites situated at at the edge of the water should be entirely restored to nature and not used again. It is a noble service to use and clean up established campsites where they are present, and to restore them to nature where called for.

Elsewhere build a small fireplace, if one is legal, and always eradicate it and restore your campsite to a natural condition before you leave. This is facilitated if you build with restoration in mind: two to four medium-sized stones along the sides of a shallow trench in a sandy place. When camp is broken the stones are returned to their places. The coals are thoroughly burned down and pulverized under a heavy foot until nothing is left but powder. The trench is filled with clean sand. *Fires should never be built against cliffs or large boulders.*

Protect the water from soap and other sources of pollution. Abundant pure water is one of the joys of the mountains. Imagine having to purify every cupful before you drank it.

Scatter organic garbage in dry, out-of-the-way places. It disappears most quickly when dry and exposed to the air. Talus slopes and dry brush are the best hiding places. Garbage should never be burned in the fireplace. Orange peels are an exception. They seem to be destructible only in a hot fire.

Thoroughly cold and pulverized charcoal may be broadcast away from camp in a fireproof site. Charcoal is part of the natural scene.

Pack cans and foil back to the roadhead. Smelly or oily cans and foil can be cleaned easily in a hot fire but please do remove them. The accumulation of garbage, cans, and charcoal around fireplaces is the principal reason campsites are abandoned and new, redundant fireplaces and campsites are created.

Latrines should be located at least 50 yards from any camping area, stream, or dry stream course. Again a little extra trouble will alleviate one of the most annoying wilderness problems. Please be willing to walk a little farther and cover up a little more carefully.

Mirror Lake before it was closed to camping   *Thomas Winnett*

Maps and Profiles

Today's Sierra traveler is confronted by a bewildering array of maps, and it doesn't take much experience to learn that no single map fulfills all needs. There are base maps (U.S. Forest Service), shaded relief maps (National Park Service), artistically drawn representational maps (California Department of Fish and Game), aerial-photograph maps, geologic maps, three-dimensional relief maps, soil-vegetation maps, etc. Each map has different information to impart (some have more information than others), and the outdoorsman contemplating a backcountry trip is wise to utilize several of these maps in his planning.

For trip-planning purposes, the reader will find a plan map in the middle of this book. Trails and trailheads used in the following trip descriptions are indicated on this map in red, and all the access roads are delineated in black.

The profile of each trip in this book gives a quick picture of the ups and downs. All profiles are drawn with the same *ratio* of horizontal miles to feet of elevation, in which the vertical scale is exaggerated by 25 times. Since carrying a pack up a hill gets to be very gruelling sometimes, this exaggeration is probably appropriate.

On the trail most backpackers prefer to use a topographic ("topo") map, because it affords a good deal of accurate information about conditions of terrain and forest cover. Topo maps come in a variety of sizes and scales, but the best, because it covers the whole Sierra in one useful scale, is the U.S. Geological Survey's 15′ Topographic Quadrangle series. The 15′ series scale is approximately 1″ = 1 mile; the contour interval (elevation difference between contour lines) is 80 feet in the Sierra; and the area covered by each map is about 14 × 17 miles. They show most of the maintained trails (exceptions are noted in the text of this book), the elevations, the relief, the watercourses, the forest cover and the works of man. Learing to read these maps takes a little practice, but the savings in shoe leather and frayed tempers make it a worthy undertaking. For the convenience of the reader, the appropriate 15′ topo maps for each trip are cited in the text.

A useful second map series is the ½″ = 1 mile series published by the U.S. Forest Service. Being base maps, they lack the contour lines, but they are revised with some frequency, and show newer roads and trails. They also include markings for water, man-made structures and some elevations.

Anglers planning a fishing trip should acquire the "Anglers' Guides" published by the California Department of Fish and Game. These include both artistically drawn representational maps and descriptions of the fishing waters. Of this in-progress series, five guides apply to the regions of the southern Sierra covered by this book ("Mono Creek," "Bear Creek," "French Canyon/Humphreys Basin," "Upper Bishop Creek" and "Mineral King").

HOW TO ACQUIRE YOUR MAPS

USFS base maps:
U.S. Forest Service,
630 Sansome St.,
San Francisco, CA 94111
An index map and one base
map per order are free.
Additional maps are
15 cents each.

DF&G "Anglers' Guides":
DF&G, Resources Building,
9th and O Sts.,
Sacramento, CA 95814
A single copy of any one guide
is free. Multiple copies are
40 cents each including tax.

USGS 15′ "Topo" maps:
U.S. Geological Survey,
Federal Center, Denver, CO
80225
75 cents each
A state index map is free.

Topo maps plus free state index maps can be obtained *in person* from USGS offices located at:

7638 Federal Building
300 North Los Angeles Street
Los Angeles, CA

345 Middlefield Road
Menlo Park, CA

504 Custom House
555 Battery Street
San Francisco, CA

Wilderness Permits and Quotas

The wilderness traveler will need a permit from the Forest Service (for federally designated wilderness areas) or from the National Park Service (for national-park backcountry). You may obtain a permit at a Park Service or Forest Service ranger station or office by indicating where you are going and when you will be there. The Forest Service requires a permit for a day hike as well as for a backpacking trip. The two services will reciprocally honor each other's permits for trips that cross a boundary between the two types of wilderness. Forest Service permits are also available by mail, and permits for the Sequoia-Kings backcountry are available by mail from February 1 through June 30. If you don't know the address of the nearest Forest Service office or station, write the Regional Forester, 630 Sansome St., San Francisco CA 94111. The address of Sequoia-Kings Canyon National Park is Three Rivers CA 93271. The Forest Service has also set up "entrance stations" on four east-side access roads leading to High Sierra trailheads—on the roads to Whitney Portal, Onion Valley, Bishop Creek and Rock Creek. Information and permits—if you make the quota—are available there.

Quotas have been established for high-use areas in the region covered by this book, including all of Sequoia-Kings Canyon National Park. For example, in 1974, 30 persons per day were allowed to go up the Bubbs Creek Trail from Cedar Grove, on a first-come, first-served basis. Those who didn't "make the cut" either had to wait until they could be one of the 30 or had to choose an alternative trip. Group size anywhere in the wilderness is limited to 25, and camping is not allowed within 100 feet of lakes and streams. There are some special regulations for particular places. For example, a person may camp only one night at each camping place on the John Muir Trail within Rae Lakes Basin. Some places are closed to wood fires, such as the Kearsarge Lakes, and some places are entirely closed to camping, such as Mirror Lake on the Mt. Whitney Trail and Bullfrog Lake, near the John Muir Trail south of Glen Pass. Copies of all these special regulations are available from the government agencies that issue Wilderness permits.

Mono Creek country

U.S. Forest Service

Mono Creek to Glacier Divide

Part of the 500,000-acre John Muir Wilderness, this region towers between Mono Creek and the northern boundary of Kings Canyon National Park. It is a roadless vastness of incredibly rugged alpine beauty composing a wilderness that beckons to the traveler. Barren summits rise above a dense mat of green conifers, and the landscape is stippled with a thousand blue-green lakes bound by connecting silver ribbons of mountain streams. Encompassing a small area of roughly 500 square miles, this section nevertheless contains enough trails and cross-country routes to satisfy the most dedicated backcountry traveler for several summer seasons.

The profile of this region is classic. It boasts the typical short, steep eastern escarpment, and the typical long, gradual western slope. The west side is cut by the drainages of Mono, Bear and Piute creeks—all tributaries of the South Fork of the San Joaquin. And the east side is cleft by the precipitous, hurrying waters of Rock Creek, Pine Creek and the North Fork of Bishop Creek—all tributaries of the Owens River. These watersheds are separated by spectacular divides, which, together with the main Sierra crest—if one uses a little imagination—form an interesting plan view. Seen from the air, the main crest and the ancillary divide spurs of this section take on the aspect of a very large frog: the head centers on Mt. Mills; Mono Divide and the Mt. Morgan/Wheeler Ridge make the forelegs; and the Mt. Hooper/Mt. Senger complex and the Mt. Tom/Basin Mountain divide compose the two lower limbs. Naturalists would hasten to render this absurd analogy more "authentic" by pointing out that the frog's back is covered with warts (17 summits exceeding 13,000'), and that this mountainous region should therefore be analogized to a toad. The reader is free to make his own Rorschach of the topography, but in any case it is vitally important—particularly in cross-country travel—for him to have a working map knowledge of the country and its terrain.

One soon learns, however, that his map knowledge never does justice to the country. This awareness comes with one's first glimpses of the majestic prominences and the awesome, blue-hazed canyons. With awareness comes wonderment—a pause to ponder the colossal forces required to move, pluck and sculpt the rock on such a scale. Clarence King, a member of the famous Brewer Survey party of 1864, was among the first white men to look at this portion of the Sierra and record his thoughts: "I believe no one can study from an elevated lookout the length and

depth of one of these great Sierra canyons without asking himself
some profound geological questions." Indeed, how did it happen?

The answer has mostly to do with ice—vast rivers of ice that
ground, scoured and scraped their juggernaut way across the
landscape. Were there an eye to witness it, in this area alone the
fields of ice would be seen to have extended over 1500 square
miles. Today there are but vestiges to mark the icefields' extent,
reminders that hang like gray ghosts on the shady northeast
faces of the higher peaks. But today's visitor has only to look
about him to understand the land-forming powers of the glaciers.
Huge U-shaped troughs mark the courses of the main glaciers
that carved the canyons of Mono, Bear and Piute creeks, and of
the South Fork of the San Joaquin River. Shallow side valleys,
usually suspended hundreds of feet above the floor of the main
canyon, mark the flow of tributary glaciers, and they have
acquired the deserved appellation "hanging valleys." Equally interesting to the traveler is the inevitable chain of lakes that stepladder down from the upper, amphitheaterlike cirque of a hanging valley. Called "paternoster lakes," they string down the valley
floor much like the beads of a rosary, and they are the joy of the
lazy angler who likes to alternate between stream and lake fishing.

Other important, but less spectacular, glacial traces include
glacial polish and glacial smoothing caused by the abrasive action
of sand and silt that moved at the bottom and sides of a glacier. In
these scoured areas one often finds long gouges or scratches rent
there by boulders caught in the flow of the ice river. The subsequent deposit of these boulders can now be witnessed in the form
of various moraines.

The landscape is still changing. Streams have cut through sediments left by glaciers. Avalanche chutes and frost nivations flute
vertical peak facades, and accumulations of scree and talus slope
away at their feet. Subtler forms of weathering continue to attack
the talus, reducing that rock to granules which then provide a
suitable habitat for hardy plants. One can observe this ecological
progression while walking the trails around timberline.

The presence of an ample and healthy plant life is necessary to
animals, and one is sure to see many animals in this region's
heavily wooded drainages. Birds are particularly plentiful, and
the lakes and streams abound with fish. Among the most commonly seen mammals are mule deer. Early-season hikers working their way up Bear Creek are almost sure to come upon a
grazing doe, and, with some luck, perhaps a pair of brand-new,
spotted-back fawns. It should be noted that any wild-animal observation requires "freezing"—not necessarily stealth, but quiet-

ness and immobility. There isn't a naturalist observer worth his salt who hasn't experienced the dilemma of a hovering mosquito and a "once in a triptime" wild-animal observation opportunity. In early and mid season both does and bucks have reddish coats, which are replaced in the fall with longer, gray hair. Because the buck is much warier, a sighting of him is rarer. One will also make trailside, passing acquaintance with the numerous squirrels that populate the heavily wooded areas, especially the fir belt. Easily recognizable because of the dual stripes running down his coppery-red back is the tiny golden-mantled ground squirrel. He is, perhaps, the most familiar squirrel, and is found in both the lodgepole and subalpine belts. His less distinguished cousin, the California ground squirrel, will be seen near the trailheads—generally below 8000 feet—and the Belding ground squirrel, or "picketpin," is seen in most of the meadows of this section. Constant companions to the high-country hiker are the cony, a small, rabbitlike creature, and the beaverlike marmot. Found in talus and other rocky areas, these somnolent rodents pipe and chirp excitedly whenever approached.

Other, less common, but consequently more exciting, sightings that one may make are of the black bear, mountain coyote, porcupine, flying squirrel and mountain lion. The black bear, contrary to impressions one might well have gathered in heavily camped national-park areas, is not often observed in the backcountry. The notable exception to this rule occurs when one leaves food lying about untended. Although this bear is more often a clown, he can be a pest, and it is always advisable to remove temptations by hoisting food up out of reach. (As the signs say, bears are wild, and it is foolish to try to pet them.) The mountain lion, coyote and flying squirrel are more often heard than seen, and the happy occasion of hearing one of these animals usually occurs while one is busy setting up camp, bedding down or cooking a daybreak breakfast. A coyote's "singing" is a familiar sound to anyone who has watched a western movie, but the habitual birdlike whistling of a mountain lion is usually unrecognized because it seems totally out of character. This cat rarely screams, but he does meow, spit and growl in unmistakable feline fashion. Hearing a flying squirrel, contradictory as it may seem, is a fairly common occurrence. It takes place at night (the squirrel is nocturnal), usually with a whhhist ... splat sound that characterizes his "flight" from one tree to another.

The most commonly seen animal in this region is man. He is usually quite domesticated, and is exceedingly easy to approach. A query like "Where've you been?" usually brings a flood of friendly information and advice that will keep the querying hiker shifting under his pack for 15 minutes or more. In the perspective of geologic time, this animal has been on the scene but a moment, and his written history consumes only a fraction of a second. Despite his relative newness, his effect has been great, and the mark of his passage is on the land—temporarily.

In this section, man's trails, usually following those of other animals, are plentiful, clearly marked and well maintained. The trail following Mono Creek and crossing Mono Pass, and the one following the South Fork of the San Joaquin River and branching over Piute Pass are old trade routes of the Mono Indian tribes. Paralleling these ancient trails is the relatively newer Italy Pass trans-Sierra crossing, and bisecting all three of these routes is the renowned John Muir Trail, which traverses the west slopes in a north-south direction.

There are seven trailhead entry points to this country that are used for trips in this book.

Mosquito Flat. Go 24 miles north from Bishop on U.S. 395 and then 11 miles on paved and dirt road to road's end in Mosquito Flat beside Rock Creek.

Pine Creek Roadend. Go 10 miles northwest from Bishop on U.S. 395 and then 10 miles on paved road to a parking area near a pack station.

Lake Sabrina. Go 16 miles southwest from Bishop on State Highway 168 to the backpackers' parking area.

North Lake. Go 16 miles from Bishop on State Highway 168 almost to Lake Sabrina and turn right on a dirt road. After a few hundred feet turn right again and go 2 miles to a backpackers' parking area just west of North Lake. You must walk the last ½ mile to the trailhead beyond the campground.

Vermilion Campground. Go east from Clovis (near Fresno) 81 miles on State Highway 168 to the Florence Lake/Lake Edison junction, then 8 miles north on a mostly paved road to Vermilion Campground.

Bear Dam Junction. Go 2¼ miles north from the Florence Lake/Lake Edison junction described above, to where the jeep road to Bear Diversion Dam leaves the oiled road.

Florence Lake. Go 6 miles east from the Florence Lake/Lake Edison junction described above.

Bear Dam Junction to Twin Falls

1

TRIP From Bear Dam Junction to Twin Falls (round trip). Topo map *Mt. Abbot*. Best early or late season; 11 miles.

Grade	Trail/layover days	Total recom- mended days
Leisurely	2/0	2
Moderate	....	....
Strenuous	....	....

HILITES Few creeks in the Sierra possess the simple, primitive appeal of Bear Creek. Never constant, it cascades, chutes and then tumbles down its rocky course, interrupted at graceful intervals by deep, slow-moving, sandy-bottomed pools. Fine brown- and golden-trout angling makes this trip a good fisherman's choice early or late season.

DESCRIPTION (Leisurely trip)

1st Hiking Day (**Bear Dam Junction** to **Twin Falls,** 5½ miles): Lichen-covered, glacially scoured granite surrounds the trailhead for this trip. The rock, fractured in many places not by nature but by man, is more precisely granodiorite, which is typically black-flecked because it contains the minerals biotite and hornblende. The first two miles (to the Bear Diversion Dam) is an unmaintained Southern California Edison Co. jeep road. After the jeep road leaves the Mono Hot Springs/Lake Thomas A. Edison road (7000′) it swings first east and then south, undulating gently as it traverses the long granite field that marks the southeast end of Bear Ridge. Rounding Bear Ridge, the jeep road ascends gently, and then drops down to the Bear Diversion Dam spillway. This particular stretch of road overlooks the gorge of the river to the south, and gives the traveler a fine opportunity to watch the abundant population of birds that frequent these broken slopes. Among the birds one is most likely to see are Steller jays, mountain chickadees, juncos, dusky and olive-sided flycatchers, cliff and barn swallows, red-tailed hawks, and a variety of sparrows. Where the jeep road starts to descend to the spillway, one can see (southeast) to Ward Mountain and Mt. Shinn, and east to Bear

Dome and the barren glacial cirques above. This route also offers the traveler on foot or on horseback a chance to absorb the feeling of this glacially scoured country. It is a feeling of openness that is emphasized by the scattering of the forest cover. The mountain juniper and Jeffrey pine occur in moderate stands amid broad expanses of granite, where they have taken root in the granular sand swales that have accumulated as a result of mechanical weathering. In turn, the network of roots sprouting from pine, willow, ceanothus and manzanita accelerates the continual process of granite breaking.

At the Bear Diversion Dam (7350') the traveler enters the mouth of the canyon whose walls rise steeply on either side of Bear Creek. The trail skirts the west and north sides of the tiny Bear Diversion Dam reservoir and strikes out east-northeast, along the north side of Bear Creek. (A signed trail begins at the road's end, about 100 feet above the reservoir. It meets the described trail about ¼ mile farther on.) It doesn't take one long to realize he has left that feeling of openness behind. The canyon walls close in, and the forest cover becomes moderate to dense.

Should one desire to try the fair-to-good fishing along the stream (they come in sizes up to 15"), he will also more than likely encounter small stands of water-loving cottonwood and aspen en route, as well as some lodgepole, oak, and the first fir. Near the creek, wildflower fanciers will relish the luxuriant growth of penstemon, lupine, paintbrush, monkey flower, and cinquefoil (pronounced "sink-foyl").

Bear Creek, in the stretch immediately above the reservoir, is a rock-bottomed, briskly flowing stream with a surprising penchant for suddenly eddying out into broad, emerald-green pools. Fortunately, the trail is never far from the creek's banks, and one can make several worthwhile forays to the water's edge without too much loss of trail time. For 1½ miles above the reservoir, the trail ascends very gradually, and then as the canyon narrows it begins to ascend more steeply. The duff trail gives way to rocky underfooting, which prevails for the rest of the trip, and about ½ mile farther this route encounters the signed boundary of the John Muir Wilderness. At the boundary, one can catch his first V-notched glimpse of Recess Peak directly up-canyon. The trail drops down for a short distance and then begins a steady, rocky ascent. Several good campsites dot the nearby banks of Bear Creek, and the traveler can take his choice of any of these primitive sites. Though the emerald-green pools occur less often, they stand in dramatic contrast to the plunging white water.

In this country slight changes in altitude entail significant changes in the plant and animal life. For example, as the trail ascends steeply, fishermen find golden trout as well as brown in their catch, and exploring naturalists discover that the predominant forest cover is now Jeffrey pine and the shrubs are now mostly gooseberry and snow brush. Arrival at the packer site is presaged by several "corduroy" bridge crossings of marshy sections, and a stock drift fence. At the improved packer campsite (8000') there is a fine, large pool offering good fishing for brown and golden trout (8"-15"). Campers in this canyon are frequently serenaded by coyotes who range Bear Ridge. Swimming in mid or late season is excellent.

2nd Hiking Day: Retrace your steps, 5½ miles.

Recess Peak over Lake Edison   *Thomas Winnett*

2 Bear Dam Junction to Upper Bear Creek

TRIP   From Bear Dam Junction to Upper Bear Creek
               (round trip). Topo map *Mt. Abbot*. Best mid or late
               season; 27 miles.

Grade	Trail/layover days	Total recom- mended days
Leisurely	4/1	5
Moderate	3/1	4
Strenuous	....	....

HILITES   This trip ascends Bear Creek beyond the densely
               forested flats at the site of Old Kip Camp. The angler
               seeking varied sport will find good fishing from the
               time he first sees Bear Creek at Bear Diversion Dam.
               Brown trout, a particular favorite of the serious
               fisherman, populate the lower waters of this trip, and
               the justly famous golden trout inhabit the upper
               waters and nearby lakes.

DESCRIPTION (Leisurely trip)

1st Hiking Day: Follow trip 1 to **Twin Falls,** 5½ miles.

2nd Hiking Day (**Twin Falls** to **Upper Bear Creek**, 8 miles): An improved packer campsite marks the point where the trail veers
north away from cascading Bear Creek. As you ascend steadily
up the north wall of the canyon, you have good views of the jumbled cirque crest on the opposite side of the canyon to the southeast. Though rocky, this trail is well maintained as it rises above
the floor of the valley. The moderate-to-dense forest cover of the
creek bottom thins as the trail climbs to the slight granite-ribbed
saddle that marks the start of the descent to a reunion with Bear
Creek.

    The floral display along this stretch of trail includes penste-
mon, larkspur, monkshood, elephant's head, lupine, goldenrod,
fleabane, paintbrush, and western mountain aster. The descent
reveals a marked change in the forest cover in that the predominant Jeffrey of the lower canyon has given way to lodgepole
and juniper. Where the views during the ascent were of the

down-canyon Bear Creek drainage, you now have views of the Mono Divide. Just above Old Kip Camp, a bend in the duff trail reveals Mt. Hilgard, and as one nears the flats of the camp he finds that the timber now includes red fir. The aspen- and cottonwood-lined banks of Bear Creek reappear on the immediate right as our route strikes the John Muir Trail and turns right. Just a few yards east of the junction lies the former site of Kip Camp (8840'), where there is fair golden- and brook-trout fishing (to 10") in nearby Bear Creek. Our route swings south through thinning forest cover on a moderate ascent that stays close to the stream. The trail passes several improved packer campsites situated near large, log-jammed pools in the stream, and the canyon takes on a valley aspect as it nears Hilgard Branch. Our route passes the Italy Pass Trail and fords by footlog several branchlets of Hilgard Branch. Near these wetter sections of trail, one will find abundant whorled blue-purple penstemon, yellow and purple shooting star, prickly red gooseberry and yellow wallflower. About 1 mile beyond the Hilgard Branch are several good campsites far enough from the creek to be legal stopping places.

3rd and 4th Hiking Days: Retrace your steps, 13½ miles.

Sign at Bear Dam Junction

Thomas Winnett

3

Bear Dam Junction
to Vermilion Campground

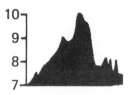

TRIP

From Bear Dam Junction to Vermilion Campground via Quail Meadows (shuttle trip). Topo maps *Kaiser Peak, Mt. Abbot*. Best early or late season; 21 miles.

Grade	Trail/layover days	Total recom-mended days
Leisurely	4/1	5
Moderate	3/1	4
Strenuous	2/1	3

HILITES

Varied scenery that ranges from the intimate confines of Bear Creek to the open expanses on Bear Ridge gives this long-weekend trip a universal appeal. The trek circumnavigates Bear Ridge, visiting the Bear and Mono Creek drainages, and the close proximity of the beginning and end of this horseshoe-shaped route makes it a potential loop.

DESCRIPTION (Moderate trip)

1st Hiking Day: Follow trip 1 to **Twin Falls,** 5½ miles.

2nd Hiking Day (**Twin Falls** to **Quail Meadows,** 10 miles): Follow the 2nd hiking day, trip 2, to the John Muir Trail and turn left. Our route follows the Muir Trail as we ascend steadily northwest, passing a stock drift fence, and then climbing steeply through a thinning forest of lodgepole and juniper. Views back into the Bear Creek drainage are excellent, including Recess Peak, Mt. Hilgard and Seven Gables. Crossing the rocky summit of Bear Ridge, we pass a trail that goes west to Mono Hot Springs. One can view the geologically more recent volcanic overlay typified by the breached crater of Volcanic Knob to the east.

As the trail begins the steep series of switchbacks that drop into the Mono Creek watershed, the traveler is treated to excellent views of the Silver Divide, the immediate Mono Creek watershed, and Lake Thomas A. Edison. This route stepladders near the foot of the descent, and then drops the final 400 feet to the steel-bridge crossing at Mono Creek. Several good campsites line the north side of Mono Creek near Quail Meadows (7760'). Additional campsites can be found along the south side of the creek. Fishing is good for brook and rainbow (to 12") in Mono Creek.

3rd Hiking Day (**Quail Meadows** to **Vermilion Campground**, 5½ miles): Our trail leaves the John Muir Trail and proceeds downstream (west) toward Lake Thomas A. Edison. This trail is relatively new, and is unmarked on the latest topo map. The first mile of level going parallels the magnificent chutes and rapids that precede Mono Creek's absorption by the Lake Edison reservoir. These white waters are periodically interrupted by sand-bottomed granite potholes that offer excellent swimming to the mid or late season traveler. One can easily imagine the members of the famous Brewer Survey Party of 1864 stopping here for a few moments of relaxation and refreshment. A few yards beyond these potholes an indistinct path branches off to the left and leads to the boat landing at the northeast tip of the lake. Here a boat-taxi service operates during the summer months, and one may obtain the ferry schedule by writing the High Sierra Resort/Lake Thomas A. Edison/Mono Hot Springs/CA 93642. The ferry service is based at a resort adjoining Vermilion Campground.

Those choosing to use the newly constructed trail along the north side of Lake Edison will find that the route undulates severely up and down the north wall of Vermilion Valley. However, the worst of these ascents and descents are over midway down the length of the lake, and the point where our trail passes the Goodale Pass Trail makes the beginning of relatively level going. Along these more level stretches the forest cover of Jeffrey, red fir, and lodgepole becomes somewhat denser. In one of these denser stands of lodgepole, a few yards from the Goodale Pass Trail junction, our route meets a second boat-landing trail. Continuing westward, our trail crosses the Cold Creek bridge, passes the trail lateral to Devils Bathtub, and winds down through a dense stand of Jeffrey to meet the Forest Service access road that leads to Vermilion Campground (7650').

Cold Creek bridge

Jeff Schaffer

4   **Bear Dam Junction to Lake Italy**

TRIP   From Bear Dam Junction to Lake Italy (round trip).
               Topo map *Mt. Abbot;* Best mid or late season; 37
               miles.

Grade	Trail/layover days	Total recommended days
Leisurely	6/1	7
Moderate	4/1	5
Strenuous	3/1	4

HILITES   This trip is tailor-made for the traveler who wants to
               experience the high, alpine country of the mid Sierra
               without having to contemplate cross-country walk-
               ing. Lake Italy, the aim of this trip, is a frequently
               used base camp for climbers, and a fine trip selection
               for the photographer.

DESCRIPTION (Leisurely trip)

1st Hiking Day: Follow trip 1 to **Twin Falls,** 5½ miles.

2nd Hiking Day (**Twin Falls** to **Hilgard Branch,** 7½ miles): Follow
the 2nd hiking day, trip 2, to the John Muir Trail and turn right
on it. From Old Kip Camp, the moderately ascending trail stays
very close to the east bank of Bear Creek. This moderate ascent
soon leaves the flats of Old Kip Camp behind, and the forest cover
changes to lodgepole. Within 2 miles after leaving the flats, one
sees the last of the familiar quaking aspen, and the canyon takes
on more of an open valley feeling. Three improved packer campsites (spaced at intervals of about 1 mile) line Bear Creek for the
first 3 miles above Old Kip Camp, and their presence indicates
the heavy use that the Muir Trail is subjected to. On the left,
below Mt. Hilgard, one can see the Hilgard Branch canyon come
into view. At the confluence of Hilgard Branch and Bear Creek
our route branches left (east) from the John Muir Trail and ascends ½ mile to the good campsites near the stream.

3rd Hiking Day (**Hilgard Branch** to **Lake Italy,** 5½ miles): The Hilgard Branch Trail ascends steadily through a thinning forest cover of lodgepole and then over large patches of glacially smoothed granite. Midway between the trail junction and Lake Italy, the trail levels out temporarily, only to begin climbing abruptly via short, rocky switchbacks. High on the left the rocky prominence of Mt. Hilgard dominates the skyline as the switchbacks temporarily end. The trail fords the stream, and then resumes its switchbacking. Just below Teddy Bear Lake, the trail passes timberline, and then crosses long granite ledges that alternate with grassy patches to the outlet of Lake Italy (11,150'). This large, bootlike lake derives its name from its similarity to the European peninsula.

Rounding the curve of the lake just above the outlet one can easily see the cirque basin where the feeder glacier had its beginnings. At the east end of the cirque, Bear Creek Spire marks the division between the western and eastern directional flows of the old glaciers. There are a number of fair exposed campsites along the turfy south shore of the lake near the outlet. However, the granitic scenery surrounding this large lake compensates for the lack of firewood and forest cover. To the west towers Mt. Hilgard; to the north, Mt. Gabb; and to the east are Bear Creek Spire and Mt. Julius Caesar. To the immediate north of Bear Creek Spire, filling the distant skyline, are Mts. Dade and Abbot. A mountaineer's heaven: every peak bordering on this lake towers well over 13,000 feet. The golden-trout fishery (8″-12″) in Lake Italy is fair-to-good—a classification that applies to the surrounding Toe, Jumble and Brown Bear and Teddy Bear lakes as well.

4th, 5th and 6th Hiking Days: Retrace your steps, 18½ miles.

Mt. Hilgard, Lake Italy (aerial view)

E.P. Pister

5 Bear Dam Junction to Lake Italy

TRIP From Bear Dam Junction to Lake Italy via Hilgard Branch, return via Vee Lake, East Fork Bear Creek (semiloop trip). Topo map *Mt. Abbot.* Best mid or late season; 41½ miles.

Grade	Trail/layover days	Total recommended days
Leisurely	7/2	9
Moderate	5/2	7
Strenuous	4/2	6

HILITES For intermediate and experienced knapsackers only, this varied and exciting cross-country trip seeks the kind of high country that is the exclusive province of the knapsacker.

DESCRIPTION (Leisurely trip)

1st, 2nd and 3rd Hiking Days: Follow trip 4 to **Lake Italy,** 18½ miles.

4th Hiking Day (**Lake Italy** to **Vee Lake,** 5 miles, part cross crountry): Our route skirts the south side of Lake Italy, following the ducked and sometimes faint Italy Pass Trail. As the trail ascends on the west side of the outlet stream from Jumble Lake, one has excellent views northeast along the Sierra Nevada crest. The trail then fords the stream, and at the east end of Jumble Lake our route branches away from the Italy Pass Trail and begins the cross-country work by traversing the granite slope on the south side of Jumble Lake to the rocky saddle that dents the ridge just above White Bear Lake. At this saddle, one can see the clear division that this ridge made between two small glaciers which once fed the main mer de glace that flowed down Bear Creek canyon. White Bear Lake and Black Bear Lake just to its east are the puddled remnants of the outermost extremities of the East Fork feeder glacier. By virtue of having come "through the back door," the hiker has the opportunity to trace the old glacier's path from its inception all the way to the main trunk. Anglers will probably want to try the fair-to-good golden-trout fishing at White Bear and Black Bear lakes before proceeding, but as a rule of thumb the fishing gets better as one descends into the East Fork drainage.

The descent to Big Bear, Bearpaw and Ursa lakes is made due south via a series of smooth granite ledges and talus. This cross-country travel requires careful route-picking and the inevitable scrambling. Hikers should take particular care in crossing these loosened talus slopes. At Big Bear and Bearpaw lakes fishermen will find some of the best fishing of the trip. Golden trout to 15″ are present in the lakes and the intervening streams, and because the fishing at Little Bear Lake is almost equally good, it isn't worth breaking down one's rod for the short walk between.

From Little Bear Lake our route veers south-southwest across an easy granite ridge that is dotted with tiny tarns. This ridge brings the traveler to a point just above the outlet of Vee Lake, and it is an easy scramble down to the turfy but forest-barren fringes of the lake (11,120′). As at Lake Italy, camping at Vee Lake is of the high, alpine, woodless variety. However, fishing on this large (50-acre) lake is good-to-excellent for golden trout (to 16″), and it is an ideal spur camp location for angling or exploratory side trips to the lakes in the upper part of the basin. From the fair campsites on the north and east sides of the lake the camper has excellent views to the east of Royce and Merriam peaks and to the west of Seven Gables.

5th Hiking Day (**Vee Lake** to **Upper Bear Creek,** 4½ miles): Keeping to the east side of the outlet stream, our route descends steeply to the Seven Gables Lakes basin. The intimate falls and chutes found along this outlet stream are a pleasant contrast to the brooding heights of Seven Gables peak to the west. At the confluence of the outlet creek and the Seven Gables branch of the East Fork Bear Creek, our route fords the Seven Gables Branch and turns downstream. However, anglers electing to first test the good fishing for golden trout at the largest of the Seven Gables Lakes will alter their route upstream—½ mile of gentle ascent. Those continuing downstream reford the Seven Gables branch just above the lovely waterfalls that precede the stream's inlet into the L-shaped lake, the lowest of the Seven Gables chain, and there pick up a faint trail. Fishing for golden (to 10″) in the L-shaped lake is good.

Descending steadily, the route continues northwest for a short quarter mile, then crosses by a shallow wade where the canyon narrows, and continues northwest to reach an obvious trail down the canyon which soon turns west. This steady descent encounters timberline just north of Seven Gables peak, and witnesses the typical hemlock-lodgepole-fir spectrum as it follows the length of a V'ed canyon and emerges into the wide, more open expanses of Bear Creek canyon. Turning northward, the trail meets and turns right onto the John Muir Trail. The descent becomes moderate to gentle as the trail winds through alternating meadow and lodgepole stands to the campsites on upper Bear Creek.

6th Hiking Day **(Upper Bear Creek** to **Twin Falls,** 8 miles): A mile of gentle descent leads to the fords of multibranched Hilgard Creek. A few yards beyond these fords the trail meets the Hilgard Branch Trail and retraces most of the 2nd hiking day, trip 4.

7th Hiking Day: Retrace the steps of the 1st hiking day, 5½ miles.

Spotted sandpiper's nest with egg

Jeff Schaffer

Bear Dam Junction to Sandpiper Lake   **6**

TRIP   From Bear Dam Junction to Sandpiper Lake
(round trip) Topo map *Mt. Abbot*. Best mid or late
season; 33 miles.

Grade	Trail/layover days	Total recom- mended days
Leisurely	5/1	6
Moderate	4/1	5
Strenuous	3/1	4

HILITES   This trip provides the unusual opportunity for knapsackers (or those with stock) to trace a river's course
from its inception. Much of this route follows the
famous John Muir Trail, but most of the campsites
avoid that trail's heavily used stopover places.

DESCRIPTION (Moderate trip)

1st Hiking Day: Follow trip 1 to **Twin Falls**, 5½ miles.

2nd Hiking Day (**Twin Falls** to **Sandpiper Lake**, 11 miles): Follow
the 2nd hiking day, trip 2, to the campsites on upper Bear Creek.
(This is a long uphill hiking day, and some people may want to
stop at upper Bear Creek and continue on to Sandpiper Lake the
next day.) The ascent is still gentle-to-moderate as it passes along
open granite slab sections with meadowy breaks, and arrives at
the trail junction where the Vee and Seven Gables Lakes Trail
branches left (east). This junction is just a few yards short of the
Bear Creek ford—a wade-across ford that is hazardous during
high water. Hikers will find the going easier by using the footlog
⅛ mile downstream (due west of the last improved packer campsite). After fording the stream via this footlog, one rejoins our
route at the west side of the wade-across ford cited above via a
short section of the Orchid Lake Trail (not shown on the topo
map). The trail then ascends steeply by switchbacks to the corduroy bridge crossing of the West Fork of Bear Creek at
Rosemarie Meadow.

At an obvious junction, our route branches left, off the John Muir Trail, eastward over an easy ridge to Lou Beverly Lake. (This well-established trail is not shown on the topo map.) The moderate forest cover of lodgepole through which the trail winds shows the effects of the higher altitude. The two-needled trees take on a stunted appearance and one begins to see clumps of red mountain heather. Lou Beverly Lake (10,050') is a tiny (5-acre), shallow, moderately forested lake with one improved packer campsite (there are other, primitive sites) at the southwest end. Fishing for golden (to 14") is good to excellent, which should be adequate reason for anglers to try their luck. For the camper who prefers a more protected and timbered lake, Lou Beverly is a fine alternative site to end this hiking day.

For the camper who prefers a high alpine feel to his campsite, the choice should be Sandpiper Lake. The signed trail to that lake crosses the marshy inlet to Lou Beverly Lake, and ascends along the north and east side of the stream connecting the two lakes. This ascent, over rough, unmaintained trail, is steady until it reaches the abrupt granite face just below Sandpiper Lake, where the going becomes very steep. The waterfall outlet of Sandpiper Lake (10450') makes a musical accompaniment to end the climb by, as one arrives at the good campsites near the outlet and along the west side of the lake. This fair-sized lake (about 25 acres) has a very sparse forest cover of stunted lodgepole but the view of the surrounding granitic peaks is excellent—particularly from the granite shoulder just southwest of the lake. Despite fairly heavy fishing pressure in the last few years, angling for golden (to 13") is often good, and this lake makes an excellent base camp for fishing and hiking excursions to the surrounding lakes on the headwaters of Bear Creek. The morning and evening sounds of Pacific tree frogs and Yosemite toads are welcome background music for the hustling cook at his chores.

3rd and 4th Hiking Days: Retrace your steps, 16½ miles.

Bear Dam Junction to Little Moccasin Lake 7

TRIP From Bear Dam Junction to Little Moccasin Lake via Sandpiper Lake, cross-country return via West Pinnacles Creek drainage, Three Island Lake (semiloop trip). Topo map *Mt. Abbot*. Best mid or late season; 47 miles.

Grade	Trail/layover days	Total recommended days
Leisurely	7/3	10
Moderate	6/2	8
Strenuous	5/2	7

HILITES Loop trips that include the variety of country this one does are rare. From the confines of Bear Creek, this route climbs above timberline, and circles two rarely visited watersheds. The cross-country work is often difficult, and this trip is recommended for intermediate and experienced hikers only.

DESCRIPTION (Moderate trip)

1st and 2nd Hiking Days: Follow trip 6 to **Sandpiper Lake**, 16½ miles.

3rd Hiking Day (**Sandpiper Lake** to **Little Moccasin Lake**, 6½ miles cross country): This rugged cross-country loop begins by rounding the west side of Sandpiper Lake (10,450′) and fording the inlet stream coming from Medley Lakes. From here the route ascends southeast by means of the granite ledge systems. Following the south fork of the east inlet stream to Medley Lakes, this route ascends steeply over smoothed, barren granite slabs and grassy pockets to a narrow unnamed lake at the head of the stream on the topo map. Views during the course of this climb include Medley Lakes, Mts. Senger and Hooper, and Seven Gables. From the unnamed lake, this route ascends up the drainage to the north-east to an obvious saddle. Just short of this saddle, one has super-lative views to the west, and these views are matched to the east when the crest of the saddle is reached.

From the saddle one can see Mts. Hilgard, Abbot, Gabb, Dade, Bear Creek Spire, Julius Caesar, Royce, Humphreys and Gemini. Route-finding on these rugged talus slopes is difficult at best, but the hiker will find the traverse around the steep north slope of Gemini a moderate one that descends to a broad saddle and down to the unnamed scree-ridden lake just north of Aweetasal Lake. This traverse offers excellent views down into the Seven Gables Lakes cirque until it crosses a saddle. The rock cairn at the saddle marks a point from which one can see the crest as it dwindles away to the southernmost skyline, including Glacier Divide, Emerald Peak, and Mts. McGee, Henry and Goddard. Immediately on the right are the twin peaks of Gemini and the spec-tacular jumbled crest of The Pinnacles. It is the latter that domi-nate the views to the west for the remainder of this hiking day's progress down the East Pinnacles Creek drainage. Descent into this drainage is first moderate (to the first unnamed, talus-cluttered lake), and then steeper as one drops down to shallow Aweetasal Lake.

Typical of most of the lakes on this drainage, Aweetasal has poor fishing and virtually no timber, but tundralike grassy spots between granite slabs. Most of these lakes were air-planted with golden trout, but lack of adequate feed and spawning areas to-gether with winter kill soon depleted the populations. This rug-ged and somewhat sterile land is the alpine Sierra at its best. Here, despite the harsh, exposed environment, the tough yet deli-cate grasses grow. Near the streams one can rediscover the yellow columbine that is found only in these rarified heights. There are, of course, the usual whorled penstemon, paintbrush, yellow cin-quefoil and shooting star, but all are dwarfed, clinging close to the turf, as though they were foreign to this clime. Here the margin for life is slim, and the hardiest knapsacker finds himself imitat-ing the plant life. When he rests or seeks sleep in the comfort of his bedroll, he instinctively curls up to conserve his precious body heat. This is perennial ice-touched land, always cold, and yet a place where one can come by a severe sunburn. Harsh and unin-viting as the land seems, the hiker soon finds a beauty to wonder at as he progresses down the drainage. Only those who dare this harshness manage to view The Pinnacles from the east side, and that rugged, spiring rock mass towers on the right as one scram-bles down the alternately moderate and steep granite slabs be-tween Aweetasal and Jawbone lakes.

Following the outlet stream from Jawbone Lake, one arrives at shallow, grassy Council Lake. Here route-finding becomes simpler as the going levels off, and by a series of grassy benches one passes Paoha and Negit lakes, and, rounding a granite shoulder, comes to Big Moccasin Lake. Stunted and solitary whitebark pines, a sure sign of high alpine country, dot the rocky fringes of this shallow lake. From Big Moccasin Lake it is an easy descent to Little Moccasin Lake, where one has fine views of the Piute Creek drainage. Above its U-shaped valley one can see Pilot Knob and the complex of avalanche chutes on the north face of Mt. Henry to the south. Majestic Mt. Humphreys dominates the Sierra crest, and the adjacent subrange is crowned by Emerald Peak. The top of Mt. Tom is visible. From this viewpoint, our route veers due west, descending a grassy chute to the campsites along the outlet streams from the upper lakes. These campsites (10,800') are good, with excellent views.

4th Hiking Day (**Little Moccasin Lake** to **Sandpiper Lake**, 7½ miles cross country): From the west fork of East Pinnacles Creek this cross-country route swings around the south end of The Pinnacles on a long talus and boulder traverse to a point just north of Pemmican Lake. This scrambling traverse offers the views described in the 3rd hiking day until the drainage of West Pinnacles Creek is reached. A slight descent past several tarns unmarked on the topo map leads to Spearpoint Lake, which, unlike the lakes of the East Pinnacles Creek drainage, is deep, and populated by a few small golden (6-8″). The rugged terrain around the edges of Spearpoint Lake determines the best feasible route to be over the easy granite ridge separating Spearpoint and Pendant lakes, and thence north across the marshy section separating Pendant and Big Chief lakes. Skirting the east side of shallow Big Chief Lake (some golden, fry), this route ascends on a moderate grade from the meadowed north end of the lake to Old Squaw Lake. This lake is barren of trout, but it offers some of the best views of The Pinnacles to be obtained on this trip. Glacially smoothed granite slabs line the lake's edge on all sides, and progress is fairly easy along the east shore. Following the inlet stream, the route ascends steadily to Wampum Lake, where anglers may try their luck for the fair fishing (golden 6-8″).

At Wampum Lake the twin peaks of Gemini once more come into view, and one has reached the cirque-basined headwaters of West Pinnacles Creek. This bowl-like cirque presents route-picking problems, and some care should be exercised in crossing the sometimes steep west wall, which divides the West Pinnacles Creek drainage from the South Fork of Bear Creek drainage. At the top of this wall one has a panoramic vista of Seven Gables,

Gemini, The Pinnacles, Emerald Peak, Mt. Henry, Mt. Senger, Mt. Hooper and the Bear Creek drainage.

Descent from this ridge presents no problems to the accomplished rock-climber, but the easiest route for the novice is to pick one's way westward around the head of the Three Island Lake cirque to the saddle just east of Sharp Note Lake, and then traverse down the steep slopes on the west side of Three Island Lake. Anglers will find fair-to-good golden-trout fishing in this large (80-acre) lake. These rockbound, deep waters provide a classic glacial setting for high-country enthusiasts, and they are a longtime favorite of camera-carrying visitors. Following the outlet stream at the north end of Three Island Lake past Medley Lake, an easy descent along a ledge system of granite leads to the inlet of Sandpiper Lake, the beginning point for this cross-country loop.

5th and 6th Hiking Days: Retrace the steps of the 2nd and 1st hiking days, 16½ miles.

Bear Dam Junction to Florence Lake 8

TRIP   From Bear Dam Junction to Florence Lake via Sandpiper Lake, Selden Pass, Blaney Meadow (shuttle trip). Topo maps *Mt. Abbot, Blackcap Mountain.* Best mid or late season; 34 miles.

Grade	Trail/layover days	Total recom- mended days
Leisurely	5/1	6
Moderate	4/1	5
Strenuous	3/1	4

HILITES   This popular shuttle trip circles the Mt. Hooper complex and visits some of the best creek and lake fishing in the Sierra. Part of this trip's popularity stems from the near proximity of the trailhead to the conclusion of this trip—making the shuttle fairly simple.

DESCRIPTION (Moderate trip)

1st and 2nd Hiking Days: Follow trip 6 to **Sandpiper Lake,** 16½ miles.

3rd Hiking Day (**Sandpiper Lake** to **Lower Blaney Meadows,** 10 miles—2 miles cross country): The first 2 miles of this hiking day are cross country. Starting from the campsites along the west side of Sandpiper Lake, this route ascends the easy, tarn-dotted swale at the southwest end of the lake and leads around the granite-slabbed nose of the ridge descending north from Mt. Senger. From this nose, one has excellent views down the Bear Creek drainage to Bear Ridge, and beyond to the barren tops of the Silver Divide. Immediately below is Lou Beverly Lake, and in its mirrorlike green surface one sees the reflection of Recess Peak. Looking north, views from left to right include Mt. Hooper, the Bear Creek drainage, and Lou Beverly Lake; and beyond, Graveyard Peak, Mt. Izaak Walton and Red and White Mountain. Given a clear atmosphere, one can see all the way north to the Minarets and the Mammoth Crest. To the immediate right is the bouldery crest of Mt. Hilgard, and to the right of that towers multipeaked Seven Gables, with Mt. Gabb peeking over its left shoulder. Turning toward the south, one looks into the immense cirque basin headed by Mt. Senger.

From the top of this ridge, it is a moderate descent west to large, granite-lined Marie Lake, where our route skirts the meadowy northern edge. Walking the turfy fringes of the lake (poor-to-fair brook and golden fishing), one will find elephant heads and western mountain aster mixed among the heather. This lake fringe marks timberline, and as our route turns south on the west side of Marie Lake, the mixed sparse forest is left behind. At the outlet of Marie Lake our route rejoins the John Muir Trail as it winds along the west banks of the lake. From the south end of the lake the trail ascends on a gentle-to-moderate grade to Selden Pass (10,873'). Breather stops on this climb offer fine views back to Mt. Hilgard and the granitic Marie Lake cirque. From Selden Pass the trail descends over short, steep switchbacks to Heart Lake. This rockbound, heart-shaped lake has a meadow-turfed fringe delicately colored with heather, primrose and yellow columbine. Fair angling for golden (6-8") makes this lake an interesting rest stop. Non-fishermen will find the views a fine way to pass the time while anglers practice their art. From the outlet, one can see Mts. Goddard and Henry to the southeast; to the southwest Ward Mountain and Mt. Shinn dominate the visible peaks. Continuing the moderate descent from Heart Lake along its outlet stream, the trail arrives at Sally Keyes Lakes. This short walk is lined with an abundance of wildflowers including corn lily, Indian paintbrush, Douglas phlox, shooting star, yellow cinquefoil, milfoil, penstemon, lupine, red heather, wallflower, nude buckwheat and western mountain aster. Fishermen who have not dismantled their rods will find the fishing here about the same as at Heart Lake.

The trail crosses the short stream joining the two Sally Keyes Lakes and descends on a duff-and-sand trail through a thickening forest cover of lodgepole. There are several good, though heavily used, campsites at the outlet and along the west shore of the lower of the two lakes. Our route crosses the outlet stream and in a long meadow ¼ mile south, a faint trail branches right, away from the John Muir Trail. Although the trail is dusty and steep, one can enjoy the unusual cross section of Sierra flora encountered in the course of its 3000-foot descent. At first, altitude-loving whitebark pines are mixed with the dense forest cover of lodgepole, but within a few miles the whitebark disappears and fir makes a brief appearance, only to be replaced by Jeffrey pine at lower altitudes. Juniper is found in both the high and low altitudes; quaking aspen are not seen until the trail nears Senger Creek, near the foot of a descent. The dry canyon walls are generally brush-covered, with heavy manzanita around the middle of the descent, but with some surprise the trail traveler will also find many wildflowers along these same stretches. In the drier regions are Douglas phlox, streptanthus and Mariposa lily; in the wetter sections are shooting star, red columbine, corn lily, cinquefoil and penstemon; almost everywhere are lupine, white Mariposa, Bigelow sneezeweed, golden brodiaea and groundsel.

The switchbacking descent ends above Blaney Meadows (visible from the trail) and then this route turns right onto the Florence Lake/Evolution Valley Trail. From this junction the duff trail descends through a moderately dense mixed forest cover of lodgepole, juniper, Jeffrey and quaking aspen, and arrives at Lower Blaney Meadows and the signed public campground (7650'). Several fair campsites, including two improved packer sites, are available. Fishing in the South Fork San Joaquin River for brook and some rainbow (to 12") is fair to good—mostly downstream.

4th Hiking Day (**Lower Blaney Meadows** to **Florence Lake,** 7½ miles): Following the well-used route west from Lower Blaney Meadows the trail ascends steadily over sand and rock to the footlog ford of the unnamed creek just east of Double Meadow. Here, the trail has been rerouted around the fringes of the grassland. Damage to fragile meadows like these, particularly during the wet early-summer months, has made a sufficient impression on the Forest Service and the National Park Service that they are now deemed worthy of appropriate conservation measures to guarantee their survival. As the trail rounds the north side of the meadow it affords excellent views of Ward Mountain and high, pointed Mt. Shinn, and then it makes a moderate descent through a forest cover of Jeffrey, juniper and white fir to an improved campground above the head of Florence Lake. From here a bridge leads over the South Fork of the San Joaquin, just above the southeast end of Florence Lake. Crossing the smooth granite west of the bridge, this trail passes a short lateral branching right to the edge of Florence Lake, and a heavily used campground. At Boulder Creek the trail fords by means of a footlog. The ford is dangerous during heavy runoff.

This route then passes the Thomson Lake/Hot Springs Pass Trail junction, and commences a series of moderate-to-steep ups and downs through a mixed forest cover of Jeffrey and juniper, with occasional aspen, white fir and lodgepole. This route skirts the west side of Florence Lake, sometimes ascending to granite ledges 300 feet above the lake's surface. Views to the southeast always include Mt. Shinn and Ward Mountain and glimpses up the South Fork San Joaquin River drainage. To the north is the Silver Divide, foregrounded by the blue waters of Florence Lake. Just before this route meets the Southern California Edison Dam Road (no public auto travel) the trail has climbed high on the ridge; it then descends steeply to the roadend. (A boat-taxi shuttles from the head of Florence Lake to the roadend in summertime, quitting around 7 p.m. each night. The cost is several dollars per person.)

Looking southeast over Florence Lake

Thomas Winnett

Bear Dam Junction to Vee Lake   **9**

TRIP   From Bear Dam Junction to Vee Lake via Sandpiper
Lake, cross country to Vee Lake, return via cross-
country route to Lake Italy, Hilgard Branch Creek,
(semiloop trip). Topo map *Mt. Abbot.* Best mid or late
season; 45 miles.

Grade	Trail/layover days	Total recom- mended days
Leisurely	8/3	11
Moderate	7/2	9
Strenuous	5/2	7

HILITES   A fine fishing trip combined with a short, rugged
cross-country segment, this route should appeal to
the intermediate knapsacker.

DESCRIPTION (Moderate trip)

1st and 2nd Hiking Days: Follow trip 6 to **Sandpiper Lake,** 16½
miles.

3rd Hiking Day **(Sandpiper Lake** to **Vee Lake,** 5 miles cross country):** This route circles the east side of Sandpiper Lake, and goes
up beside the eastern inlet stream to the elbow of this stream and
fords it. Shortly beyond, our route meets and follows the south
fork of the east inlet stream to Medley Lakes. This cross-country
route crosses steep, glacially smoothed granite that is interspersed with grassy, wildflower-colored pockets, and arrives at
the narrow, barren unnamed lake that lies at the head of this
stream fork. Along with the rarified air of the climb (crossing the
12,000′ level) the route brings fine views of Mts. Senger, Hooper
and Seven Gables. A rest break is probably in order before beginning the final flower-lined ascent to the obvious saddle on the
northeast horizon. The climb begins easily, soon becomes steep,
and concludes with a scramble to the crest.

At this saddle, one has unmatched views to the east. Besides the immediate summits of Seven Gables and the twin spires of Gemini, one can see Mts. Hilgard, Abbot, Gabb, Dade, Bear Creek Spire, Julius Caesar, Royce and Humphreys. Every one of these peaks towers over 13,000 feet. Also from this saddle, one can pick out the natural route to the southernmost of the Seven Gables Lakes. Though steep, this descent is made mostly over glacially smoothed rock. Route-picking, however, is sometimes made difficult by interruptions of talus and scree slides.

The upper lakes of the Seven Gables chain are talus-bound, shallow bodies of water having no fish, but anglers will want to try the good fishing on the lower lakes (golden trout to 12″) before making the final ascent to Vee Lake. These lower lakes and the intersecting stream are a fly fisherman's paradise. The ascent to Vee Lake is made over granite and talus along the outlet stream from that lake. The ascent terminates at the turfy east end (11,120′), where there are fair campsites. Hikers who do not care for the high, alpine kind of camping should plan on ending their day at the lowest of the Seven Gables Lakes, where there are several good campsites. Fishing on large Vee Lake (50 acres) is good to excellent for golden (to 16″). Views from the campsites on the east and north sides of the lake are excellent of the striking, white-granite faces of Royce and Merriam peaks.

4th Hiking Day (**Vee Lake** to **Lake Italy,** 5 miles cross country): Beginning at the north side of the north arm of Vee Lake, this hiking day's route ascends the granite shoulder to the string of rockbound tarns just south of Little Bear Lake. This moderate ascent is accomplished over a granite ledge system broken by talus. Fishing on tiny Little Bear Lake for golden is fair to good, and this evaluation holds for Big Bear and White Bear lakes upstream. Following the inlet stream of Little Bear Lake, the route ascends to the outlet of Big Bear, Ursa, Bearpaw Lake basin, crosses the stream joining Big Bear and White Bear lakes, and ascends steeply along the eastern side of this stream. Above the abrupt northeast side of White Bear Lake one can make out the obvious saddle that separates the drainage of the East Fork of Bear Creek from that of Hilgard Branch. Our route crosses this saddle, traverses the southeast end of the Jumble Lake cirque, and strikes the Italy Pass Trail, where it turns left.

The saddle and the traverse offer unusual end-on views of Mts. Julius Caesar, Dade, Abbot, Mills and Bear Creek Spire. Descending the moderate-to-steep slopes above Jumble Lake, one cannot help feeling awed by the forces that carved this basin. The smoothed rock is mute testimony to the grinding action of the glaciers that found their start here, and, as the trail continues to descend along the north shore of Jumble Lake, one pursues the course of the glacier as it forged its way into the much larger Lake Italy cirque. This descent fords the stream that joins Jumble Lake and Lake Italy, and drops down to the shores of the lake about a mile above the outlet (11,150'). This very large lake (124 acres) is granite-enclosed, with narrow, meadowed fringes. Fair campsites that are quite exposed can be found along the south shore near the outlet, and there are superlative views of the surrounding peaks. Fishing for golden (8-12″) is fair.

5th, 6th and 7th Hiking Days: Reverse the steps of trip 4, 18½ miles.

Douglas phlox

Jeff Schaffer

10   Bear Dam Junction to Second Recess

TRIP From Bear Dam Junction to Second Recess via Hilgard Branch, Lake Italy, cross-country route to Lower Mills Creek Lake, Second Recess, return via Fish Camp, Quail Meadows (semiloop trip). Topo map *Mt. Abbot*. Best late season; 48½ miles.

Grade	Trail/layover days	Total recommended days
Leisurely	9/3	11
Moderate	7/2	9
Strenuous	5/2	7

HILITES Another fine cross-country route, this trip is frequently used by climbers making ascents of the cluster of peaks that line the route. Anglers, photographers, naturalists and garden-variety trailpounders will all find something to excite them en route. Because of the cross country, this route is recommended for intermediate and experienced knapsackers only.

DESCRIPTION (Moderate trip)

1st, 2nd and 3rd Hiking Days: Follow trip 4 to **Lake Italy,** 18½ miles.

4th Hiking Day (**Lake Italy** to **Lower Mills Creek Lake,** 5 miles cross country): This scenic cross-country route rounds the granite-bound north side of Lake Italy to Toe Lake, and then ascends the increasingly steep north cirque wall to 12,250-foot Gabbot Pass (the saddle between Mt. Gabb and Mt. Abbot). The ascent involves a strenuous workout, but does not require rock-climbing skills. As a reward, the hiker acquires some of the finest views obtainable in this part of the Sierra. This route is generally considered a climber's access route for ascents of Mts. Gabb and Abbot, and is seldom used by casual hikers. Parts of it are slippery in early summer. Peaks in line of sight during the ascent and at the pass include, to the west, Mts. Hilgard and Gabb; to the south, Mt. Julius Caesar and Royce Peak; to the east, Mts. Dade, Abbot and Mills, and Bear Creek Spire; and to the north, the crest of the Silver Divide.

From the pass, this ducked route descends just east of the Mt. Gabb glacier to the steep headwall of the Upper Mills Creek Lake cirque. Traversing the east side of this cirque, the route becomes a trail as it continues down the east side of the cascading creek between the lakes to the good campsites at the timberlined outlet of Lower Mills Creek Lake (10,840'), an outstandingly pretty lake. Both Upper and Lower Mills Creek lakes are meadow-fringed, though mostly rockbound, and offer good-to-excellent golden fishing (to 13"). Views from the campsites are excellent of the Mono and Silver divides.

5th Hiking Day (**Lower Mills Creek Lake** to **Quail Meadows,** 9½ miles): Staying on the east side of Mills Creek, a faint fisherman's trail descends the sparsely timbered slopes below Lower Mills Creek Lake past two small lakelets (good fishing for golden to 10"). At the final drop into Second Recess Creek canyon, this faint, often washed-out trail switchbacks down steeply to the confluence of the two creeks. The forest cover alters during the course of this descent from stunted lodgepole and some whitebark to flat-needled fir, lodgepole pine, and occasional quaking aspen and Jeffrey pine. This route, now following a distinct trail, descends on a moderate slope along the east side of Second Recess Creek. As one nears the brink of Mono Creek canyon one gets a clear picture of the glacial story that left these spectacular landforms. It is evident that the valley of the Second Recess was a secondary (or feeder) arm of the greater ice mass that once filled the deeper Mono Creek canyon. After accomplishing the moderate-to-steep descent to the log crossing of Mono Creek, the traveler can look back whence he came and fully understand the nature of the geologic term "hanging valley." The greater ice mass of the main trunk ground deeper, leaving these valleys literally hanging.

At Fish Camp this route passes several improved packer camp-sites and turns left (west) onto the Mono Creek Trail. This creek-side trail descends moderately, offering between-the-trees views into First Recess, and of the abrupt, dark, north face of Volcanic Knob. Frequent groves of quaking aspen line this route, and late season sees the banks of Mono Creek clad in golden hues. In mid-summer one may sample the odor of the highly fragrant Kelley's lily. At the point where the canyon walls appear to be closing in, about 3 miles below Fish Camp, the trail veers away from the creek on a steep, switchbacking ascent that crosses the long-nosed ridge that separates the North Fork from the main canyon of Mono Creek. On the west side of this ridge, our route descends a short distance to the John Muir Trail junction, and turns left along the east side of the North Fork of Mono Creek. The trail then switchbacks down steeply to ford the North Fork a few yards above its confluence with the main stream. From this ford it is less than a mile of relatively level going through a dense lodgepole forest cover to the good campsites above Quail Meadows (7760'). Here fishing for brook and some golden (to 14") is good.

6 and 7th Hiking Days: Reverse the 2nd and 1st hiking days, trip 3, 15½ miles.

Running Mono Creek below Quail Meadows   *Jeff Schaffer*

Mosquito Flat to Second Recess   **11**

TRIP From Mosquito Flat (Rock Creek) to Second Recess via Mono Pass (round trip). Topo maps *Mt. Tom, Mt. Abbot.* Best mid or late season; 32 miles.

Grade	Trail/layover days	Total recommended days
Leisurely	6/2	8
Moderate	5/2	7
Strenuous	4/2	6

HILITES The exciting eastern escarpment makes the first part of this trip a memorable experience. The trail to Mono Pass offers sweeping vistas that vie for the traveler's consideration with the intimacy of the beautiful, cirque-bound lakes of Second Recess.

DESCRIPTION (Leisurely trip)

1st Hiking Day (**Mosquito Flat** to **Ruby Lake,** 2½ miles): The magnificent Sierra crest confronts the traveler at the very outset of this trip. From the trailhead at Mosquito Flat (10,300′) the wide, rocky-sandy trail starts southwest toward the imposing skyline dominated by Mts. Mills, Abbot and Dade and Bear Creek Spire. A short distance from the trailhead, our route tops a low rocky ridge just west of Mack Lake. From this ridge one has good views of the green-clad Little Lakes Valley, and cannot help but feel a sense of satisfaction that this beautiful valley enjoys protection as part of the John Muir Wilderness. Aside from some early, abortive mining ventures, this region remains relatively unspoiled. The trail crosses the ridge and in a short distance meets the junction of the Little Lakes Valley Trail.

Here our route branches right (west) and ascends steeply over rocky switchbacks. In the course of this switchbacking ascent, the traveler will see the moderate-to-dense forest cover of whitebark and lodgepole diminish in density as we near timberline. Views during the climb include the glacier-fronted peaks named above, and, midway up the ascent, Mt. Morgan. Immediately below to the east, the deep blue of Heart and Box lakes and some of the Hidden Lakes reflects the sky above, and the viewer looking at the panorama of the valley can readily trace the glacial history that left these "puddles" behind.

Near the meadowed edge of the outlet stream from Ruby Lake is a junction, where we turn left. It becomes apparent that a cirque basin is opening up, although one cannot see Ruby Lake, which completely fills the cirque bottom, until one is actually at water's edge (11,000'). This first breathtaking view of the lake and its towering cirque walls makes the climb worth the effort. Sheer granite makes up the upper walls of the cirque, and the crown is topped by a series of spectacular pinnacles, particularly to the west. To the north, also on the crest, a notch indicates Mono Pass, and close scrutiny will reveal the switchbacking trail that ascends the south ridge of Mt. Starr. The lower walls of the cirque are mostly made up of talus and scree that curve outward to the lake's edge, and it is over this jumbled rock that ambitious anglers must scramble to sample the fair fishing for brook, rainbow and brown (to 12"). Good campsites can be found below the outlet of the lake. Lakeside campsites are exposed and usually windy.

2nd Hiking Day (**Ruby Lake** to **Fish Camp,** 9 miles): First retrace your steps ¼ mile to the Mono Pass Trail. Following a general east-to-west course, the trail climbs by long, steady switchbacks up the north wall of the cirque, and after a long steady traverse veers northward by steeper switchbacks to the summit of Mono Pass (12,000'). The best views from the pass area are obtained by climbing the easy granite shoulder of Mt. Starr, to the east. Views from this shoulder include: Mts. Stanford, Huntington, Crocker and Hopkins and Red and White Mountain to the north; and Mts. Abbot and Dade, Bear Creek Spire, and Mt. Humphreys to the south.

The trail continues north from the pass, descending steadily over granite. It traverses the west side of rockbound Summit Lake (poor fishing), and then descends more steeply to the slopes above Trail Lakes (poor-to-fair brook fishing). The westerly descent around Trail Lakes turns northward, and the trail drops to the Golden Creek ford. Here, this route re-enters forest cover (moderate stands of lodgepole), and it continues to descend as it passes by the lateral to Pioneer Basin and the lateral to Fourth Recess Lake. Serious anglers may wish to alter their hiking plan with a rewarding excursion to the excellent brook (some rainbow and golden) fishing obtainable at the lower Pioneer lakes. Fishing at nearby Fourth Recess Lake is good for brook (to 14"). Beyond these laterals, the trail fords the outlet streams from Pioneer Basin.

Mono Rock towers on the left as our route passes the Third Recess Trail lateral, and, about a mile farther, the lateral to Hopkins Lakes and Hopkins Pass. Anglers who wish to sample the good fishing for brook, rainbow and occasional golden will find many fine, deep holes along this stretch of trail. For the most part, Mono Creek rushes along briskly, but occasional potholes and level stretches in the stream bed contribute to the good spawning areas that any good Sierra trout stream requires. Anglers and hikers alike will appreciate the colorful abundance of quaking aspens that line Mono Creek. For those with color film in their cameras, the best time to capture the aspen color is usually late September or early October. This route then passes the Grinnell Lakes lateral, and descends to the good improved campsites on both sides of the log spanning Mono Creek at Fish Camp (8550').

3rd Hiking Day (**Fish Camp** to **Lower Mills Creek Lake,** 4½ miles): Retrace the steps of part of the 5th hiking day, trip 10.

4th, 5th and 6th Hiking Days: Retrace your steps, 16 miles.

Bear Creek Spire   *Thomas Winnett*

12   Pine Creek Roadend to Honeymoon Lake

TRIP From Pine Creek Roadend to Honeymoon Lake (round trip). Topo map *Mt. Tom.* Best midseason; 11 miles.

Grade	Trail/layover days	Total recom- mended days
Leisurely	2/2	4
Moderate	2/0	2
Strenuous	....	....

HILITES The steep, winding ascent to Honeymoon Lake offers breathtaking over-the-shoulder views of the Pine Creek watershed, and the Honeymoon Lake campsite views of the Sierra crest make this one of the best choices for a base camp location on the east side of the Sierra.

DESCRIPTION (Leisurely trip)

1st Hiking Day (**Pine Creek Roadend** to **Honeymoon Lake,** 5½ miles): The trailhead (7400') is located at the pack station just south of Pine Creek. The dusty duff trail ascends gently from the pack station through a dense, mixed forest cover of Jeffrey pine, juniper, red fir, quaking aspen, and birch, and fords several branchlets of an unnamed creek that feeds Pine Creek. These fords are decorated by blossoms of wild rose, dogwood, columbine, tiger lily and Queen Anne's lace. A few yards beyond these fords, the trail emerges from the forest cover, directly opposite the Union Carbide tungsten mill, and then merges with a recently rebuilt mining road. This tortuously twisted, rocky road is used for access to the Brownstone Mine, where new drilling was commenced in 1974. Although the slope into the Pine Creek canyon is steep, the road's grade is, for the most part, moderate, and this segment is simply a matter of slog-and-pant. Two welcome streams break the monotony of the climb, and the view (despite the ugly tramway that scars Morgan Creek) is spectacular. Through the Pine Creek valley that slopes away to the northeast, one can look across the Owens River drainage to the volcanic tableland and White Mountain (14,242') on the skyline.

The road ends just above the clapboard and corrugated shacks marking the Brownstone Mine.

There is one advantage to the presence of the mining activities in this canyon—and that is the dramatic contrast between industrial and recreational use of wilderness country. Coincident to this is the contrasting tempi of the lower and upper parts of the valley. One has only to watch the juggernaut flow of the tramway buckets and the antlike scurrying of trucks and people across the way to fully appreciate the slow, peaceful pace of the wilderness traveler. From the mine, the trail ascends over talus and scree by short, steep switchbacks. The trees along this ascent include juniper, limber pine and lodgepole pine. The juniper have left beautiful, weathered snags of a dramatic golden hue that are a constant delight to color photographers.

With the steepest part of the ascent behind, the trail fords another unnamed tributary and veers north to join Pine Creek just below Pine Lake. Here, the creek alternates cascades, falls and chutes in a riot of white water. The trail fords the stream, and amidst a moderate forest cover of lodgepole arrives at the northeast end of Pine Lake. This medium-sized lake (16 acres) is a popular overnight camping place (campsites along the northeast shore), and fishermen may wish to tarry here to sample the fair brook (to 12″), but fishing is generally better at Upper Pine Lake.

The trail to Upper Pine Lake proceeds by skirting the rocky northwest side of Pine Lake and ascending the sometimes marshy section that crosses the seepage flow from Birchim Lake. Leveling out, the trail parallels the outlet stream from Upper Pine Lake (excellent campsites) and arrives at the west side of the lake (10,200'). Anglers will find that brook and rainbow (to 12″) frequent these waters, and angling is good. At the southwest inlet, the trail ascends moderately, crosses the muddy, boggy, multibranched inlet stream, and presently arrives at the Pine Creek Pass/Italy Pass Trail junction. Our route turns right, away from the Pine Creek Pass Trail and onto the Italy Pass Trail, and ascends to the rockbound shores of Honeymoon Lake (10,440'). This moderate-sized lake (10 acres) has good campsites near the outlet stream, and excellent meadowed sites above the head of the waterfall on the inlet stream on the west side. Fishing for brook and rainbow (to 10″) is good. This lovely lake makes an excellent base camp for side excursions to 40 surrounding lakes in four drainages, or for climbing of five nearby peaks that exceed 13,000' in elevation.

2nd Hiking Day: Retrace your steps, 5½ miles.

13   Pine Creek Roadend to Moon Lake

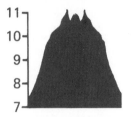

TRIP
From Pine Creek Roadend to Moon Lake via Pine Creek Pass (round trip). Topo map *Mt. Tom.* Best midseason; 20 miles.

Grade	Trail/layover days	Total recom- mended days
Leisurely	4/1	5
Moderate	3/1	4
Strenuous	2/1	3

HILITES
The juggernaut tramways and snarling trucks that surround the trailhead belie the primitive country that lies beyond the first climb. Pine Creek, from its lower aspen-clad banks to its tundra-meadow birthplace, is a kind of stream that hiker, angler, photographer and naturalist can take a fancy to. At Moon Lake the visitor will experience memorable open, alpine surroundings at their finest.

DESCRIPTION (Leisurely trip)

1st Hiking Day (**Pine Creek Roadend** to **Upper Pine Lake,** 5 miles): Follow most of the 1st hiking day, trip 12.

2nd Hiking Day (**Upper Pine Lake** to **Moon Lake,** 5 miles): From the junction of the Italy Pass and Pine Creek Pass trails, our route bears left on a steady ascent toward Pine Creek Pass. Originally a Mono Indian trading route, this trail and pass have been used by man for almost five hundred years. The moderate forest cover of lodgepole thins as the trail climbs, and soon emerges above timberline. Tiny, emerald-green, subalpine meadows break the long granite slabs, and wildflower fanciers will find clumps of color that include wallflower, shooting star, penstemon, lupine, primrose, and yellow columbine. The trail parallels a seepage making up the headwaters of Pine Creek as it ascends a long swale between two white granite walls, and then makes the final steep rocky climb to Pine Creek Pass (11,100'). From the vicinity of the pass, one has excellent views to the north of Mt. Julius Caesar (with Bear Creek Spire protruding over the right shoulder); to the northwest of Merriam and Royce peaks; to the south of Pilot Knob, Glacier Divide, and parts of the great Humphreys Basin; and to the southeast of Four Gables and Mt. Humphreys. This pass marks the division between the east and west drainage flows at the Sierra crest. The trail to French Canyon then descends steeply to a long, fairly level, rocky bench, and then drops again over talus and slab ledges for about ¼ mile, to meet the signed trail branching left to Elba and Moon lakes.

Our route leaves the main trail, following this fisherman's trail as it ascends the fairly steep south wall of French Canyon. This 400-foot climb brings one to fair-sized Elba Lake (unnamed on the topo map). Typical of these high, montane lakes, Elba seems virtually devoid of vegetation and life. It is understandable that the first-time visitor to this country often refers to it as "moon country," but those who come to know and love the high country soon discover the beauty that hides close beneath the sterile veneer. Spots of green between the tumbled talus blocks indicate grassy tundra patches or clumps of willows, and occasionally the weathered landscape is broken by a dwarfed lodgepole or whitebark pine. Steady, silent scrutiny will usually discover movement that indicates life. A bird is usually the first to be detected, and most likely it will be either a rosy finch or a hummingbird. Four-footed movement among the rocks is most likely a cony or a marmot, or it just might be a wolverine or a bushy-tailed wood rat. Fishermen will soon find life in the lake, for Elba Lake has a good population of golden and golden hybrids (to 12″). Following the inlet stream, our route then ascends steadily to larger Moon Lake (10,998'). Fair campsites can be found along the southeast side of the lake. Fishing for golden (to 12″) is excellent, and, using Moon Lake as a base, anglers can explore eight more fishing lakes sharing this same bench system.

3rd and 4th Hiking Days: Retrace your steps, 10 miles.

14 Pine Creek Roadend to Bear Dam Junction

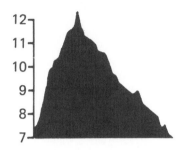

TRIP   From Pine Creek Roadend to Bear Dam Junction via
             Honeymoon Lake, Italy Pass, (shuttle trip). Topo
             maps *Mt. Tom, Mt. Abbot.* Best mid or late season; 30
             miles.

Grade	Trail/layover days	Total recom- mended days
Leisurely	5/2	7
Moderate	4/1	5
Strenuous	3/1	4

HILITES This is one of the best and shortest routes for an am-
             bitious intermediate desiring to get the "feel" of a
             trans-Sierra crossing, for the route embraces the
             steep eastern escarpment; the barren, glaciated
             granite of the Sierra crest; and the long, densely
             wooded slopes of the west side.

DESCRIPTION (Leisurely trip)

1st Hiking Day: Follow trip 12 to **Honeymoon Lake,** 5½ miles.

2nd Hiking Day (**Honeymoon Lake** to **Lake Italy,** 6 miles): The faint
trail from Honeymoon Lake ascends steadily along the north side
of the North Fork of Pine Creek through thinning lodgepole
forest, and emerges on a rocky ridge dividing two lake basins
composing the headwaters of Pine Creek. On the right, to the
north, Chalfant Lakes (fair fishing for rainbow to 10″) sparkle at
the foot of Mt. Julius Caesar. On the left, the Granite Park lakes
invite one to make little cross-country detours. Scooped, scoured
and scarped by a river of ice, the granite of the upper cirque was
left massive and smooth. Subsequent prying by expanding ice
widened tiny crevices until chunks of granite broke loose and
tumbled to the foot of the slope. Talus slopes born of this ice ero-

sion are added to each year, and the occasional passerby who witnesses the thunderous crash of a large slab of freed granite can count himself lucky. Among large boulders, across talus, and along smoothed granite this trail—scarcely more than a ducked route except in its steeper parts—ascends steadily to the east side of the uppermost lake in the Granite Park chain. From this lake, the route ascends steeply on short switchbacks to Italy Pass (12,300'). Views from this notch are dominated by massive Mt. Julius Caesar immediately to the northeast, but there is an excellent view back to the east of an unusual, unnamed chocolate-layer-cake peak (so typified because of the light dikes striating the mountain face) just east of Chalfant Lakes.

From the pass, the ducked, faint trail descends steeply into the Jumble Lake basin, traverses the north slope above the lake, and then drops over the lip of the hanging valley into the Lake Italy basin. This large lake (124 acres) lies at the foot of seven of the highest peaks in the Sierra. It was named Lake Italy by the USGS in about 1907 because of its resemblance to that country in shape. Our descending route fords the outlet stream from Jumble Lake, strikes the "Italy" profile just above the "heel," and then parallels the south shore to the fair campsites there and at the outlet. Although the population of golden trout is somewhat depleted, their size (sometimes up to 12") makes this a fair lake for angling.

3rd, 4th and 5th Hiking Days: Reverse the steps of trip 4, 18½ miles.

Chalfant Lakes, Mt. Tom   *Thomas Winnett*

15 Pine Creek Roadend to Sandpiper Lake

TRIP   From Pine Creek Roadend to Sandpiper Lake via Honeymoon Lake, Italy Pass, Sandpiper Lake, Selden Pass, Hutchinson Meadow, French Canyon, Pine Creek Pass (loop trip). Topo maps *Mt. Tom, Mt. Abbot, Blackcap Mountain.* Best mid or late season, 53½ miles.

Grade	Trail/layover days	Total recommended days
Leisurely	9/2	11
Moderate	7/2	9
Strenuous	5/2	7

HILITES   The intermediate trail traveler (or the ambitious beginner) will find this long trip a rewarding choice. After leaving beautiful Pine Creek, this trail route tours Granite Basin and Italy Pass, and then joins the John Muir Trail. Traveling south, this singular trail crosses Selden Pass, and ascends the South Fork of the San Joaquin River watershed. Leaving the Muir Trail at Piute Creek, this route then loops back to rejoin the Pine Creek Trail via Pine Creek Pass.

DESCRIPTION (Moderate trip)

1st and 2nd Hiking Days: Follow trip 14 to **Lake Italy,** 11½ miles.

3rd Hiking Day (**Lake Italy** to **Sandpiper Lake,** 11½ miles): The trail descends along the east bank of Hilgard Branch past the low ridge behind which lie Teddy Bear and Brown Bear lakes (fair fishing for golden to 12″) and then switchbacks down steeply to a ford of the creek. Then the trail levels out as it winds through a sparse forest cover of lodgepole. About a mile farther, it descends steeply once more, via rocky switchbacks, and after losing 500 feet levels out. The loss of altitude brings an increase in density of the forest cover—mostly lodgepole—and the individual trees no longer appear gnarled and stunted. The route then fords the outlet stream draining Hilgard Lake, and presently we make a final switchbacking drop into the main canyon of Bear Creek. Here we turn right on the Muir Trail and follow the second part of the 2nd hiking day, trip 6.

4th Hiking Day (**Sandpiper Lake** to lower **Sally Keyes Lakes,** 5 miles): Follow the first part of the 3rd hiking day, trip 8.

5th Hiking Day (**Lower Sally Keyes Lake** to **Hutchinson Meadow,** 12½ miles): An early start for this hiking day is advisable in order to complete the long, sometimes steep, always dusty descent into the South Fork of the San Joaquin River drainage. From Sally Keyes Lakes (10,200'), the duff trail descends through heavy stands of lodgepole interspersed with tiny meadows. Colorful wildflowers, often in patches, dot this stretch of trail: Indian paintbrush, Douglas phlox, shooting star, yellow and white cinquefoil, penstemon, lupine, red heather, western wallflower, buckwheat, and western mountain aster. This route passes the (faint) first of two trail laterals to Blaney Meadows, swings eastward, and crosses two terminal moraine ridges. The sometimes rocky trail then descends to ford Senger Creek in a lovely forested flat, where it leaves the heavy concentrations of lodgepole behind. Alternately steep and moderate descents characterize the southeastward course of the trail, and the traveler soon finds that he is entering a drier area of manzanita and fractured granite. Views are excellent to the south and west of the resistant granite slopes of Mt. Shinn and Ward Mountain. To the southeast, the skylined peaks of the LeConte Divide and Emerald Peak dominate the view until the trail passes the second lateral to Blaney Meadows, where it makes the final descent to the junction with the main Florence Lake Trail. A prelunch swim in the nice holes on the South Fork of the San Joaquin River to the west of the junction is in order, and fishermen will find fair fishing for brook in the same vicinity. Several fair-to-good primitive campsites and one packer campsite are near the junction.

From this junction, our route continues east on a duff and granite sand trail through a mixed forest cover of Jeffrey pine and juniper interspersed with occasional red and white fir. The trail crosses an easy series of ridges and descends past several good campsites to the Piute Canyon Trail junction, where our route branches left, away from the John Muir Trail. Sporadic appearances of quaking aspen (in the wetter spots) line this rocky ascent up Piute canyon. The trail keeps to the west side of briskly flowing Piute Creek, and fords the multibranched Turret Creek. This climbing, rocky trail affords excellent views of highly fractured Pavilion Dome and the surrounding, unnamed domes composing the west end of Glacier Divide. The trail then swings easterly through a narrowing canyon, fords tiny West Pinnacles Creek, and pursues a rocky course until it enters a moderate lodgepole forest cover before reaching the East Pinnacles Creek ford. Views of the cascading tributary streams are frequent along this trail section. From the ford, the trail ascends gently to beautiful Hutchinson Meadow (9439'), where travelers will find excellent campsites near the Pine Creek Pass Trail junction. Fishing for golden and brook is good-to-excellent (to 9"). The lovely meadow setting provides excellent campsite views of several granite peaks (Pilot Knob and Peak 12432) to the east and west, and of the lower south slope of Merriam Peak to the north.

6th Hiking Day (**Hutchinson Meadow** to **Upper Pine Lake**, 8 miles): This hiking day's route leaves the Piute Pass Trail and ascends moderately up French Canyon. Rocky stretches alternate with the soft underfooting of grassy sections. Fishing along these upper reaches of French Canyon Creek is good to excellent, despite the diminishing size of the stream. The trail crosses several unnamed tributaries draining the east and west slopes of Royce and Merriam peaks, and soon climbs above timberline. The character of the canyon walls reflects the increase in altitude. Barren granite, mostly white and heavily fractured, scoops away to the east, making a broad-headed, typical cirque basin. The footing becomes very rocky as the trail passes the faint fisherman's trail to Moon Lake, and then veers northerly, climbs steeply, and crosses a long granite bench. From the bench, it is but a short, easy climb to the summit of Pine Creek Pass, where there are excellent views to the north of Mt. Julius Caesar and the tip of Bear Creek Spire.

Directly ahead, the trail descends a long, talus-ridden swale. This descent soon enters a sparse forest cover of lodgepole, winding between large slabs of granite. Tiny subalpine meadows fill the gaps in the rock, and the traveler is sure to encounter western wallflower, shooting star, penstemon, lupine, primrose, and yellow columbine. The trail veers away from the trickling Pine Creek seepage, crosses a slight rise, and then drops to the hard-to-see junction with the Italy Pass Trail. Our route keeps to the right, fords the North Fork of Pine Creek just above the cascading inlet to Upper Pine Lake, and arrives at the excellent campsites along the west side of the lake and below the outlet (10,200'). Good fishing for brook, rainbow, and some golden (to 12") can be had on Upper Pine Lake.

7th Hiking Day: (**Upper Pine Lake** to **Pine Creek Roadend**, 5 miles): Retrace most of the steps of the 1st hiking day, trip 12.

North Lake to Piute Lake   **16**

TRIP   From North Lake to Piute Lake (round trip). Topo
map *Mt. Goddard.* Best mid or late season; 7 miles.

Grade	Trail/layover days	Total recom- mended days
Leisurely	2/0	2
Moderate	....	....
Strenuous	....	....

HILITES   This trip offers an easy walk into the high country
and a lake with large trout. It is an excellent choice
for beginning knapsackers who want to sample the
high country with a modest effort.

DESCRIPTION (Leisurely trip)

1st Hiking Day: (**North Lake** to **Piute Lake,** 3½ miles): Shortly after
leaving the trailhead (9360'), this route enters the John Muir
Wilderness and then ascends gently along slopes dotted with
meadowy patches, aspen groves and stands of lodgepole pine. In
season the traveler will find a wealth of wildflowers in these little
meadows and in the sandy patches among the granite slabs, including: paintbrush, columbine, tiger lily, spiraea and penstemon. After the trail fords the North Fork of Bishop Creek several
times, the ascent becomes moderate. Aspen is left behind, the
lodgepole becomes sparse, and some limber pine is seen. The
glaciated canyon is flanked by slab-topped Peak 12707 on the
south and rust-colored, 13,225-foot Mt. Emerson on the north.
The newcomer to the High Sierra will marvel at how the great
granite slabs maintain their precarious perches atop Peak 12707,
seeming to be almost vertically above him. But they all topple
eventually, due to the action of frost wedging, and add to the piles
of talus at the foot of the peak. Approaching Loch Leven Lake, the
trail levels off, and the angler may wish to try the lake waters for
rainbow and brown trout (to 10"). The trail then ascends moderately again, through a cover of sparse lodgepole and whitebark,
winds among large, rounded boulders, and skirts a small lake
before arriving at the next bench up the canyon, which contains
this day's destination, Piute Lake (10,950'). The traveler may

wish to consider the wind in selecting a campsite, as it often blows stiffly in this Piute Pass country. There are good campsites on the north side close to the water. Fishing for brook and rainbow is fair (to 18″). Those who would go out of their way to find seclusion may elect to scramble southeast up a fairly steep slope to granite-bound Emerson Lake.

2nd Hiking Day: Retrace your steps, 3½ miles.

Mt. Humphreys   *E.P. Pister*

North Lake to Hutchinson Meadow   **17**

TRIP From North Lake to Hutchinson Meadow via Piute Lake, Piute Pass (round trip). Topo maps *Mt. Goddard, Mt. Tom, Mt. Abbot*. Best mid or late season; 22 miles.

Grade	Trail/layover days	Total recom- mended days
Leisurely	4/1	5
Moderate	3/1	4
Strenuous	2/0	2

HILITES Hutchinson Meadow is one of the finest in the High Sierra, and the trail to it beside Piute Creek takes the traveler through several miles of wild mountain "lawns" and gardens, where Sierra wildflowers are at their best. Add the views of Mt. Humphreys and the spectacular Glacier Divide, and this trip becomes one of the most scenic in all the Sierra. Yet the Humphreys Basin is equally famous for its golden trout.

DESCRIPTION (Moderate trip)

1st Hiking Day: Follow trip 16 to **Piute Lake,** 3½ miles.

2nd Hiking Day: (**Piute Lake** to **Hutchinson Meadow,** 7½ miles): The trail ascends an open, rocky slope to timberline, and switchbacks up to the last traverse before Piute Pass (11,423′). Here the traveler in midsummer will probably pass through a "road cut" in a snowbank, created by packers using sand and shovels. At the pass there are grand views west to the canyon of the South Fork San Joaquin River, south to Glacier Divide (the north boundary of King's Canyon National Park) and north to Mt. Humphreys, highest peak this far north in the Sierra. (If it could acquire 14 feet from somewhere, Bishop residents would have their own 14,000-foot Sierra peak.) The rocky trail descends moderately to Summit Lake, and levels off as it fords a stream and enters the great, high lake bowl called Humphreys Basin, which contains 31 lakes that have golden trout. The sandy trail contours through alpine grasses and then descends to ford the outlet stream of Big and Little Desolation lakes. There is good fishing in Big Desolation for golden to 20", reached by going 2 miles north on the trail that turns right from our route shortly after this ford. Or the angler may wish to sample the waters of Golden Trout Lake, just south of the trail, for the fair fishing for golden (to 10"). About ¼ mile before Golden Trout Lake the trail forks. The newer trail, to the right, is not shown on the topo map. Either one will take you to Hutchinson Meadow. Entering timber, the route begins a moderate descent on a rocky trail through sparse lodgepole which soon becomes moderate. Breaks in the timber cover afford views of the residual glaciers that give the Glacier Divide its name.

About 4 miles from Piute Pass the display of flower-studded green "lawns" begins, and from here to Hutchinson Meadow the traveler is seldom out of sight of these subalpine gardens. The amateur botanist will discern paintbrush, shooting star, fleabane, swamp onion, red mountain heather, buttercup, cinquefoil, penstemon, buckwheat, yarrow milfoil, groundsel and Douglas phlox, along with Labrador tea, lemon willow and alpine willow. Rollicking Piute Creek is always close at hand, lending its music to complete this scene of mountain beauty. The trail levels out and fords the distributaries of French Canyon Creek, arriving at the good campsites at Hutchinson Meadow (9439'). Here beneath Pilot Knob and Peak 12432 the angler will find the riffles of Piute Creek good to excellent fishing for brook and some golden (to 9"), or he may cautiously approach the little pools on the distributaries of French Canyon Creek, which spread out through the east side of the meadow and offer equally good fishing.

3rd Hiking Day: Retrace your steps, 11 miles.

Aspen trees   *Don Denison*

North Lake to Florence Lake **18**

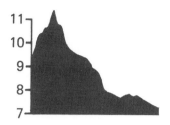

TRIP   From North Lake to Florence Lake via Piute Lake, Piute Pass, Hutchinson Meadow, Lower Blaney Meadows (shuttle trip). Topo maps *Mt. Abbot, Blackcap Mountain, Mt. Tom, Mt. Goddard*. Best mid or late season; 27½ miles.

Grade	Trail/layover days	Total recommended days
Leisurely	4/1	5
Moderate	3/1	4
Strenuous	3/0	3

HILITES   Following an old Indian trade route, this trip tours nearly every life zone and type of forest belt found in the Sierra. Well suited to foot or stock travel, the trail crosses Piute Pass and descends the west slopes via the San Joaquin drainage. Good angling in the Humphreys Basin waters, fine views of the Sierra crest and Glacier Divide, and well-maintained trails make this a good, solid beginner's trip.

DESCRIPTION (Leisurely trip)

1st and 2nd Hiking Day: Follow trip 17 to **Hutchinson Meadow,** 11 miles.

3rd Hiking Day: (**Hutchinson Meadow** to **Lower Blaney Meadows,** 9 miles): Staying on the north side of Piute Creek, the alternately duff and rocky trail descends gently through a moderate forest cover of lodgepole. After the easy ford of East Pinnacles Creek, the timber thins, and the precipitous valley walls begin to close in. There are excellent views of the cascading tributaries, and the green rock around Pavilion Dome in the southwest is but one of many beautiful parts of these canyon walls. Meadowy patches of grass lace the rockier sections of trail, and it drops over a moderate slope to a tiny lakelet that interrupts the brisk, bouncing flow of Piute Creek. Although the fish are somewhat smaller than in the lakes passed on the 2nd hiking day, they are plentiful, and anglers may wish to sample some of these pan-sized golden.

Our route then swings westerly to ford West Pinnacles Creek, and southerly as it approaches the ford of multibranched Turret Creek. Crossing the easy granite nose protruding from the west wall of the canyon, the trail descends over steep and then moderate slopes to the junction with the John Muir Trail. Our route turns right (west), and undulates via rocky trail down the South Fork San Joaquin River drainage. The mostly sparse forest cover has changed from a predominance of lodgepole to Jeffrey, juniper, some red and white fir, and the seepage-loving quaking aspen. The underfooting of this trail exhibits the effects of both chemical and physical weathering of the granite walls, with its deep pockets of heavy, coarse quartz sand. Where this sand has mixed with alluvial deposits, trees and shrubs have taken root, and along these stretches the ground is frequently carpeted with a shallow layer of duff.

The trail junction where our route leaves the John Muir Trail, keeping to the left, makes an excellent lunch or swimming stop. However, those desiring their water on the warmer side can wait until they reach the public hot springs 2 miles down the trail. In a forest cover that has become heavy, the trail from the junction continues by a series of moderate ups and downs past a second short lateral (ascending northward to join the John Muir Trail) to the Hot Springs campground. Here, a signed trail leads off to the left to the public hot springs less than ¼ mile away (via a wide, fast-water ford). A few yards beyond the campground, the trail meets the fenced boundary of the Diamond D Guest Ranch. Several of the outbuildings of this commercial establishment are in view as the trail skirts the boundaries and fords the noisy branchlets of Senger Creek. The heavy traffic (both stock and mechanical conveyance) that is the spoor of the guest ranch upstream interrupts the primitive appeal of the subsequent trail.

Our route winds through the heavy forest cover surrounding Blaney Meadows, and strikes the Sally Keyes "short-cut trail," then continues past this trail and around the fringes of the meadow to the fair campsites at Lower Blaney Meadows (7650'). Fishing for brook and some rainbow is fair to good (mostly downstream).

4th Hiking Day: (**Lower Blaney Meadows** to **Florence Lake,** 7½ miles): Follow the 4th hiking day, trip 8.

Lake Sabrina to Midnight Lake   **19**

TRIP From Lake Sabrina to Midnight Lake (round trip). Topo map *Mt. Goddard*. Best mid or late season; 11 miles.

Grade	Trail/layover days	Total recom- mended days
Leisurely	2/0	2
Moderate	....	....
Strenuous	....	....

HILITES The sparkling blue lakes near the head of the Middle Fork of Bishop Creek, nestled close under 13,000-foot granite peaks, are among the most scenic on the Sierra Nevada's east slope. The favorite lake of all these, among many old Sierra trompers, is Midnight Lake.

DESCRIPTION (Leisurely trip)

1st Hiking Day (**Lake Sabrina** to **Midnight Lake**, 5½ miles): From the designated backpackers' parking area below Lake Sabrina, the route follows the Lake Sabrina road ½ mile to the trailhead, on the left about 200 yards below Lake Sabrina dam. The trail leads south from the road to aspen-covered slopes. We round a point just above the dam and suddenly are rewarded with one of the finer panoramas in the Sierra: the shining waters of Lake Sabrina in the foreground, the Middle Fork of Bishop Creek cascading into the southwest end of the lake, and the jagged spires and ridges of the Sierra crest, often snow-streaked until late summer, as a backdrop. The trail contours around the southeast shore of the lake, crossing open slopes spotted with dwarf aspen, mountain mahogany, sagebrush and a few magnificently gnarled junipers. About midway around the lake, we begin to climb, passing an unmarked trail leading left up the slope to George Lake and crossing two small creeks. Then the route enters a lodgepole forest and climbs steadily, emerging from the forest cover now and then for splendid views down over the Lake Sabrina basin. After threading an open area of jumbled boulders, we reach the north end of Blue Lake. This spot is a photographer's delight, with lodgepoles crowding the uneven shoreline and the rugged Thompson Ridge reflected in the clear waters of the lake.

The trail turns right and crosses the outlet creek via some well-placed logs, then cuts left and traverses over and around a number of granite outcroppings just above the west shore of the lake. (The trail here is not obvious; watch for ducks.) About midway around the lake is an unmarked trail junction. The left fork goes to Baboon Lake, but we turn right and follow the trail—once again distinct—over a low saddle, down across a rocky slope and back up granite ledges into a grassy valley spotted with lodgepoles. Just before reaching the northernmost of the Emerald Lakes, we turn right and climb a boulder-strewn ridge. The trail crosses the ridge and descends through broken terrain to the east shore of Dingleberry Lake, where there are several excellent campsites just beyond the south end of the lake.

Just above the campsites is a boulder-hop ford of the Middle Fork Bishop Creek, and then we ascend a picturesque, grass-floored valley, dotted with lodgepole and whitebark pines. After climbing over several small granite benches, we reach the marked junction of trails to Midnight Lake (right) and Hungry Packer Lake (left). Moonlight Lake is a short cross-country jaunt to the southeast, across granite slabs and boulder fields. The backdrop of the campsites is truly magnificent, with the jagged white peaks of the Sierra crest, dominated by 13,830-foot Mt. Darwin and steeple-spired 13,435-foot Mt. Haeckel, towering almost directly above. Fishing is fair-to-good for rainbow and brook trout (to 10″).

2nd Hiking Day: Retrace your steps, 5½ miles.

Bishop Lake, Saddlerock Lake   *Thomas Winnett*

Lake Sabrina to Baboon Lakes   **20**

TRIP   From Lake Sabrina to Baboon Lakes (round trip).
Topo map *Mt. Goddard*. Best mid or late season; 9
miles.

Grade	Trail/layover days	Total recom-mended days
Leisurely	2/0	2
Moderate	....	....
Strenuous	....	....

HILITES   Sooner or later, everyone who returns to the High
Sierra will want to try a little cross-country hiking.
This fairly short trip is a fine choice for the traveler
who has reached that point in his career.

DESCRIPTION (Leisurely trip)

1st Hiking Day (**Lake Sabrina** to **Baboon Lakes,** part cross country,
4½ miles): Follow the 1st hiking day, trip 19 to the trail junction
on the west shore of Blue Lake. Here we turn left (south) and
walk through granite-slab terrain under a forest of lodgepole pine,
passing the south end of Blue Lake (not visible) and crossing the
stream on a large log. The trail becomes difficult to follow as it
traverses a series of granite outcroppings, but it continues southward to an overlook above Donkey Lake. Here we bear left and
descend to some small campsites above the western shore. From
Donkey Lake to lower Baboon Lake, the trail is almost nonexis-
tent, but is marked by a line of ducks. The route is not difficult,
however, as the country is open granite slabs dotted with
lodgepoles and a few whitebark pines. Bearing southwest for a
half mile, we reach the bouldery north shore of lower Baboon
Lake and some fine open campsites. Upper Baboon Lake is a
short, easy scramble to your left (southeast). One mile southeast,
cross-country, is icy-cold Sunset Lake, close under the glaciated
ramparts of Mts. Powell and Thompson. Fishing in Baboon Lakes
is fair-to-good for rainbow trout (to 12″).
2nd Hiking Day: Retrace your steps, 4½ miles.

21   Florence Lake to Lost Lake

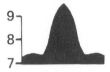

TRIP   Florence Lake to Lost Lake (round trip). Topo maps
Mt. Abbot, Blackcap Mountain. Best early or mid
season; 18 miles.

Grade	Trail/layover days	Total recom- mended days
Leisurely	2/1	3
Moderate	2/0	2
Strenuous	....	....

HILITES   Almost every "Lost Lake" in the Sierra Nevada is
somewhat lost in the sense that there is no regular,
maintained trail to it, and the Lost Lake of Florence
Lake country is no exception. This trail situation always makes for seclusion and solitude, which are becoming ever more valuable.

DESCRIPTION (Leisurely trip)

1st Hiking Day (**Florence Lake** to **Lost Lake,** 9 miles): From the foot
of Florence Lake, the hiker has a choice of walking the trail
around the west side of the lake or taking the ferry to the
lakehead ($2.00/person; 8 a.m. to 6 p.m. weekdays/ 7 a.m. to 7
p.m. weekends). The description in this book covers the trail route
from the parking area at the foot of the lake. Leaving the parking
area at the roadend, the trail follows a maintenance road (closed
to public vehicles) for 1/8 mile as it skirts the west side of the lake,
before giving way to a trail which undulates over granite ridges
that form a series of spines down to the lake. Some of these rises
are as much as 300 feet, as the trail rolls through a mixed forest of
Jeffrey pine, juniper, aspen, white fir and lodgepole pine. Pre-
views of the kind of country to come are provided by views southeast of Ward Mountain and Mt. Shinn, north of the Silver Divide
across the lake, and glimpses of the San Joaquin drainage to the
east. About halfway to the head of the lake this route passes a
junction with a Thomson Lake/Hot Springs Trail (not maintained). Just before the ford of Boulder Creek, a second, unsigned
lateral to Thomson Lake takes off to the right (south). From the

west side of the log crossing of Boulder Creek this trail climbs steeply, and some fallen trees, which appear to be the result of recent beaver activity, provide only minor inconveniences. Boulder Creek is forded three times, the second time about 15 feet below where an old bridge has washed out, and the third time by a junction where the right fork, a jeep trail, leads to Summit Lake and Hot Springs Pass, while the Thomson Lake Trail continues to climb left. Beyond a creek not shown on the topo map, the route becomes more moderate; then an unsigned trail branches left to Lost Lake. This route crosses the outlet stream from Thomson Lake and parallels the outlet of Lost Lake to the campsites on the lake's northern edge.

2nd Hiking Day: Retrace your steps, 9 miles.

Florence Lake *Thomas Winnett*

22 Florence Lake to Courtright Reservoir

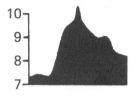

TRIP From Florence Lake to Courtright Reservoir (shuttle trip). Topo maps *Mt. Abbot, Blackcap Mountain.* Best early or mid season; 21 miles.

Grade	Trail/layover days	Total recom- mended days
Leisurely	2/1	3
Moderate	2/0	2
Strenuous	....	....

HILITES Those who hate to retrace their steps are always looking for good trips that have a roadhead at both ends. This mid-Sierra shuttle should be a valuable addition to their collections.

DESCRIPTION (Leisurely trip)

1st Hiking Day: Follow trip 21 to **Lost Lake**, 9 miles.

2nd Hiking Day (**Lost Lake** to **Courtright Reservoir**, 12 miles): We begin this hiking day by contouring at 9,600 feet from Lost Lake west to the outlet of Thomson Lake. A packer campsite is located at the outlet, while several others are found on the south side, bearing the spoor of the vehicles that come up the jeep road from Dusy Meadows. Angling southeast, our trail climbs steeply to Thomson Pass, enters the John Muir Wilderness above the headwaters of Burnt Corral Creek, and then descends to Burnt Corral Meadow. About 40 yards northeast of where the trail fords the West Fork of Burnt Corral Creek, several very cold springs provide a refreshing reason for the thirsty hiker to pause before continuing down to the Long Meadow/Chamberlain's Camp junction. Taking the right fork at this junction, we make a gentle-to-moderate ascent to serene Hobler Lake, where good campsites can be found among the giant red firs and the lodgepole pines. Ascending gently, the trail then leaves the Muir Wilderness, crosses the outlet of a tiny lake to the west, and meets the Courtright/Blackcap Basin Trail on a ridge above Chamberlain's Camp. From here we retrace part of the 1st hiking day, trip 23.

Glacier Divide to Bubbs Creek

This area is bounded by Glacier Divide on the north, the Owens Valley on the east, Courtright and Wishon reservoirs on the west, and Bubbs Creek on the south, and it contains the greatest single block of unbroken wilderness in the southern Sierra. Still untainted by roads, the core of it enjoys the protection of National Park status, and the adjacent peripheral zones to the west, north and east are declared Wilderness Areas. Spread out over an area of roughly 1200 square miles, it boasts some of the most remote and scenic sections of the Sierra, and it is replete with scores of peaks that soar above 13,000 feet, hundreds of lakes and thousands of miles of sparkling streams. Were the hiker able to take every trip suggested in this section, he would have a solid sampling of four life zones ranging in altitude from 5000 feet to well over 12,000 feet. Further, he would have crossed ten major divides, visited three major watersheds, and enjoyed a wilderness experience perhaps unequaled anywhere in the world.

Topographically, the country divides neatly into three disparate types: the west slopes, Kings Canyon National Park, and the eastern escarpment. The Park, the heart of the high country, was established in 1940 when the Congress recognized the obvious need to protect this fragile wilderness from the increasing encroachment of stockmen and local, shortsighted business interests. Although the Park makes up the largest part of this section, the potential visitor should not ignore trips into the wilderness areas on the east and west sides of the Park.

The Park "heartland" is the rugged, comparatively barren, mostly alpine zone that lies between the Sierra crest and the LeConte/White Divide. Here are the headwaters of the South Fork of the San Joaquin and the Middle and South Forks of the Kings River. The latitudinal watershed divides, within the Park, are Goddard Divide (separating the South Fork of the San Joaquin River from the Middle Fork of the Kings River), and the Monarch/Cirque Crest divide (splitting the watersheds of the Middle Fork and the South Fork of the Kings River). Within the Park are several longitudinal divides that serrate the topography into a complex ridge-chasm conformation. Most outstanding among these secondary divides are White Divide, Ragged Spur, Black Divide and the King Spur.

In contrast to the Park, the east escarpment enjoys a diverse and sometimes dense forest cover—a cover that diminishes as it rises to the Sierra crest. All of the many eastside streams flow into the Owens River, and they are separated by towering spur ranges that protrude from the backbone of the crest. The escarpment is nowhere more severe and forbidding than the stretch from South Lake to Onion Valley—accounting in part for the absence of heavily used trailheads in this interval. Peculiar also to the east side is the lower juniper woodland belt replete with the scattered grasses, pinon pine, Utah juniper (sometimes mistakenly referred to as Utah Cedar) and brush plants associated with the Great Basin. Fortunately, for those of us who enjoy and would preserve the east escarpment's native primitive appeal, this region is protected by a long, narrow belt of Wilderness Area designation.

Similarly, the west slopes (west of the Park boundary) enjoy this immunity, but it is a sad political commentary that policy-makers and boundary-setters did not initially establish the Wilderness Area limit along the obvious demarcation indicated by the present roadends at Courtright and Wishon reservoirs. The terrain of these western slopes is remarkable for its absence of outstanding peaks. In general it is a gradual, steady ascent to the LeConte/White Divide and the timbered rise of Kettle Ridge. The pleasant, rolling landscape of Woodchuck Country and the several alpine basins nestled at the foot of the LeConte Divide make up the headwaters of the North Fork of the Kings River, the sole drainage of this particular area.

Looking at topo maps of this section (Blackcap Mountain, Mt. Goddard) one can readily ascertain the comparative heavy forestation of the region west of the LeConte Divide. Travelers working their way up any one of the various dendritic tributaries of the North Fork of the Kings River will discover for themselves the magnificent spectrum of Sierra flora that attends these west-side entries to the high country. Beginning in the lower elevations around 6500 feet are the stately mixed confiers such as the sugar pine, ponderosa pine, and incense-cedar. The ponderosa pine, with its distinctive bark plates and its long needles, is frequently mistaken for its close cousin the Jeffrey pine which is of a higher elevation but sometimes found in the same locale. There are many distinguishing characteristics, but the surest is the difference in their cones. The naturalist's rule of thumb is, "If you can comfortably catch a tossed cone, it is a cone of the Jeffrey pine." This differentiation arises from the fact that the prickle found on the end of each scale of the Jeffrey cone is turned inward, whereas the prickle on the ponderosa cone turns outward. But the most distinctive cone of all belongs to the sugar pine. Sometimes as long as a man's arm, it is an impressive fruit whether it be found on the ground or seen hanging in clusters at the ends of massive branches.

Climbing a little higher, one enters the fir belt. First comes the

white fir, along with occasional groves of Jeffrey pine, and finally
the noble stands of red fir. Being rather brittle, red firs are frequently associated with a heavily littered forest floor, but the atmosphere engendered by their open, parklike groves is entirely
unique. Perhaps it is the soft, filtered green light that sifts
through their dense, short-needled crowns, or it may be the gentle
line of their graceful, down-sweeping branches. Whatever the
reason, there are a hush and a feeling of needing to tip-toe
through these stands that do not exist in other kinds of forests.
Standing in one of these cathedral-like groves, it is the easiest
thing in the world to empathize with John Muir's bitterness when
he wrote:

> Any fool can destroy trees. They cannot run away; and if they could,
> they would still be destroyed—chased and hunted down as long as
> fun or a dollar could be got out of their bark hides, branching horns,
> or magnificent bole backbones. Few that fell trees plant them; nor
> would planting avail much toward getting back anything like the
> noble primeval forests. During a man's life only saplings can be
> grown, in the place of the old trees—tens of centuries old—that have
> been destroyed. It took more than three thousand years to make
> some of the trees in these Western woods—trees that are still stand-
> ing in perfect strength and beauty, waving and singing in the mighty
> forests of the Sierra. Through all the wonderful, eventful centuries
> since Christ's time—and long before that—God has cared for these
> trees, saved them from drought, disease, avalanches, and a thousand
> straining, leveling tempests and floods; but he cannot save them
> from fools—only Uncle Sam can do that.

The "gentle country" of the trees continues as the trails wind
upward through dense groves of the two-needled lodgepole pine.
Near timberline, solitary gnarled sentinels in the form of Sierra
juniper guard the ridges, and cling tenuously to rocky slopes. The
slim lodgepole pine no longer appears in tall, dense stands—now
its trunk is bent to the unchecked winds of alpine country. Occasional clumps of whitebark pine and mountain hemlock dot those
spaces among the granite that are not already filled with the
tender-yet-tough grasses of an alpine meadow.

This is the land and the forests of the west slopes—an environment that has nurtured and awed man since his first acquaintance with it. It is an often-ignored fact that the first visitor to
these slopes was the Indian, and there is adequate evidence to
show that he was leaching his ground acorn meal at the sites of
Simpson and Zumwalt meadows long before the white man had
settled the eastern shores of America. While Englishmen and
Spaniards fought sea battles for supremacy of ocean trade routes,

Our National Parks, by John Muir.

the Indians of the Mono and Monache groups were peacefully plying their primitive trade routes over Piute, Bishop and Kearsarge passes. Using laurel-wood bows and cane arrows that were dipped in a poison concoction of crushed, rattlesnake-venomed deer liver, Indian hunting parties ranged the upper watersheds of the Kings and San Joaquin rivers—this, while the white man was establishing the first Presidio-Mission complexes in Alta California. In Philadelphia, civilized men of 1776 used a bird feather and decomposed animal fat to paint their names on a piece of wood pulp—historians now refer to it as an historic document. At almost the same time, in Tehipite Valley, an unknown Indian artisan using a similar stain produced a series of amebalike figures—and today's archeologist-historian refers to them as primitve graffiti.

The first meetings of these original inhabitants and exploring white men had the seeds of disaster. Gabriel Moraga, among the first white men to penetrate this country, was called "the greatest pathfinder and Indian fighter of his day." Subsequent incursions by trappers, pioneer settlers and gold seekers brought the inevitable confrontation, and, to the white man's discredit, the inevitable eradication of the red man. Like the grizzly bear, he was judged a nuisance, and was considered "fair game." Today, both species are extinct in this region.

Early exploratory ventures from west to east into the heartland of this region were so arduous as to render their continuation impractical. This is quite understandable, as any examination of the topography will show. Numerous divides, nearly all exceeding 12,000 feet, cross-hatch the landscape, making passage even to this day lengthy and arduous. Fremont, in December 1845, endeavoring to carry out a rendezvous with Talbot and Walker on the westside river they called "Lake Fork," led an unsuccessful sally into the reaches of the North Fork of the Kings River. He was turned back by snow and "impossible" going. Jedediah Smith's party, in an earlier attempt during spring, had suffered the same travails, and the subsequent annals of the Brewer Survey parties of 1864 and 1870 tell a similar story.

The actual trail-blazers of currently used trails were, however, not the Spaniards or the trappers. The earliest trails were usually those of the sheepherders who grazed their flocks in the backcountry during the last half of the 19th century. Among the better known of these sheepherders were Bill Helm and Frank Dusy, whose early exploratory efforts on the west slopes culminated in the discovery of the Tehipite Valley and in the building of the Tunemah Trail. W. Baird, operating in the same vicinity, established what is now known as the Hell-for-Sure Pass Trail, and although the 1864 Brewer Survey party was the first to visit the area, it is assumed that Portuguese sheepmen were the first to establish the current western access route to the Evolution region. No route in the Sierra has received more attention than the comparatively recently established John Muir Trail. This scenic route traverses the Park just west of the Sierra crest.

The locations of the trailheads for this part of *Sierra South* are given below

South Lake. Go 12 miles southwest from Bishop on State Highway 168 to the South Lake turnoff, and then 7 miles to the South Lake parking area.

Big Pine Creek Roadend. Go west from U.S. 395 in Big Pine 11 miles on a paved road to the roadend to deposit passengers and packs, but drive back 2 miles to old Glacier Lodge to park.

Taboose Creek Roadend. Turn west on a dirt road that leaves U.S. 395 12 miles south of Big Pine. Go right at a fork at 1.7 miles, pass through a gate at 2.4 miles, and continue to the roadend at 5.8 miles.

Sawmill Creek Roadend. Turn west on a dirt road that leaves U.S. 395 18 miles south of Big Pine and go west on Black Rock Spring Road 1 mile to a junction. Turn north and follow Old U.S. 395 0.2 mile to an unmarked dirt road leading west. Pass through a gate and follow this poor road 2.3 miles to its end just north of Sawmill Creek.

Oak Creek Roadend. Turn west from U.S. 395 2.3 miles north of Independence onto the paved Fish Hatchery Road and go 1.3 miles to a junction. Go right here, passing Oak Creek Campground, 5.8 miles to the roadend.

Onion Valley. Drive west from Independence on U.S. 395 15 miles to the roadend parking lot.

Courtright Reservoir. Drive northeast 42 miles from Clovis (near Fresno) on State Highway 168 and turn right onto the Dinkey Creek Road, following it 28 miles to the Courtright/Wishon "Y," from where Courtright Reservoir is 7½ miles north, and there is a large parking area at the south end of the reservoir.

Wishon Reservoir. Follow the directions above to the Courtright/Wishon "Y" and from there drive east 2 miles to the Wishon Dam and across the dam to the trailhead parking lot.

Crown Valley Trailhead. From Wishon Village go 6 miles south on paved road almost to the roadend, to a large parking lot on the west side of the road.

Lewis Creek Trailhead. Go 77 miles east from Fresno on State Highway 180, to a parking area 5 miles east of the bridge of the Kings River.

Cedar Grove Roadend. Go 85 miles east from Fresno on State Highway 180 to the roadend.

23 Courtright Reservoir to Post Corral Meadows

TRIP   From Courtright Reservoir to Post Corral Meadows (round trip). Topo map *Blackcap Mountain*. Best early to mid season; 16 miles.

Grade	Trail/layover days	Total recom- mended days
Leisurely	2/0	2
Moderate	....	....
Strenuous	....	....

HILITES   A fine weekend selection, this two-day trip visits enchanting Long and Post Corral Meadows. Dense forests of fir and lodgepole that line the trail route are a pleasant habitat for a variety of wildlife. This trip is an excellent selection for the beginning knapsacker.

DESCRIPTION (Leisurely trip)

1st Hiking Day (**Courtright Reservoir** to **Post Corral Meadows,** 8 miles): From man-made Courtright Reservoir (8170') the route crosses the dam and, following a brief section of maintenance road, skirts the granite shoulder of the ridge that lines the east shore of Courtright Reservoir. Excellent views to the north of spectacular Maxson Dome greet the traveler crossing the dam, and the view down the Helms Creek gorge just below the spillway is a dizzying one that leaves the traveler feeling as though he were treading the brink of hell's abyss. A few yards down the rocky maintenance road, the trail branches left (north), descending at first through an area of granite slabs, and then leveling out. This leveler section offers fine views of Long Top mountain and the East Fork of Helms Creek watershed.

The trail descends past the meadowed foot of a long sheet of glacially smoothed granite on the left that sports numerous spectacular glacial erratics, then it fords the East Fork of Helms Creek, and winds through a dense forest cover of young lodgepole around the east side of Maxson Meadows. Ascending gently, the trail passes Chamberlain's Camp (a Forest Service trail-maintenance camp that is manned intermittently) and the Dusy Meadows jeep road. Just beyond the Chamberlain's Camp cabin, the trail ascends steeply by short, dusty switchbacks, and then tops this climb in a beautiful mixed stand of red fir and lodgepole. This rocky slope reveals the typical rounded boulders set in a dusty silt matrix of a glacial moraine. After passing the first of two trails to Burnt Corral Meadow, the trail then fords an un-named, intermittently flowing stream, and descends gently to the head of beautiful Long Meadow. Aptly named, this grassland stretches away to the northeast for about a mile, and the route winds through the middle—seldom more than a few yards away from the sluggishly flowing South Fork of Post Corral Creek.

Our route passes a second Burnt Corral Meadow Trail midway through through the meadow, fords the South Fork of Post Corral Creek, and then leaves the sandy-surfaced trail of the meadow behind as it swings east. Through the moderate-to-dense forest cover one can occasionally hear Post Corral Creek, and although it is out of sight, one can clearly hear the sound difference due to the increased volume of water resulting from the contribution of Burnt Corral Creek. Our route passes a faint trail branching left to a privately owned line cabin (Forest Service Multiple-Use land policy allows cattlemen to graze these lands), and then descends gently to the excellent campgrounds at the head of Post Corral Meadows (8201'). There are several primitive campgrounds at the head of the meadow, and one packer site. Other sites can be found at the foot of the meadow (ford Post Corral Creek) adjacent to the trail junction of the Hell-for-Sure Pass Trail. Fair-to-good fishing for pan-sized brook trout and some rainbow (to 7") can be had along Post Corral Creek.

2nd Hiking Day: Retrace your steps, 8 miles.

Don Denison

24   Courtright Reservoir to North Fork Kings

TRIP   From Courtright Reservoir to North Fork Kings
                River via Post Corral Meadows (round trip). Topo
                map *Blackcap Mountain*. Best early to mid season;
                24 miles.

Grade	Trail/layover days	Total recom- mended days
Leisurely	4/1	5
Moderate	3/1	4
Strenuous	2/1	3

HILITES   The winding, horseshoe-shaped route-plan of this
                trip tours magnificent backcountry meadows and
                lush forests, and terminates alongside the racing,
                pothole-dotted North Fork of the Kings River. Excel-
                lent fishing and swimming on the Kings River make
                this a good trip selection for the beginner desiring
                maximum wilderness exposure for a minimum of
                hiking days.

DESCRIPTION (Leisurely trip)

1st Hiking Day: Follow trip 23 to **Post Corral Meadows,** 8 miles.

2nd Hiking Day (**Post Corral Meadows** to **North Fork Kings River,** 4
miles): From the campsites at the lower end of Post Corral
Meadows (8201') , the trail passes the Hell-for-Sure Pass Trail
(branching left), and winds through a densely forested stretch of
mixed stands of red fir, lodgepole, and silver pine. The duff-and-
sand trail surface makes for very pleasant walking, and the relatively level going allows the trail traveler to keep a sharp eye out
for the commonly seen mule deer and the sometimes seen black
bear. Tiny meadowy sections interrupt the dense forest sections,
and the experienced silent hiker will pause at the fringe of these
fens to watch for betraying movement. The general southward
progress of the trail changes to an upward slog eastward as the
trail ascends a rocky, moderate slope, and finally emerges on an
open, manzanita-covered ridge above the North Fork Kings River
drainage. This open slope is a fine point from which to view the
unfractured granite river chasm to the west and the dramatic
U-shaped valley to the southeast.

From this point, it is interesting to speculate on the probably route followed by Captain John Fremont, the "Pathfinder." Historians are still speculating on this subject, but on one thing they do agree—Fremont's party got lost in the upper reaches of the North Fork of the Kings River. They suffered terribly during an early winter storm, were forced to eat their saddle stock, and finally retreated. From this ridge, the trail descends on a traverse over infrequently jointed granite to the banks of the river (8029'). Excellent campsites can be found a short distance up or downstream, but one should remember that it is illegal to camp within 100 feet of the stream. Angling for brook, rainbow and some brown (to 12") is excellent. Swimming in some of the finest sand-bottomed potholes in the Sierra is available just downstream, and photographers seeking a worthy subject will find Sue Falls about ¼ mile downstream.

3rd and 4th Hiking Days: Retrace your steps, 12 miles.

Sierra juniper

David Beck

25 Courtright Reservoir to Rae Lake

TRIP   From Courtright Reservoir to Rae Lake via Post
              Corral Meadows (round trip). Topo map *Blackcap
              Mountain*. Best mid to late season; 26 miles.

Grade	Trail/layover days	Total recommended days
Leisurely	4/2	6
Moderate	3/2	5
Strenuous	2/2	4

HILITES   Rae Lake, an alpine gem surrounded by meadow on
              two sides and tumbled granite slopes on the other
              two, has long been a favorite of anglers and other
              high-country visitors. Situated beneath Fleming
              Mountain, this lake's innate beauty and its proxim-
              ity to 25 other lakes and the intervening streams
              make it a choice base camp for discovery explorations
              of Red Mountain Basin.

DESCRIPTION (Leisurely trip)

1st Hiking Day: Follow trip 23 to **Post Corral Meadows,** 8 miles.

2nd Hiking Day (**Post Corral Meadows** to **Rae Lake,** 5 miles): Our
route leaves the Blackcap Basin Trail at the campground at the
foot of Post Corral Meadows (8201') just beyond the crossing of
Post Corral Creek, and ascends the divide separating the Fleming
Creek and Post Corral Creek drainages. The ascent climbs eastward, passes a Forest Service spur-trail maintenance camp
(sometimes manned), and then crosses several unnecessarily
dynamited sections of granite. To dynamite these granite slabs is
a policy decision—an unfortunate and unrepresentative policy
that sees the Forest Service maintaining backcountry trails for
horses and pack animals when the overwhelming use of the trails
is by those on foot.

The trail crosses the John Muir Wilderness boundary, switchbacks over the crest of a divide, and begins a long, steady, rocky
ascent through a moderately dense forest cover of lodgepole,
incense-cedar and red fir. As the trail nears Fleming Creek it
climbs steeply, and there are spots along this ascent from which
the passerby has beautiful views of the long, silver chutes of the

West Fork of Fleming Creek as it plunges over the glacially smoothed, unfractured granite of this upper basin. The lodgepoles begin to take on the stunted look characteristic of high country as the trail emerges at the subalpine meadows surrounding Fleming Lake. Itchy anglers may wish to sample the fair-to-good brook-trout fishing (to 10″) at Fleming Lake, but fishing is generally better as one ascends the drainage.

The trail passes a packer campsite at the outlet of Fleming Lake and crosses a lovely subalpine meadow to Indian Lakes Trail junction. Here, our route branches left and ascends steeply to the spur trail to Rae Lake. This rocky, morainal trail brings us to the excellent campsites along the south and east sides of Rae Lake (9894′). Almost ringed by meadow, this charming lake exhibits a timbered east wall, a mostly meadowed south side, and precipitous rocky faces on the west and north sides. Originally named "Wolverine Lake", 13-acre Rae Lake makes a fine base camp for day-hiking excursions to Lower Indian Lake, Upper Indian Lake, and the lakes of the Red Mountain Basin. Fishing for brook (to 12″) is good.

3rd and 4th Hiking Days: Retrace your steps, 13 miles.

Woolly sunflowers

Thomas Winnett

26 Courtright Reservoir to Devils Punchbowl

TRIP From Courtright Reservoir to Devils Punchbowl return via Meadow Brook and North Fork Kings River (semiloop). Topo map *Blackcap Mountain*. Best mid to late season; 35 miles.

Grade	Trail/layover days	Total recommended days
Leisurely	6/2	8
Moderate	5/2	7
Strenuous	4/2	6

HILITES Traveling what was originally known as the "Baird Trail" (an old sheepherder's trail that remained for years the primary access to the Evolution Valley country) this route culminates at regal Devils Punchbowl Lake. Here, excellent fishing and magnificent views greet the visitor, and a prolonged stay—using the lake as a base camp—will compensate the hiker with excellent fishing and views from the surrounding lakes.

DESCRIPTION (Leisurely trip)

1st and 2nd Hiking Days: Follow trip 25 to **Rae Lake,** 13 miles.
3rd Hiking Day (**Rae Lake** to **Devils Punchbowl,** 4 miles): Descending from Rae Lake (9894″), the trail meets and joins the trail from Lower Indian Lake, and a few hundred yards farther (in the meadow) joins the Hell-for-Sure Pass Trail. Our route turns left, fords the West Fork of Fleming Creek, and ascends the steep moraine divide to the east. The forest cover diminishes as the trail ascends, and through the thinning timber one has good views of the northern reaches of the LeConte Divide and of Fleming Mountain. Then the trail veers somewhat more southward, and rounds a granite-nosed ridge before ascending a grassy swale to the Devils Punchbowl Trail junction. From this junction, one can look up the benched drainage containing Hell-for-Sure Lake to the notch that marks Hell-for-Sure Pass.

Our route turns right onto the Devils Punchbowl Trail, skirts a ridge, and descends past several streamside campsites ·at the headwaters of the East Fork of Fleming Creek. Climbing out of this drainage, the rocky trail reaches the good campsites at the north end of Devils Punchbowl Lake (10,100'). Timber cover on three sides of this charming, fairly large (33-acre) lake is moderate-to-sparse lodgepole mixed with willow in the wetter areas. Firewood is ample, and fishing for brook (to 13") is excellent. Anglers with extra layover days may wish to use this lake as a base camp for further angling adventures in the Red Mountain Basin. Angling varies from excellent at Horseshoe and Hell-for-Sure lakes to fair at Blackrock Lake. Equally varied is the range of trout. At Blackrock Lake there is a fair population of rainbow, while Horseshoe has a mixed fishery of brook, rainbow and (says the DF&G) golden hybrids. Whether the reason for excursions into the Red Mountain Basin be angling or just enjoying the rugged, alpine country, the basin merits investigation.

4th Hiking Day (**Devils Punchbowl** to **North Fork Kings River**, 6 miles): Walking around the west fringe of Devils Punchbowl Lake, the hiker should take time out to step a few yards to the right of the trail for the breathtaking view west to the two tiny lakes ("Tall Jigger" and "Short Jigger") and the wooded upper drainages of the East Fork of Fleming Creek. The trail then becomes somewhat faint as it crosses the rocky saddle at the southwest end of Devils Punchbowl, and descends the heavily timbered slopes to the rolling meadows of Meadow Brook. These meadows exhibit an unusual amount of seepage, and it is well that the winding, duff trail keeps to the lodgepole forest fringe on the west side. Along the trail and on the fringes of the stream, one will find a luxuriant growth of shooting star, swamp onion, and knee-high lupine. There is a serene quality to a rolling alpine meadow that touches all who visit it, and the meadows that stepladder down with Meadow Brook are a particular delight. The brief 2 miles of trail that wind in and out of these grasslands are a rare pleasure. There is, however, a disturbing factor, which grates on the sensitivities of all experienced high-country travelers. That factor is the presence of privately owned cattle that summer-graze here. Because of the heavy seepage, these grasslands are vulnerable, and they are undergoing irremediable harm. A close-up examination will reveal the torn turf and polluted waters caused by this stock. Further, the presence of these domestic bovines dramatically detracts from the meadow's magical wilderness quality.

The trail passes a second large meadow section, and then swings away from Meadow Brook. It then makes a final, steep descent into the North Fork of the Kings River valley. Views during this descent include large segments of Woodchuck Country, Nichols Canyon, and the U-shaped contour of the North Fork

Kings River valley. On the descent, the dusty, down-winding trail reflects the lower altitude, with the reintroduction of the golden, shaggy-barked incense-cedar and the vanilla-scented Jeffrey pine. Our route then meets and turns right onto the Blackcap Basin Trail. A short distance downstream, the trail crosses granite slabs, and then passes a snow-survey cabin with a nearby waterfall and a fine, deep pool (good swimming). Immediately leaving the vicinity of the river, the trail swings right, crosses a rocky granite ridge, and then descends through a heavy stand of lodgepole, Jeffrey, and occasional red fir and incense-cedar. This route fords Fleming Creek and arrives at the excellent riverside campsites situated at the point where the trail begins to climb out of the North Fork Kings River watershed. Fishing for brook (to 12″) is excellent, and swimming in the nearby potholes (just downstream) is also excellent.

5th and 6th Hiking Days: Reverse the steps of trip 24, 12 miles.

Guest Lake   *U.S. Forest Service*

Courtright Reservoir to Guest Lake   **27**

TRIP   From Courtright Reservoir to Guest Lake (Bench Valley) via Post Corral Meadows, North Fork Kings River (round trip). Topo map *Blackcap Mountain.* Best mid to late season; 37 miles.

Grade	Trail/layover days	Total recom- mended days
Leisurely	6/3	9
Moderate	5/2	7
Strenuous	4/2	6

HILITES   Of the three lake basins lying close under towering LeConte Divide, Bench Valley is the least known and least-visited. This is surprising in view of the excellent angling available at McGuire Lakes and Guest Lake. The other lakes of this basin are among the most picturesque in the Sierra, and the angler with an inclination to visit stirring subalpine scenery en route should give this trip serious consideration.

DESCRIPTION (Leisurely trip)

1st and 2nd Hiking Days: Follow trip 24 to **North Fork Kings River,** 12 miles.

3rd Hiking Day (**North Fork Kings River** to **Guest Lake,** 6½ miles): From the river's edge, the trail swings left through a dense stand of lodgepole, Jeffrey, and occasional red fir and incense-cedar, and fords Fleming Creek just above its confluence with the North Fork Kings River. In these shady timber stands, heavy coats of green moss cover rock and tree alike; bright orange shelf bracts flash like great eyes against the forest green; and sounds seem muted on the carpet of pine needles. But the soft duff trail is soon left behind as the route climbs above the river valley over the granite nose of a ridge, and then descends to the snow-survey cabin nestled in granite slabs at river's edge. A nearby waterfall on the river and the pool below makes a nice spot for a fast pre-lunch swim, and anglers will find good fishing for brook trout (to 11″) immediately up or downstream. The trail then passes the Meadow Brook Trail branching left to Hell-for-Sure Pass and the Nichols Canyon Trail branching right, before fording an unnamed tributary and Meadow Brook. Ascending gently, this trail route winds through moderate-to-dense stands of lodgepole and red fir.

After fording Fall Creek, the route leaves the Blackcap Basin Trail by branching left onto an unmaintained shortcut trail (signed) that ascends along the south side of Fall Creek. The route is gentle at first, and easy to follow, but this condition changes as soon as the area of the broad granite walls is reached. Here, the hiker keeps on course by staying close to the creek on the south side. This is a pleasant chore, for the creek forms a lovely silver ribbon as it chutes hundreds of feet across glacially smoothed granite. Where ledges interrupt the flow, pockets of wildflowers have taken root, and a well-deserved lunch break is in order here.

Our ascending route meets another trail lateral at the foot of the valley, and joined as one they wind alongside the luxuriantly foliaged banks of Fall Creek. Wildflowers fill the valley floor: shooting star, penstemon, larkspur, monkshood, monkey flower, columbine, wallflower, and Indian paintbrush. Frequently the trail is overhung by rank, fast-growing false solomon's seal, which, because of soaked pant legs, is considered an annoyance by walkers. The trick to keeping one's pants legs dry is: (1) travel in a party of two or more; (2) finagle to be the last person in the walking file.

After traveling a short distance along the river, the trail begins a steep ascent of the valley's east wall. Short switchbacks, which soon become rocky and steep, mark this strenuous climb, and the first, water-level view of lower McGuire Lake comes a a welcome and pleasant surprise. The lake's waters appear suddenly only a few feet from the precipitous drop-off, and from this point one can indeed ascertain the true meaning of the term "hanging valley." Our route passes several primitive and packer campsites as it rounds the north side of lower and upper McGuire Lakes. Both of these lakes afford excellent fishing for brook (to 18"). Through moderate-to-sparse timber, the trail crosses an easy ridge to the fisherman's lateral that turns off the main trail and leads to Guest Lake (10,160'). Excellent packer and primitive campsites with unobstructed views of Blackcap Mountain line the north shore of this lovely granite-lined lake, and it is a fine choice as a base camp for excursions to 20 nearby lakes in this basin. At Guest Lake fishing for brook trout (to 12") is good. Fishing in the lakes of the upper Bench Valley Basin varies from good to excellent, and offers the angling sportsman a creel of both brook and rainbow trout.

4th, 5th and 6th Hiking Days: Retrace your steps, 18½ miles.

Courtright Reservoir to Guest Lake   **28**

TRIP   From Courtright Reservoir to Guest Lake via Post
                 Corral Meadows, North Fork Kings River, and re-
                 turn via cross-country route to Devils Punchbowl,
                 then by trail to North Fork Kings, Post Corral
                 Meadows (semiloop trip). Topo map *Blackcap
                 Mountain*. Best mid or late season; 43 miles.

Grade	Trail/layover days	Total recommended days
Leisurely	7/3	10
Moderate	5/3	8
Strenuous	4/2	6

HILITES   This looping trip traverses two of the finest angling
                basins found on the west side of the Sierra. The rug-
                ged cross-country route between the basins makes it
                a choice limited to intermediate and experienced
                knapsackers, and the grand vistas encountered along
                this route more than compensate for the skill and
                energy required. The return leg of this trip through
                Meadow Brook valley is an exposure to subalpine
                meadows that will kindle an appreciation of and a
                dedication to preserving these beautiful grasslands.

DESCRIPTION (Leisurely trip)

1st 3 Hiking Days: Follow trip 27 to **Guest Lake**, 18½ miles.

4th Hiking Day (**Guest Lake** to **Devils Punchbowl** via cross-country
route, 6½ miles): The trail from Guest Lake is a fisherman's trail
that joins the main Bench Valley Basin Trail ascending to
Horsehead Lake. This ascent winds north through sparse,
stunted lodgepole and alpine meadows. Mostly rocky, the trail is
sometimes faint, but in the grassy sections it is easy to follow.
When the trail arrives at the grassy fringes of open Horsehead
Lake, the traveler has excellent views to the east and northeast of
the barren crest of the LeConte Divide. From this lake's open
shores one can readily see that he has surmounted a series of

hanging valleys, and that this hanging-valley chain continues in the tiny cirques carved out of the granite divide to the east and northeast.

Beyond the marshy inlet to Horsehead Lake, this route rounds the east side of the lake, fords the east inlet (from Filly Lake), and parallels the north inlet stream as it ascends above timberline. Faint fisherman's routes crisscross this drainage, and the conflicting ducks placed by misguided but well-meaning visitors should be taken with a grain of salt. Anglers passing through this country will be able to sample the brook and rainbow (to 10″) at Horsehead Lake; brook (to 8″) at Roman Four Lake; rainbow (to 11″) at West Twin Buck Lake (East Twin Buck Lake is barren); and rainbow (to 7″) at Schoolmarm Lake.

From the west side of Twin Buck Lakes we ascend northward to the outlet of Schoolmarm Lake. Our route crosses the outlet and leads northwest, then north, ascending steeply over heavily fractured granite and talus. Maintaining elevation, this route traverses the rugged, fractured, talus-ridden headwaters basin of Fall Creek in an east-to-west fashion above a series of chutes. This traverse brings one to a point above the jumbled granite and metamorphic rock divide between the Fall Creek and Meadow Brook watersheds, just north of Point 11398. From this point, the route descends the long cirque basin directly to the west down the steep east side of the cirque basin. *This descent should be undertaken only by experienced hikers with rudimentary climbing skills.* The foot of this descent is a long, sloping cirque bench that is easily negotiated. Then it is another steep climb northwest down to the north side of the lakelets just above Devils Punchbowl. This final steep descent brings one to the sparse-to-moderate lodgepole forest cover at the north end of Devils Punchbowl Lake (10,100′). There are several excellent campsites here, and fishing for brook (to 13″) is excellent. This lake is a perennial choice among anglers as a base camp for further side trips into Red Mountain Basin.

5th Hiking Day (**Devils Punchbowl** to **North Fork Kings River**, 6 miles): Follow the 4th hiking day, trip 26.

6th and 7th Hiking Days: Retrace the steps of the 2nd and 1st hiking days, 12 miles.

Courtright Reservoir to Portal Lake

29

TRIP From Courtright Reservoir to Portal Lake (Blackcap Basin) via Post Corral Meadows, North Fork Kings River (round trip). Topo map *Blackcap Mountain.* Best mid or late season; 45 miles.

Grade	Trail/layover days	Total recom- mended days
Leisurely	6/4	10
Moderately	5/4	9
Strenuous	4/4	8

HILITES Portal Lake lives up to its name. It is indeed the door to Blackcap Basin, a beautiful, austere, granite basin forming the headwaters of the Middle Fork of the Kings River. This trip boasts an encompassing look at west-slope ecology over a 2500-foot elevation span.

DESCRIPTION (Leisurely trip)

1st Hiking Day: Follow trip 23 to **Post Corral Meadows,** 8 miles.

2nd Hiking Day (**Post Corral Meadows** to **Big Maxson Meadow,** 8 miles): Follow the 2nd hiking day, trip 24, to North Fork Kings River. Then proceed to the junction of the trail to Bench Valley as described in the 3rd hiking day, trip 27. From this junction, the Blackcap Basin Trail continues south along the North Fork of the Kings River. Fishing along the river continues to be good for brook and rainbow (to 12″), and occasional pools, usually located at the foot of a chute or a fall, make for fine late-season swimming. The narrowing canyon walls open briefly as the trail reaches wide Big Maxson Meadow (8480′). Formerly a sheepherders' camp, and more recently grazed by cattle, this meadow offers fair-to-good campsites at its northwest and southeast ends. If used as a base-camp location, these meadow campsites are central for side trips to Halfmoon Lake and to the alpine lakes of upper Bench Valley. The trail to Halfmoon Lake, not shown on the topo map, leaves the meadow just upstream from a cabin.

3rd Hiking Day (**Big Maxson Meadow** to **Portal Lake,** 6½ miles): As the trail leaves the open flats of the meadow, the traveler has excellent views east-southeast to the glacially smoothed, narrowing walls of the canyon. Bearing in the direction of these canyon narrows, our duff trail passes the second of the Bench Valley Trail laterals and the first of the Scepter Pass Trail laterals. The louder river sounds on the right reflect the steepening slopes as our trail begins a steady-to-steep climb, which levels out as its direction turns south through a thinning lodgepole forest cover. This direction soon brings the trail back to the river, which it fords, and subsequently passes the second Scepter Pass Trail lateral. Staying close to the south side of the river, our trail swings east beneath the steep granite south wall of the canyon. This steady, often rocky ascent offers excellent views eastward into great Blackcap Basin. Obviously glacial in origin, the basin shows the usual smoothed granite, striae, hanging valleys and morainal debris. Rimmed by Blackcap Mountain on the northwest, LeConte Divide on the east and Kettle Ridge on the south, this basin encloses over 50 alpine lakes. Nestled against basaltic-lava-topped cirque walls and peaks, these deep, dark-blue lakes fill hanging valleys which lie waiting for geological processes to crumble their retaining walls and spill their contents into the high basin below.

Our trail ascends through thinning lodgepole forest and reaches the head of a small basin, where it passes two packer campsites, the first of them located at a junction with a disappearing lateral into Crown Basin to the south. Just beyond the second campsite, in a marshy meadow, is the ducked but easy-to-miss ford of the outlet of Portal Lake. A short, switchbacking climb up from this ford brings one to the jewellike setting of this small lake (10,300'), with two good campsites on its north shore.

4th, 5th and 6th Hiking Days: Retrace your steps, 22½ miles.

Courtright Reservoir to Florence Lake   30

TRIP   From Courtright Reservoir to Florence Lake via Post Corral Meadows, Hell-for-Sure Pass, John Muir Trail, Blaney Meadows (shuttle trip). Topo maps *Blackcap Mountain, Mt. Abbot*. Best mid or late season; 39½ miles.

Grade	Trail/layover days	Total recommended days
Leisurely	7/3	10
Moderate	5/2	7
Strenuous	4/2	6

HILITES   Crossing the LeConte Divide at Hell-for-Sure Pass, this fine shuttle trip tours the headwaters of two major Sierra drainages—North Fork of the Kings River and South Fork of the San Joaquin. Unparalleled scenery and excellent angling earmark this trek for hiker and angler.

DESCRIPTION (Moderate trip)

1st and 2nd Hiking Days: Follow trip 25 to **Rae Lake**, 13 miles.

3rd Hiking Day (**Rae Lake** to **Lower Goddard Canyon**, 11 miles): Proceed to the Devils Punchbowl Trail junction as described in the 3rd hiking day, trip 26. From this junction, our trail ascends steadily above the meadowed basin to the barren granite bench north of Disappointment Lake. Far from being a disappointment, anglers will find the brook-trout fishing in this lake to be good to excellent (to 15″).

The trail winds across slab granite, talus and turfy patches to the east end of the bench, and then ascends steeply to the north end of barren Hell-for-Sure Lake. This large (58-acre) lake with its narrow northern meadow fringe is a long-time favorite of people using this three-quarters-of-a-century-old sheep trail. A fine fishing spot for rainbow trout (to 10″), this lake takes up the largest part of the upper cirque of Red Mountain Basin. Smoothed and polished slab granite issues from the lake's waters, broken only by an occasional glacial erratic or a lonesome, dwarfed lodgepole. Just beyond the slab granite the broken slopes of talus and scree lead up to the abrupt, metavolcanic-topped LeConte Divide. The notch to the northeast of Hell-for-Sure Lake marks Hell-for-Sure Pass (11,297'), and the climb to this saddle is a steep, switchbacking, rocky slog. The traveler arriving at the summit of Hell-for-Sure Pass inevitably agrees with the thousands who have gone before who pantingly said, "Ain't it though?" From the pass, Hell-for-Sure Lake takes up most of the immediate scenery to the southwest, but one can see a good part of the way down the Fleming Creek drainage. The most impressive view, however, is that of Goddard Canyon, Emerald Peak, Peter Peak and Mt. McGee to the east and northeast. Virtually naked of vegetation, the incredibly steep canyon walls plunge uninterrupted to the valley floor nearly 2500 feet below. This breathtaking view lasts most of the switchbacking way down to the ford of the first unnamed tributary feeding the South Fork of the San Joaquin. From this ford (about halfway down the vertical distance) the trail traverses the west canyon wall on a long, rolling descent that crosses two more tributaries, and then doubles back along the South Fork of the San Joaquin. The subsequent steady-to-moderate descent stays on the west side of the river and refords the tributaries cited above. The trail crosses over mostly rock, some talus and scree, and occasional meadowy sections. Willow clumps along the river always indicate the presence of birdlife, and the passerby is sure to encounter Brewer blackbirds, hummingbirds, flycatchers, fox sparrow, Lincoln sparrow, nuthatches, robins, and an occasional finch. Among the flowers and shrubs seen along this section of trail are sagebrush, Labrador tea, monkey flower, yellow cinquefoil, shooting star, milfoil, tiger lily, red columbine, buckwheat, penstemon, western mountain aster, camas, red heather, and the ubiquitous lupine. This descent, leveling near the confluence with Evolution Creek, reenters forest cover with the appearance of lodgepole and aspen. The trail then passes the drift fence a short way upstream from the John Muir Trail junction, and arrives at the fair-to-good campsites (both packer and primitive) south of the bridge (8600'). Fishing for brook and some rainbow on the river remains fair-to-good despite heavy angling pressure.

4th Hiking Day (**Lower Goddard Canyon** to **Lower Blaney Meadows,** 8 miles): The trail descends to the junction with the John Muir Trail, and turns left onto that trail. This is a steady descent over a dusty trail through stands of quaking aspen, lodgepole and some juniper. Underfoot, almost continuous gardens of wildflowers line the trail, including sneezeweed, penstemon, yellow cinquefoil, pennyroyal, Mariposa lily and lupine. As the trail approaches the suspension bridge ford of the South Fork of the San Joaquin River, the canyon walls narrow and rise V-shaped from the canyon floor. On the north wall one can make out the unmistakable striations carved there by ice-driven rocks in the last glacial stage. Our route passes by several more campsites just before crossing the bridge, and then descends a rocky stretch over morainal debris. This steady descent levels out through a densely forested flat ("Aspen Flat") that is made up of postglacial alluvial deposits. An occasional Jeffrey and juniper add variety to the forest cover as the route leaves the flat and descends steeply on a rocky, dusty trail. Looking back, one has a last look at Emerald Peak, Veed by the steep canyon walls, and ahead one catches his first glimpse of imposing Ward Mountain. Our route fords Piute Creek and passes the Hutchinson Meadow Trail that branches to the right. From this junction one has good views of the domes to the east, the most notable being Pavilion Dome. Passing several campsites, this route continues as described in the 3rd hiking day, trip 18.

5th Hiking Day (**Lower Blaney Meadows** to **Florence Lake**, 7½ miles): Follow the 4th hiking day, trip 8.

Bigelow sneezeweed

Thomas Winnett

31   Courtright to Crown Valley Trailhead

TRIP   From Courtright Reservoir to Crown Valley Trailhead via Post Corral Meadows, North Fork Kings River, Portal Lake (Blackcap Basin), cross country to Blue Canyon, then by trail over Kettle Ridge to Cabin Creek (shuttle trip). Topo maps *Blackcap Mountain, Mt. Goddard, Marion Peak, Tehipite Dome.* Best mid or late season; 49 miles.

Grade	Trail/layover days	Total recommended days
Leisurely	....	....
Moderate	8/4	12
Strenuous	6/3	9

HILITES   Employing a challenging cross-country route *(for experienced knapsackers only)*, this trip joins Blackcap Basin with Blue Canyon. Where it crosses the LeConte Divide, it traverses the spine of that divide, offering breathtaking views to either side. The trailed segments of this trip touch a full range of flora and fauna representative of the exciting west slopes.

DESCRIPTION (Strenuous trip)

1st 3 Hiking Days: Follow trip 29 to **Portal Lake**, 22½ miles.

4th Hiking Day (**Portal Lake** to **Blue Canyon Cabinsite**, 7 miles cross country): Staying on the south side of the inlet stream from Portal Lake (10,300′), our route ascends the steep fractured granite slope to Midway Lake. One must take great care on this ascent, especially in the wet places. Then, on a gentler ascent, this route follows up Midway Lake's inlet stream past several rocky tarns to large (30-acre) Cathedral Lake. Fair fishing for rainbow and some brook trout (to 10″) is available here. This high, alpine lake is typical of the lakes of Blackcap Basin. Situated in a granite pocket, ringed by cirque walls on three sides, characterized by deep, cold waters, and relieved only by an occasional clump of willow, heather or stunted lodgepole, the lake hugs the White Divide. Our route skirts the north side of the lake, then turns southeast and climbs the talus and steep granite slabs to the crest of the White Divide just north of distinctive Finger Peak. After contouring beneath the steep north face of Finger Peak, this route crosses the saddle between Finger and Blue Canyon peaks. Views from this saddle are superlative of the White Divide, Goddard Divide, and Ragged Spur, and down into the Blue Canyon Creek drainage. Thence, our route descends by chutes to the northernmost, unnamed lakes of the Blue Canyon Creek drainage, and follows the southwest course of this drainage over slab granite that is broken by welcome grassy pockets. The route veers left and drops down to the west side of granitoid Lake 10364. At the outlet of this lake, our route crosses the stream and descends steeply to the moderately forested (lodgepole, quaking aspen, some hemlock) flats at the head of Blue Canyon. Staying on the south side of the creek, this route meets the fisherman's trail that descends steadily over a jumbled, rocky slope. From the slopes on the left, the hiker is very apt to hear the piping of a marmot as he rounds the turn in the canyon that gives him the view of the lovely, open meadows below. This trail scrambles down to the head of these meadows, skirting the eastern fringe, and arrives at the log ford leading to the good campsites up and downstream from the landmark cabinsite. Fishing for brook (to 10″) on Blue Canyon Creek is good.

5th and 6th Hiking Days: Reverse the steps of trip 35, 19½ miles.

Granite fractured by frost wedging   *Thomas Winnett*

32   Wishon Reservoir to Halfmoon Lake

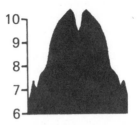

TRIP   Wishon Reservoir to Halfmoon Lake (round trip). Topo map *Blackcap Mountain*. Best early or mid season; 22 miles.

Grade	Trail/layover days	Total recommended days
Leisurely	4/1	5
Moderate	3/0	3
Strenuous	2/0	2

HILITES   Halfmoon Lake, at the end of an unnamed trail, nestled in a cirque below an unnamed peak, can serve as a hideout for the city-dweller who—temporarily—has had it. On the way to this fine lake, Mooreboys Meadow offers a campsite where the flora and fauna are plentiful and fascinating.

DESCRIPTION (Leisurely trip)

1st Hiking Day (**Wishon Reservoir** to **Mooreboys Meadow**, 5½ miles): From the east side of the dam, the trail angles northeast up a ridge on steep, dusty switchbacks under a mixed forest cover of pines, firs, cedar and occasional black oak. As views back down to Wishon become less frequent, the trail crosses a jeep road and passes into deep forest. Two tiny streamlets provide thirst-quenching relief on this strenuous climb, and a continuous band of wildflowers periodically expands into gardens in open spots, enhanced by many species of butterflies in an aerial array of blues, oranges and yellows. We descend from the ridge to Woodchuck Creek (good campsites) where a wade-across ford brings us to the junction of this newer section of trail with the pre-Wishon Woodchuck Trail. We ascend northward from the creek for a short distance, then veer east, climbing a manzanita-covered ridge under a moderate forest cover.

Past the sometimes muddy confluence of the branches of Woodchuck Creek, the trail passes a lateral leading to Indian Springs and Chuck Pass, then ascends to beautiful Mooreboys Meadow (not named on the topo map), which is filled with thousands upon thousands of shooting stars and corn lilies. The quiet hiker will be entertained by the antics of the very large marmot colony in the rocky ledge on the right, and the photographers may wish to camp at the north end of the meadow, along the creek, to take advantage of the large plant and animal populations.

Second Hiking Day (**Mooreboys Meadow** to **Halfmoon Lake**, 5½ miles): A short distance above the meadow, the trail passes a lateral leading left across the creek and up to Woodchuck Lake. Our trail bears right and ascends a ridge to a junction where another lateral goes left, this one passing Chimney and Marsh Lakes on its way to Woodchuck Lake. Another mile brings us to yet a third lateral up to Woodchuck. From this junction we ascend east gently to moderately, and climb the southeast ridge of an unnamed granite dome, where the sparseness of scattered lodgepole and whitebark pines allows broad views in all directions. Only the hiker totally dedicated to pushing down the trail can pass up the exhilirating panorama from the top of this island: an east-west spectrum from the LeConte Divide and Kettle Ridge down to the forested slopes beyond Wishon, and a north-south range from the Minarets to the high peaks in the southeast.

The trail drops steeply to the saddle of Crown Pass (Point 10188), where the vestiges of an unmaintained trail down Nichols Canyon go left and the Crown Lake/Crown Valley Trail goes right. Past these junctions, we follow the ridge north to a beautiful overlook of Halfmoon Lake before descending steeply down a densely forested lodgepole slope to the north end of the lake. Good campsites are on the north and east sides of this striking lake.

3rd and 4th Hiking Days: Retrace your steps, 11 miles.

33   Wishon Reservoir to Portal Lake

TRIP   From Wishon Reservoir to Portal Lake via Halfmoon Lake (round trip). Topo map *Blackcap Mountain.* Best mid season; 35 miles.

Grade	Trail/layover days	Total recom- mended days
Leisurely	6/1	7
Moderate	4/1	5
Strenuous	3/0	3

HILITES   Blackcap Basin is a worthy goal of any vacation trip, but this long route to it offers additional attractions along the way, from the serene forests of Woodchuck country to the dramatic cliffs surrounding Halfmoon Lake.

DESCRIPTION (Leisurely trip)

1st and 2nd Hiking Days: Follow trip 32 to **Halfmoon Lake,** 11 miles.

3rd Hiking Day (**Halfmoon Lake** to **Portal Lake,** 6½ miles): From the muddy junction north of Halfmoon Lake, our trail leads north down the valley of the lake's outlet. As the trail steepens, the forest cover thickens, and we begin to lose the sweeping views of the LeConte Divide, Bench Valley and aptly named Blackcap Mountain that have enhanced the walking to this point. After a wading ford our trail plunges in earnest down to the North Fork Kings River at Big Maxson Meadow. The sound of the river heralds the approach to a ford (difficult in early season) which takes us across to a junction with the Courtright/Blackcap Basin Trail at the northwest end of the meadow, from where we follow the 3rd hiking day, trip 29, to Portal Lake.

4th, 5th and 6th Hiking Days: Retrace your steps, 17½ miles.

Wishon Reservoir to Crown Lake   **34**

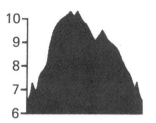

TRIP   From Wishon Reservoir to Crown Lake (semiloop trip). Topo maps *Blackcap Mountain, Tehipite Dome.* Best early or mid season; 24 miles.

Grade	Trail/layover days	Total recom- mended days
Leisurely	4/1	5
Moderate	3/1	4
Strenuous	2/0	2

HILITES   Everybody wants to get off the beaten path, but if everybody goes to the same unused place, it will be beaten. This guidebook attempts to offer a number of selections for solitude, so that your chances of being alone, when you go to one of them, will be pretty good. This excursion touches a number of such places.

DESCRIPTION (Leisurely trip)

1st Hiking Day: Follow trip 32 to **Mooreboys Meadow,** 5½ miles.

2nd Hiking Day (**Mooreboys Meadow** to **Crown Lake,** 5 miles): Follow the 2nd hiking day of trip 32 to the junction of the Crown Lake Trail and turn right (south) on it.

From the junction, the trail descends steeply south to the large, lodgepole-ringed meadow of Crown Lake. Viewed from the pass, the lake does have a crownlike shape, but its west side, containing several small pools, can be quite marshy at times, and campsites are best on the east side of the lake, where the trail skirts it.

3rd Hiking Day (**Crown Lake** to **Indian Springs,** 6 miles): The trail becomes somewhat indistinct as it crosses the marshy south end below Crown Lake, but it can easily be located as it follows along the east side of the outlet creek. Here we descend easily in moderate forest, at first lodgepole, but mixed with western white pine

nearer Scepter Creek. Intermittent marshy patches interrupt the
duff trail as it descends gently southward, crossing the creek
shortly beyond a junction with a trail back up the East Fork of
Scepter Creek. The Crown Valley Trail continues downstream,
swinging a bit west of the creek, so that it is out of sight and
sound.

We continue south to a junction with the Chuck Pass/Indian
Springs Trail in Large Meadow and turn right (west) onto it. This
level trail leads west to a ford of the unnamed stream draining
Chuck Pass and then climbs moderately up the west side of the
creek. The forest-bordered meadows along the creek headwaters
are, in the mountain springtime, narrow emerald ribbons interspersed with lush gardens. From Chuck Pass our trail leads down
through heavy, parklike pine forest on a set of steep switchbacks.
The path then threads a rocky, snag-strewn meadow and descends to a series of sweeping green meadows on the south, where
the wildflower population boasts dozens of species. Descending
gently, the trail reaches Indian Springs and some good campsites
near Woodchuck Creek.

4th Hiking Day: (**Indian Springs** to **Wishon Reservoir,** 7½ miles):
The trail down the valley of Woodchuck Creek, often soft and
muddy from the seepage of springs, penetrates a dense forest of
lodgepole pine and reaches a junction with the Hoffman Mountain Trail. Here it veers north and passes the ruins of an old
cabin. This sandy forest path then dips west to meet the
Wishon/Halfmoon Trail at a junction passed on the first hiking
day. From here we retrace the steps of part of that hiking day to
the roadend.

Crown Valley Trailhead to Blue Canyon   **35**

TRIP   From Crown Valley Trailhead to Blue Canyon via
Cabin Creek, Crown Creek, Kettle Ridge (round
trip). Topo maps *Tehipite Dome, Marion Peak, Mt.
Goddard.* Best mid or late season; 39 miles.

Grade	Trail/layover days	Total recommended days
Leisurely	8/2	10
Moderate	6/2	8
Strenuous	4/2	6

HILITES   This trip winds through magnificent stands of fir and
lodgepole before crossing lofty Kettle Ridge to Blue
Canyon. Naturalists will find that the ecological contrast between the west and east slopes of Kettle
Ridge almost coincides with that found when crossing the Sierra crest. Wildflowers abound around the
many tributary crossings, and fishing is excellent.

DESCRIPTION (Leisurely trip)

1st Hiking Day (**Crown Valley Trailhead** to **Cabin Creek,** 5½ miles):
From the trailhead parking lot, this route crosses an easy rise to
the east, passing through a magnificent forest of sugar, lodgepole,
Jeffrey, white fir and incense-cedar. Mostly duff, the trail becomes very dusty owing to heavy stock usage as the summer
progresses. The trail then fords Little Rancheria Creek, and continues its gentle ascent past the Spanish Lake Trail, where the
ascent becomes steeper. Short switchbacks bring one to the lush,
wildflower-filled seepage area surrounding Three Springs. Here,
fresh, cold water gushes from the ground in a dainty meadow. A
dense fir forest pushes against the edges of the lush meadow, and
wildlife tracks abound in the vicinity of the spring. Among the
tracks one is very apt to find those of the mule deer, porcupine,
black bear, meadow mouse, skunk, squirrel, and any number of a
variety of birds including pygmy nuthatch, robin, bluejay, junco,
horned owl and woodpecker. After leaving the springs, the ascent
levels off gradually until it reaches the top of the ridge, and it

passes the first of three laterals to Hoffman Mountain. Tiny tributaries repeatedly cross the trail, making the top of this climb a lovely wildflower garden that includes lupine, monkey flower, golden brodiaea, currant, gooseberry and larkspur. As the trail turns somewhat southerly, it begins to descend, and, through the trees, one has limited views to the southeast of Spanish Mountain, Rodgers Ridge and the Obelisk. The duff trail then descends through a moderate-to-dense forest cover of lodgepole, red fir, and some Jeffrey to a ford of a tributary of Cabin Creek. About ¼ mile beyond, the trail dips to the good campsites at Cabin Creek (8240'). The creek is a tiny stream of water, but its diminutive size does not hide its irrepressible nature as it tumbles down with a riot of sound. Brook trout abound in this little creek, but fishermen will find them generally very small. The better campsites are located just upstream.

2nd Hiking Day (**Cabin Creek** to **Crown Creek,** 6 miles): Leaving Cabin Creek the trail continues easterly and passes the second lateral to Hoffman Mountain branching off to the left. Gradually ascending over a rock and duff surface, the trail tops an easy saddle that is distinguished by its stands of the smooth, pale-barked quaking aspen. From the saddle the trail descends gently through a dense forest cover of red fir and lodgepole past the last trail lateral to Hoffman Mountain (not shown on the topo map). (Most of the signing in Woodchuck Country is long out of date, and, except for indicating general directions, is dangerously misleading.) A few yards beyond, our route passes the Statum Meadow Trail branching right, and continues on past Cow Meadow to Summit Meadow (incorrectly labeled as "Wet Meadow" on the topo map). Views on the left include the jumbled granite landmark of Crown Rock, and a few yards farther on our trail passes another trail lateral to Spanish Lake. The duff-and-sand trail winds through a dense timber cover on a gentle descent to the uniquely constructed Crown Valley Guard Station, where emergency services are available when it is manned. Turning somewhat northerly, the trail descends to the willow-infested and ghost-snagged west end of the Crown Valley meadows, and in the course of this descent passes several primitive campsites situated next to the small stream on the right. The trail fords this tributary at the head of the meadow, and winds around the fenced southern edge of the grasslands. The dozen or so buildings of the Crown Valley Ranch, a recently active "guest ranch," come into view as the trail winds the length of the valley. Just beyond the ranch clearing our trail passes the Tehipite Valley Trail and the John Muir Wilderness boundary sign, and then winds through a dense forest of red fir, white fir, lodgepole and Jeffrey. Descending gently, the trail affords occasional, tree-shrouded views of the Monarch Divide, and in the more open sections one can see Spanish Mountain and the Obelisk to the southwest. Increasing amounts of manzanita, snowbrush and willow can be seen from the trail as it descends more steeply into the tributary drainages of Crown Creek, and the trail surface becomes very sandy as it traverses a long slope to Crown Creek itself. A few yards above the creek bed, a sign reading "campsite" points along a trail lateral branching left. This lateral ascends the Crown Creek drainage for about 1 mile, and then descends to a long, wade-across (dangerous in high water) ford. On the east side of the creek, the lateral terminates at several excellent meadowed campsites (7040') where firewood is abundant. Anglers will delight in the excellent rainbow fishing (to 16") to be found along the creek, and naturalists will find the natural salt lick at the creek ford a superlative spot for quiet wildlife watching.

3rd Hiking Day (**Crown Creek** to **Kettle Dome Campsite,** 4½ miles): Retrace your steps to the main trail, and turn left toward Crown Creek. A few descending steps from this junction, the trail fords Crown Creek and continues eastward in fairly level fashion. As the trail nears the foot of Kettle Ridge, Kettle Dome comes into view as a two-pronged granite finger. The trail crosses several small run-off streams (not all are indicated on the topo), and at the Kings Canyon National Park boundary begins a steady climb. For those who are interested, the 7500-foot contour marks the best place to begin a side excursion to ascend Tehipite Dome. It is an interesting historical sidelight that Frank Dusy, a local sheepherder, around the turn of the century pursued a wounded grizzly bear approximately along this route. Further exploration by Dusy for grazing areas resulted in the blazing of this crossing of Kettle Ridge and the old Tunemah Trail (leading to Simpson Meadow). It is interesting to note that the lower slopes have some sugar pine, John Muir's favorite Sierra tree. The trail soon becomes very steep, with exceptionally few switchbacks, and this poor trail construction results in the trail's being heavily washed—a condition not helped by the heavy stock traffic it suffers. As the trail ascends, the forest cover thins somewhat, but still includes sugar pine, red fir, lodgepole and Jeffrey. The underbrush, for the most part, is manzanita and snowbrush. At the top of the ridge, it is time well spent to detour off to the right of the trail for the unsurpassed views of Monarch Divide and the Middle Fork Kings River watershed. The panorama of the Monarch Divide encompasses Goat Crest, Slide Peak, Kennedy Mountain and Hogback Peak. Slide Peak, with its clearly defined avalanche chutes, is particularly interesting, and above the

canyon's blue haze one can trace the glacial paths on the far side
that left the remarkable, unnamed, finlike ridge to the east-
southeast. The trail crosses a tiny, incongruous stream right on
top of the ridge, and then descends steeply. This descent offers a
different set of views, including Tunemah Peak, Burnt Mountain,
Blue Canyon, Marion Peak, parts of Cirque Crest, Goat Crest and
the rest of the Monarch Divide. The initial descent levels off in a
meadowed bench containing a good tributary stream (unnamed)
and several excellent campsites (8200'). These campsites are due
east of Kettle Dome, and approximately 1000 feet above the Blue
Canyon floor.

4th Hiking Day (**Kettle Dome Campsite** to **Blue Canyon Cabinsite,**
3½ miles): The dusty and rocky trail descends by steady, steep
switchbacks the remaining 1000 feet to the canyon floor. This
descent parallels the tributary on which the campsites for the
previous hiking day were situated until it nears Blue Canyon
Creek. The flora of Blue Canyon differs markedly from that of
Crown Creek, and the combination of sagebrush, quaking aspen,
and rushing creek gives the impression of being alongside one of
the plummeting streams on the east side of the Sierra. Ascending
the rocky slopes of Blue Canyon, the trail alternates between
steady and steep climbing through a sparse-to-moderate forest
cover that includes lodgepole, aspen and some juniper. Looking
back down Blue Canyon, one has Veed views across the Middle
Fork Kings River to the Monarch Divide and the pinnacle formations that constitute Kennedy Peak. Flowers along this ascent
include Indian paintbrush, pennyroyal, Mariposa lily, pussy
paws, scarlet gilia and larkspur. Just north of the large packer
site, the trail crosses to the east side of the creek via a deep
wade-across ford, and then continues its steady climb. Above this
ford, Blue Canyon Creek exhibits some of the most spectacular
granite-bottomed chutes in the Sierra. The water shoots at an
incredible velocity down these chutes, which are sometimes ¼
mile long. They are marked at either end by cascades and water-
falls. At the head of one of these series, the trail emerges at Blue
Canyon meadows. Here, in contrast to the white-water mael-
strom below, Blue Canyon Creek winds docilely in typical
meadow-meandering fashion, and immediately on the left one
can see the old notched-log sheepherder cabin across the creek.
Good campsites lie just south of the cabin. Angling for brook and
rainbow (to 10") in Blue Canyon Creek is good. These campsites
make a good base camp for angling and discovery side trips to the
head of Blue Canyon basin, and to the adjoining watershed of
Alpine Creek (to the east—see trip 36).

5th, 6th, 7th and 8th Hiking Days: Retrace your steps, 19½ miles.

Crown Valley Trailhead to Alpine Creek   **36**

TRIP From Crown Valley Trailhead to Upper Alpine Creek via Cabin Creek, Crown Creek, Kettle Ridge, Blue Canyon, Tunemah Trail (round trip). Topo maps *Tehipite Dome, Marion Peak*. Best mid or late season; 47 miles.

Grade	Trail/layover days	Total recommended days
Leisurely	10/3	13
Moderate	8/3	11
Strenuous	5/2	7

HILITES Traversing mostly wooded slopes, this trip crosses Kettle Ridge and descends to captivating Blue Canyon. The excellent fishing on Crown and Blue Canyon creeks might understandably warrant making this trip, but the subsequent cross-country travel adds a dash of spice that makes this a must for intermediate hikers.

DESCRIPTION (Leisurely trip)

1st, 2nd, 3rd and 4th Hiking Days: Follow trip 35 to **Blue Canyon Cabinsite,** 19½ miles.

5th Hiking Day (**Blue Canyon Cabinsite** to **Upper Alpine Creek,** 4 miles cross country): This hiking day's route follows parts of the old Tunemah Trail. Originally a sheepherder's route to Simpson Meadow, this route then became a heavily used stock trail, but with the advent of Kings Canyon National Park and the subsequent exclusion of grazing rights, the trail fell into disuse. Today the only mark, other than that of the abundant wildlife, which one sees on this trail is the boottrack of the adventurous knapsacker. The derivation of the name "Tunemah," as described in an old magazine article, is "a Chinese 'cuss-word' of very vivacious connotation."*

The point where the Tunemah Trail branches east from Blue Canyon is due east of the cabinsite described in the previous hiking day. Unsigned, this trail is marked only by two ancient rock cairns. The old Tunemah Trail left the canyon about 1½ miles down-canyon. Once found, however, the trail remains remarkably clear as it ascends the east wall of the canyon. The initial section is ducked over open, rocky terrain but it soon resolves into a long, steady traverse that parallels a stream not shown on the topo map, about ⅛ mile north of the stream. This first rise terminates at a small meadow where the hiker can see a marked change in the forest cover, as dense stands of lodgepole, silver pine and some juniper line the wild pasture. The trail then continues to climb steadily. This well-ducked ascent keeps to the left of the stream that empties this long, timbered cirque, and as the hiker rises above the cirque floor, he has fine views southwest to Tehipite Dome, Tombstone Ridge, and the timbered east face of Kettle Dome. This steady ascent terminates at a moderately timbered saddle just north of Burnt Mountain. On the east side of the saddle, one has fine views ranging from the northeast to the southeast of White Divide, Tunemah Peak, Observation Peak, Red Point, Marion Peak, State Peak, Dougherty Peak, Dead Pine Ridge and Kennedy Mountain.

From this saddle our route descends past the wet-meadowed site of a snow-survey tower, where the hiker must choose between two alternatives. One way is to scoot northwest up and over a prominent timberline spur leading down from Peak 11448, and then dip slightly over talus to a meadowed bench and brook. A short, enjoyable stab at ascending granite slabs to the 10,400-foot level and a scramble down a rocky gulley lead to the outlet of Lake 10450, where tracks of bear and deer abound. A steep boulder-hop will get the hiker back up to 10,400 feet on a nose to the northeast, from which point the undulations that must be traversed to reach the fine campsites on Alpine Creek are insignificant. The other possible route from the snow-survey tower contours around the upper Rattlesnake Creek drainage, where all vestiges of a trail disappear. Finding the route is no problem, as it continues due east across the moderately timbered divide separating the Rattlesnake and Alpine Creek drainages. Contouring around the head of the steep west wall of the Alpine Creek drainage entails some bouldering and traversing of granite slabs to the creek, where our route fords. This ford is best made

*"Unexplored Regions of the High Sierras," T. S. Solomons, Overland, Nov. 1896.

above the picturesque waterfall and chute. Staying on the east side of Alpine Creek, a faint trail ascends to open, alpine tundra-meadows and the excellent campsites (10,400′) just west of Tunemah Peak. Those interested in these fragile, high-country meadows will find the typical red-flowered primrose and the clustered, much-tufted, white-flowered alpine saxifrage underfoot. Good fishing for brook trout (to 10″) is available on Alpine Creek. These campsites provide a splendid alpine setting for further excursions to Tunemah Lake and ascents of nearby Tunemah, Blue Canyon and Finger peaks.

6th Hiking Day (**Upper Alpine Creek** to **Blue Canyon Cabinsite,** 4 miles cross country): Retrace the steps of the 5th hiking day, or ascend the Alpine Creek drainage ½ mile and cross the divide between the Alpine and Blue Canyon Creek drainages at saddle 11046. Because this route is frequently touched with snow until late in the season, care should be exercised. This route descends via chutes to the wooded head of Blue Canyon Creek, and then proceeds as described in the 4th hiking day, trip 31.

7th, 8th, 9th and 10th Hiking Days: Reverse the steps of the first 4 hiking days, 19½ miles.

Corn lilies sprout in wet ground   *Thomas Winnett*

37 Crown Valley Trailhead to South Lake

TRIP   From Crown Valley Trailhead to South Lake via Crown Valley, Blue Canyon, Tunemah Trail, Simpson Meadow, Middle Fork Kings River, Dusy Basin, Bishop Pass (shuttle trip). Topo maps *Tehipite Dome, Marion Peak, Mt. Goddard*. Best mid or late season; 56 miles.

Grade	Trail/layover days	Total recommended days
Leisurely	11/4	15
Moderate	9/3	12
Strenuous	6/3	9

HILITES   Experienced backpackers who like their country "high and wild" will find this remote trans-Sierra route to their liking. The fine fishing at the beginning and end of this long trip justifies taking a rod along, and the photographer will find ample cause to use several rolls of film on the abundant wildlife and landscapes he will encounter. The cross country composing the midsection of this trip is sufficient challenge for the hardiest hiker.

DESCRIPTION (Moderate trip)
1st, 2nd, 3rd, 4th and 5th Hiking Days: Follow trip 36 to **Upper Alpine Creek,** 23½ miles.
6th Hiking Day (**Upper Alpine Creek** to **Simpson Meadow,** 8 miles cross country): The hiker breaking camp is confronted with two alternatives. He can climb to Tunemah Pass by way of Tunemah Peak (Peak 10985) and the White Divide (excellent views, but no

water) or descend to the route of the old Tunemah Trail and climb it via Bunchgrass Flat (less elevation gain, plentiful water, but difficult route-finding). The White Divide route descends slightly east of Alpine Creek (remember to fill two quart canteens with water before you leave) to a meadowed bench, which it contours to a sidehill moraine. Note the prominent unforested spur of Tunemah Peak to the south; the route ascends diagonally between it and the cliffs to the north. The footing is sometimes treacherous on scree-covered slabs until the route tops the skyline seen from the bench and swings east up steep slopes of stunted whitebark pine to the summit ridge. Patience and practice in boulder-hopping will get one to the 11,894-foot summit from here. After a pause to take in the magnificent view, pick your way down a steep talus slope to a saddle immediately east of the peak. Proceed southeast down the White Divide, keeping to the right to avoid minor peaks on the ridge. Thickets of stunted whitebark hamper progress along the way and may necessitate some climbing to escape them. Bunchgrass Flat can be seen deep in the canyon of Dog Creek as a steep green pasture. A short pull brings the hiker to Peak 10985. From this point, not Simpson Meadow but the slopes farther up the Middle Fork Kings River that were ravaged by a 1948 fire are visible. Descend east-northeast on talus to the sloping forested plateau seen from above, keeping close to the northeast spur of Peak 10985. Remnants of the old Tunemah Trail, and the other alternate route, are soon met contouring in from the south.

The Tunemah Trail route from the campsite on upper Alpine Creek descends the east side of the creek, then starts to contour along the Alpine Creek drainage just below the chutes and water-falls cited in the previous hiking day. This contouring traverse fords the tiny East Fork of Alpine Creek amid a moderate forest cover of lodgepole and red fir, and then rounds the rocky nose of the watershed divide above Bunchgrass Flat. After fording Dog Creek, the route ascends steeply to a timbered depression just south of Peak 10985, from which one obtains sweeping views northward of the Goddard Creek drainage, including Ragged Spur and portions of the Black Divide. Directly east-northeast, towering Mt. Woodworth tops the horizon, and the barren heights of the Monarch Divide and Cirque Crest dominate the south and southeast, with the impressive avalanche-chute-scarred Windy Peak in the foreground. From this point, the route contours, and even climbs somewhat to avoid drop-offs to the south, to join the alternate route in descending the pronounced east-northeast spur of Peak 10985. Where the going gets steeper, vestiges of the old Tunemah Trail may be followed traversing, plummeting down chutes, and traversing yet again, always heading more or less northeast. Beguiling game trails cross the route, seemingly headed straight south for Simpson Meadow. Don't trust them—they peter out in dense brush and leave the exhausted hiker hung up among numerous cliffs. Halfway down, water can be found by making a short northward traverse to the mapped creek. At 8000 feet it is safe to turn due east and begin the bushwhack in earnest, unhampered by cliffs. The rattlesnakes commonly found in this area occupy the hiker's mind as his legs sink into waist-deep brush, although presumably he had lost his fear of death long before selecting this trip. Where Goddard Creek drools over the lip of its hanging valley, the cross-country route from the Enchanted Gorge (see the High Sierra Hiking Guide to *Mt. Goddard*) is met.

Down at the banks of the Middle Fork Kings River the problem is to find logs or boulders in any combination suitable for crossing. Traces of the old Tunemah Trail may be followed to a high trail bridge a mile downstream if attempts to ford are frustrated. Across the bridge one turns upstream on the Middle Fork Trail. At Dougherty Creek (log crossing) and a half mile beyond in Simpson Meadow there are several good packer campsites. In between are a junction with the Granite Pass Trail, a perhaps-staffed ranger station, and a ford of Horseshoe Creek. The timber cover on this flat includes lodgepole, fir, Jeffrey and quaking aspen; and the predominant shrub is sagebrush. The brook and rainbow fishing (to 16″) in the Middle Fork is good to excellent. For those interested in reliving bits of history, this meadow site and the flats of Tehipite Valley were a favorite campsite of the Indian tribe of the Monache (the mountain men of the Yokuts tribe). A little casting around on the granite slopes above the trail will reveal several examples of bedrock mortars in which the Indians ground seeds and tanned hides.

7th, 8th and 9th Hiking Days: Follow trip 56, days 4, 5 and 6, 24½ miles.

South Lake to Treasure Lakes   **38**

TRIP   From South Lake to Treasure Lakes (round trip). Topo map *Mt. Goddard*. Best mid or late season; 5 miles.

Grade	Trail/layover days	Total recom- mended days
Leisurely	2/0	2
Moderate	....	....
Strenuous	....	....

HILITES   This short trip is a fine "weekender." Touching the upper reaches of the South Fork of Bishop Creek, it exposes the traveler to three life zones with a very limited expenditure of energy and time.

DESCRIPTION (Leisurely trip)

1st Hiking Day (**South Lake** to **Treasure Lakes,** 2½ miles): From the roadend (9760') the trail climbs steadily along the east side of South Lake. A moderate-to-dense forest cover of lodgepole pine and fir lines the rocky route as it meets and turns onto the Treasure Lakes Trail. Mostly over duff and sand, the trail descends, fording Bishop Creek's South Fork and a tributary. This descent affords good views of Hurd Peak and the backgrounding, glacially topped Sierra crest. The trail then fords another tributary and the outlet from the largest of the Treasure Lakes. After this ford we begin a moderate-to-steep ascent on a duff-and-sand trail that swerves somewhat north before doubling back and continuing the ascent in a southward direction. In the higher elevations, the forest cover shows increasing whitebark pine mixed with the lodgepole, and there is an abundance of wildflowers lining the trail and clustered in the grassy sections that seam the granite. Although this trail does see some stock traffic, it is, for the most part, a hiker's trail. The ascent steepens, crosses an area of smoothed granite slabs dotted with glacial erratic boulders, and after fording the outlet stream from Lake 10646, arrives at the good campsites on the northeast side of that lake. This lake, the largest in the Treasure Lakes basin (12 acres), affords fair-to-good

fishing for golden (to 12″). Anglers who wish to spend a layover day here will find that, contrary to the usual rule of thumb, the fishing gets better as one tries the lakes of the upper basin.
2nd Hiking Day: Retrace your steps, 2½ miles.

Golden trout from Granite Park

Thomas Winnett

South Lake to Treasure Lakes **39**

TRIP   From South Lake to Treasure Lakes, return via cross-country route to Long Lake (semiloop trip). Topo map *Mt. Goddard*. Best mid or late season; 8 miles.

Grade	Trail/layover days	Total recommended days
Leisurely	2/0	2
Moderate	....	....
Strenuous	....	....

HILITES   Like the previous trip, this two-day trek explores the Treasure Lakes chain, but, unlike the previous trip, it returns by an easy cross-country route to the Bishop Pass Trail. Thus it makes a fine, easy semiloop that should be investigated by all, regardless of experience.

DESCRIPTION (Leisurely trip)

1st Hiking Day: Follow trip 38 to **Treasure Lakes,** 2½ miles.

2nd Hiking Day (**Treasure Lakes** to **South Lake** via Long Lake, 5½ miles, part cross country): Following the faint fisherman's trail that ascends from the south end of the largest of the Treasure Lakes (10,646'), one follows the intervening stream to the cirque-basined three upper lakes. This ascent sees the timber cover thinning until, at the upper triad, all that remains is low-lying whitebark pine. Like the lower Treasure Lakes, these three lakes contain a good population of golden trout (to 15"). These trout were originally backpacked in by A. Parcher, son of the pioneer resort owner W. C. Parcher, and the spawn of that initial plant provide good fishing for today's anglers. From the upper lake, our route crosses the outlet and ascends the moderate slopes to the saddle just east of the lake. This ascent crosses easy ledges and some loose rock just south of the gray fractured slopes of Hurd Peak. Grand views from this saddle include Mts. Gilbert, Johnson and Goode to the south and southwest; and the spectacu-

lar comb ridge of the Inconsolable Range lining the South Fork
Bishop Creek drainage to the east.

Our route then follows the natural, moderate-sloped descent to
lovely Margaret Lake (brook trout, to 8″). Thence it descends
along the tarn-dotted slopes northeast of Margaret Lake, and,
after fording tumbling South Fork Bishop Creek just north of
Spearhead Lake (rainbow, to 16″), meets and turns left onto the
South Lake/Bishop Pass Trail. After fording the willow-infested
outlet of Ruwau Lake, it passes the lateral trail to that lake, and
circles very close along the east shore of Long Lake (brook, rainbow, brown, to 17″). At the tail of Long Lake, the trail refords the
South Fork Bishop Creek. Our route then passes the Bull and
Chocolate Lakes Trail lateral. The moderate descent changes to a
steep switchbacking downgrade before recrossing the South Fork
of Bishop Creek for the last time. As it levels out, it passes the
Treasure Lakes spur trail, and retraces a portion of the 1st hiking
day's route to South Lake.

Dusy Basin, the Black Divide   *Thomas Winnett*

South Lake to Dusy Basin **40**

TRIP   From South Lake to Dusy Basin via Bishop Pass (round trip). Topo map *Mt. Goddard*. Best mid or late season; 14 miles.

Grade	Trail/layover days	Total recommended days
Leisurely	....	....
Moderate	2/0	2
Strenuous	....	....

HILITES   A popular route, the Bishop Pass Trail climbs the scenic course of the South Fork of Bishop Creek. At Bishop Pass, the trail enters King Canyon National Park, but, more significantly, it begins the adventure of the high, barren, granitoid country of Dusy Basin. Grand side-trip possibilities are sufficient reason for planning layover days on this trip.

DESCRIPTION (Moderate trip)

1st Hiking Day (**South Lake** to **Dusy Basin**, 7 miles): Starting from the roadend (9760′)—about ¼ mile above the South Lake dam—the trail ascends through a moderate-to-dense forest cover of lodgepole and fir on a somewhat rocky trail. This ascent traverses the morainal slope on the east side of South Lake, bearing toward Hurd Peak, and then passes the junction with the Treasure Lakes Trail. The trail shifts direction somewhat eastward as it slopes upward along the South Fork Bishop Creek, and passes the Bull and Chocolate Lakes Trail junction. Frequent patches of lupine, forget-me-nots, wallflowers, and swamp onions delight the traveler as he fords tributaries and crosses swampy sections. The trail then fords the South Fork Bishop Creek and switchbacks up to the islet-dotted north end of Long Lake. After recrossing South Fork Bishop Creek, it undulates along the east side of beautiful Long Lake (brook, rainbow, brown, to 17″) and passes the junction with the Chocolate and Ruwau Lakes Trail. The memorable vistas of the wooded and meadowed shores of

Long Lake stay with the visitor as he crosses the cascading Ruwau Lake outlet stream and ascends through sporadic subalpine tarn-dotted meadows. Sometimes steep, this steadily ascending trail climbs past spectacular Saddlerock Lake (rainbow to 10″), and the unmarked fisherman's trail spur to Bishop Lake (brook to 14″).

Beyond Saddlerock Lake, the trail passes timberline and begins a series of steep switchbacks at the head of a spectacular cirque basin. Excellent views of Mt. Goode appear on the right, and the incredible comb spires of the Inconsolable Range on the left accompany the panting climber, making his breather stops unforgettable occasions. Glacially smoothed ledge granite and quarried blocks on every hand line this well-maintained trail as it passes the unmarked and unmaintained Jigsaw Pass route, visible as a steep, nearby, talus-bottomed col at the head of the Inconsolable Range. Occasional pockets of snow sometimes blanket the approach to Bishop Pass (11,972′) late into the season, and care should be exercised in the final ascent to the summit. Views from the pass are excellent of the Inconsolable Range to the north; the Palisades to the southeast; Dusy Basin immediately to the south, flanked by Columbine and Giraud peaks; and the Black Divide on the distant western skyline. From the pass our route descends on a sometimes switchbacking southwestern traverse. This rocky descent contours over rock-bench systems some distance north of the basin's northernmost large lake (11,300′), fording its inlet stream. Just below this stream ford, our route branches left, leaving the trail and crossing smooth granite and tundra to the good campsites at the west end of this lake. Other good campsites can be found a few yards to the southwest, along the outlet stream. Fishing for golden and brook trout on this northernmost lake is fair, but anglers should try the good-to-excellent golden and brook angling (to 22″) at Lake 11393 and the lake just west, along with the connecting stream.

Alpine scenery from the above campsites is breathtaking in its vastness. One can see the Inconsolable Range as it rises behind Bishop Pass, and the climber's Mecca, the Palisade crest, fills the eastern skyline. Also to the east towers symmetrical Isosceles Peak. A very sparse forest cover of gnarled whitebark pine dots the granite landscape on all sides, and the fractures in the granite are filled with grassy, heather-lined pockets.

2nd Hiking Day: Retrace your steps, 7 miles.

South Lake to Big Pine Creek Roadend **41**

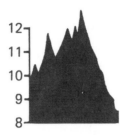

TRIP

From South Lake to Big Pine Creek Roadend via Treasure Lakes, Dusy Basin, cross country to Jigsaw Pass, Fifth Lake (shuttle trip). Topo maps *Mt. Goddard, Big Pine.* Best mid or late season; 20 miles.

Grade	Trail/layover days	Total recommended days
Leisurely	....	....
Moderate	4/1	5
Strenuous	2/0	2

HILITES

This unusual route is a fine selection for the intermediate backpacker who is looking for an interesting and challenging route with some cross-country work. The scenery en route is claimed by many to be the most impressive in the Sierra, and the angling varies from good to excellent, mostly on lakes. Camera buffs who neglect to bring along color film will regret it.

DESCRIPTION (Moderate trip)

1st Hiking Day: Follow trip 38 to **Treasure Lakes,** 2½ miles.

2nd Hiking Day (**Treasure Lakes** to **Dusy Basin,** 6½ miles, part cross country): Proceed cross country to the South Lake/Bishop Pass Trail as described in the 2nd hiking day, trip 39, where our route turns right onto the South Lake/Bishop Pass Trail and continues as described in the 1st hiking day, trip 40.

3rd Hiking Day (**Dusy Basin** to **Fifth Lake,** 5 miles, part cross country): Retrace the steps of the 2nd hiking day to Bishop Pass. As the trail descends east from the pass, it levels out somewhat and then swings north. Where the trail changes direction, our route branches right (unsigned) over granite ledges and boulders to the heavy talus pile that marks the foot of the Jigsaw Pass col. This cross-country boulder-hopping requires concentration, but even the most absorbed hiker will hear the underground tributary stream flowing several feet beneath the rock underfooting. Occasionally, between the large boulders, the beautifully built, now-landslide-covered Jigsaw Pass Trail, can be seen. This old trail once was traveled by stock (believe it or not!). The top of the col is cairned (12,622'), and taking a breather stop at this cairn affords excellent views west to Mt. Goode and the upper South Fork Bishop Creek drainage. Views to the south and north are restricted, but one can see down the steep North Fork Big Pine Creek drainage occupying the precipitous canyon to the east. Our route descends from the pass over talus and scree, and, keeping to the right, climbs down over stepladdering bench systems of fractured granite. Some sections of this steep downgrade entail difficult route-picking over huge boulders and "greasy rock," and care in one's footing is a must. Spectacular, knife-edges ridges line this descent on either side, but the steep watershed opens as it approaches the final, stiff climb down to the sparse-to-moderate forest cover at the southeast end of Fifth Lake. The best route keeps to the right to avoid the final steep bluffs above (immediately south of) Fifth Lake. Excellent campsites can be found near the outlet and along the east side of this fine lake. Fishing for rainbow, brook and brown (to 18″) is good.

4th Hiking Day (**Fifth Lake** to **Big Pine Creek Roadend,** 6 miles): From the outlet of Fifth Lake a faint fisherman's trail descends along the east side of the stream, turns east and, near the west side of Fourth Lake, strikes the Sixth Lake Trail, branching left, and the Black Lake Trail, continuing east. Our trail route turns right and descends along the east side of North Fork Big Pine Creek toward Third Lake.

An interesting side trip that requires an extra hiking day can be taken to Palisade Glacier. This cross-country route fords North Fork Big Pine Creek and ascends the Sam Mack Lake outlet stream. Keeping left of the stream, the route veers away from the lake on an easy ascent over granite and wildflower-filled grassy pockets to the foot of this algae-reddened ice mass.

Our trail route continues down the North Fork Big Pine Creek drainage through a moderate forest cover of whitebark pine and lodgepole. The trail is frequently rocky, particularly in the steeper stretches, as it switchbacks down the slope above Third Lake. Geologically interesting views to the south and east, of the differing granites of Temple Crag and Mt. Alice, make the traveler's rest breaks educational as well as pleasurable. Fair fishing for rainbow (to 12″) characterizes the waters of Third Lake, and this description holds for Second and First lakes as well. Wildflowers seen along this descent include Indian paintbrush, pussy paws, red columbine, wallflower, lupine, fireweed, tiger lily and shooting star. After passing man-enlarged Second and natural First lakes, the trail fords the North Fork Big Pine Creek and passes the trail lateral to Black Lake branching left. From that junction the trail continues to descend on a rocky slope, staying close to the north side of the North Fork Big Pine Creek. The decrease in altitude is reflected in the changing forest cover, which includes the lower-altitude-loving Jeffrey pine and fir, mixed with lodgepole, as it passes the large stone cabin marking Cienega Mirth flats. Descending past dashing Second Falls, the trail makes several long traverses, and en route passes the High Meadows Trail (branching left). A few yards past that junction our route meets the Big Pine Creek Roadend (8400′), about 1 mile above the confluence of the North and South forks of Big Pine Creek.

Red columbine

Jeff Schaffer

42 South Lake to Chocolate Lakes

TRIP   From South Lake to Chocolate Lakes (round trip).
Topo map *Mt. Goddard.* Best mid season; 6 miles.

Grade	Trail/layover days	Total recom- mended days
Leisurely	2/0	2
Moderate	....	....
Strenuous	....	....

HILITES   The barren heights of the Inconsolable Range mir-
rored in the lakes of the Chocolate chain make this
trip one to be remembered. The good fishing on the
lakes is a bonus, and the package ties up as a grand
"warm-up" for the hiker starting his season late.

DESCRIPTION (Leisurely trip)

1st Hiking Day (**South Lake** to **Chocolate Lakes,** 3 miles): Proceed to
the Bull Lake Trail junction as described in the 1st hiking day,
trip 40. Here our route turns left, away from the South
Lake/Bishop Pass Trail. Ascending moderately, the trail refords
the South Fork Bishop Creek, and arrives at sparsely timbered,
moderate-sized (10-acre) Bull Lake. Rock-encircled clumps of willows alternate with grassy sections as the trail skirts the north
side of the lake. Fishermen may wish to sample this lake's fair
brook-trout fishing (to 9″) before continuing up the lake's inlet
stream to the lower Chocolate Lakes. This ascent crosses rocky
talus stretches as it fords and refords the stream. Breather stops
offer sweeping views back across the South Fork Bishop Creek
drainage to Mts. Goode, Johnson, Gilbert and Thompson.
Dominating all views to the east are the barren, pinnacle-comb
formations of the somber Inconsolable Range. The granitic Chocolate Lakes chain consists of three lakes that are progressively
larger as one ascends the basin. Necklaced together, they hang
like sapphire jewels around the northeast side of red-rocked
Chocolate Peak. The trail passes several good campsites at lower
Chocolate Lake. All these lakes have a fair fishery of brook (to
10″), and the upper, larger lake (11,100′) affords good campsites.

2nd Hiking Day: Retrace your steps, 3 miles.

South Lake to Chocolate Lakes   **43**

TRIP   From South Lake to Chocolate Lakes return cross country to Treasure Lakes (semiloop). Topo map *Mt. Goddard*. Best mid or late season; 9½ miles.

Grade	Trail/layover days	Total recom- mended days
Leisurely	3/1	4
Moderate	2/1	3
Strenuous	....	....

HILITES   A premium added to the previous trip, this route returns via Ruwau Lake and Treasure Lakes. The short cross-country stretch of the second hiking day is a good test for novices who want to try their skills.

DESCRIPTION (Leisurely trip)

1st Hiking Day: Follow trip 42 to **Chocolate Lakes,** 3 miles.

2nd Hiking Day (**Chocolate Lakes** to **Treasure Lakes**, 4 miles, part cross country): From the upper Chocolate Lake (11,100′), the trail ascends southward up the easy ridge joining Chocolate Peak with the main crest of the Inconsolable Range. This rocky, sometimes faint trail then turns west as it descends steeply to the north shore of large (25-acre), deep Ruwau Lake. Fishing on this lake is fair to good for rainbow (to 16″). The trail then turns northwest and switchbacks down the steep, rocky valley wall to the South Lake/Bishop Pass Trail. Our route turns left onto this trail, fords the outlet creek from Ruwau Lake and leads around the south end of Long Lake, fording the South Fork Bishop Creek. Then it climbs southwest, up the easy sloping basin to Margaret Lake (brook trout, to 8″). Above Margaret Lake, the obvious route ascends the rocky talus basin to the southwest and crosses the divide south of Hurd Peak. Barren except for occasional whitebark pine, this cross-country route ascends by glaciated granite ledge systems to a rock-ribbed saddle. Views from this saddle are good of Mts. Goode, Johnson and Gilbert to the south and west, and the Inconsolable Range to the east. In addition to the boot track of the occasional cross-country walker, this saddle also sees the track of

deer, fox, marmot and cony. The steep descent route from this
saddle to the Treasure Lakes chain is easily ascertained, and the
traveler meets a faint fisherman's trail at the east side of the
upper of these lakes. This trail crosses talus and ledges around
the east side, fords the outlet, and follows the stream down
through moderate stands of whitebark pine to Lake 10646, the
largest of the Treasure Lakes chain. The hiker will find good
campsites on the northeast side of this lake. Fishing on this lake
is fair-to-good for golden (to 12″), and anglers investigating the
fishing on the upper Treasure Lakes will find good-to-excellent
angling for golden ranging in length from 8″ to 15″.

3rd Hiking Day: Reverse the steps of trip 38, 2½ miles.

Palisade Crest from the air (looking west)   *E.P. Pister*

South Lake to Palisade Basin   **44**

TRIP   From South Lake to Dusy Basin, return via Palisade Basin, Deer Meadow, Middle Fork Kings River, Bishop Pass (semiloop trip). Topo maps *Mt. Goddard*, *Big Pine*. Best mid or late season; 37½ miles.

Grade	Trail/layover days	Total recom- mended days
Leisurely	7/3	10
Moderate	6/2	8
Strenuous	4/2	6

HILITES   Those who yearn to go "high and light" will find this rugged route to their liking. For scenery the incomparable Palisade crest dominates the route, excepting along the short looping section on the John Muir Trail down Palisade Creek and up LeConte Canyon.

DESCRIPTION (Moderate trip)

1st Hiking Day: Follow trip 40 to **Dusy Basin, 7 miles.**

2nd Hiking Day (**Dusy Basin** to **Glacier Creek**, 6 miles cross country): The backpacker can contemplate crossing to Palisade Basin via any one of three foot-walkers' passes: Knapsack Pass; the unnamed pass between Columbine Peak and Isosceles Peak; and what has come to be known as "Thunderbolt Pass," just southwest of Thunderbolt Peak. Our route uses Knapsack Pass (11,673'). Leaving our campsite at the northernmost large lake of Dusy Basin, we descend on the trail and ford Dusy Branch Creek at 10,900 feet, just above (north of) the lowest lakes of the basin. From here our cross-country route boulder-hops southeastward on a steady ascent. The footing is mostly rock, broken by occasional pockets of granite sand, and the forest "cover" consists of very sparse clumps of the five-needled, stunted whitebark pine. These lower lakes contain golden and brook trout (to 12"). The well-ducked steady ascent over heavily fractured rock becomes steeper on the final climb to the pass. Impossible as it may seem, there are recorded visits to Palisade Basin via this pass with stock! Views from the pass include Black Giant, Mt. Powell and Mt. Thompson to the northwest, and the Palisade Basin and Crest to the east. From this vantage point, the vast expanses of Palisade Basin appear totally barren of life except for an isolated whitebark pine or a spiring snag, but a closer examination later in this hiking day will reveal much more. The continuing bracing views of the Palisade Crest, as our route descends from Knapsack Pass, stir the most blasé non-mountain-climber. These peaks look, as one climber expressed it, "like mountain peaks are supposed to look." Precipitous faces composed of relatively unfractured granite, couloirs, buttresses and residual glaciers combine to make this crest one of the finer climbing areas in the Sierra Nevada.

Our well ducked route keeps to the left as it descends over a moderate-to-steep ledge system to the westernmost lake of the Barrett chain. Passing around the south end of this rockbound lake, this route crosses the easy saddle east of the lake to the largest lake of the chain, and follows a fisherman's trail around the north end. From this lake the sheer cliffs of the west face of North Palisade dominate the skyline, and our route continues eastward past several tiny, rockbound lakelets. In contrast to the granite of lower Dusy Basin, this granite looks "newer," since it shows much less fracturing and exfoliation, but both were formed at the same time. After contouring around the head of the drainage at the east end of Palisade Basin, our route crosses the definite saddle between Point 12692 and the main Palisade Crest. Among climbers this saddle is called "Potluck Pass." Along with the continuing views of the Palisades, this vantage point also looks across the Palisade Creek watershed to Amphitheater Lake. To the southwest the glacially sculpted terrain has an appearance similar to the top of a meringue pie. The descent from Potluck is a scramble over a steep, smoothed granite ledge system, keeping to the right. This downgrade continues over scree and then levels out at Lake 11672, and our route follows the west shore of the lake to the good campsites on that edge of the lake and along the outlet creek just below the lake. Fishing at this lake is poor-to-fair for golden (to 8"). Grassy sections around the sandy-bottomed lake provide a foothold for colorful alpine wildflowers, including yellow columbine, sturdy white heather, and the blue sky pilot.

3rd Hiking Day (**Glacier Creek** to **Deer Meadow**, 5 miles, part cross country): After fording Glacier Creek, our route ascends the sloping basin east to a saddle overlooking the Palisade Lakes basin.

Views from this saddle are good of Devils Crags and Mt. McDuffie to the west, North Palisade to the north and Middle Palisade to the east. Sometimes over snow, this route descends past several tiny glacial tarns, across fractured granite as it veers westward. Part way down this moderate-to-steep grade, Palisade Lakes and the glacially smoothed bowl-like cirque surrounding the lakes come into view. Then, by route-finding down a ledge system, this route encounters sparse whitebark pine just before it meets the John Muir Trail just west of lower Palisade Lake. Anglers, and those wishing to view the lovely Palisade Lakes cirque basin, should walk the short distance to the northernmost of these lakes. Angling on these large lakes is fair-to-good for rainbow and golden (to 15″).

Continuing west on the John Muir Trail, the route descends by zigzagging switchbacks along the north side of Palisade Creek. Wildflowers seen along the creek include wallflower, shooting star, white cinquefoil, Indian paintbrush and penstemon. The head of these switchbacks is an excellent vantage point from which one can see the crest of Middle Palisade peak to the northeast, and, west beyond Deer Meadow lying immediately below, Devils Crags, Wheel Mountain, and Mt. McDuffie. Slopes on both sides of this steep descent are dramatically glacially smoothed. As the trail reaches the head of the flats above Deer Meadow, it enters a moderate stand of lodgepole and silver pine. Abundant wildflowers, including western mountain aster, Douglas phlox, pennyroyal, red columbine and tiger lily, appear as the trail comes close to the creek, and red fir, juniper and aspen occasionally mingle with the predominant lodgepole forest cover. The trail then passes several good campsites before fording Glacier Creek via several step-across branchlets. There are excellent views across the Palisade Creek canyon to the cascading falls of Cataract Creek as they tumble down the steep south wall. Through a heavily ferned area, the trail reaches the Amphitheater Lake Trail junction (unmarked except for a sign reading, "Deer Meadow, John Muir Trail"). Here amid a dense grove of lodgepole are several excellent campsites (8870′), where firewood is abundant, and fishing for golden and brook is excellent (to 12″). Hikers having a layover day here will find the steep climb up the unmaintained trail to Amphitheater Lake a rewarding one. Fine views, excellent angling for brook and golden, and evidence of abandoned mining ventures make this side trip an intriguing one.

4th Hiking Day (**Deer Meadow** to **Grouse Meadows**, 5 miles): About 100 yards below these campsites, the trail fords the unnamed drainage creek (multibranched) of Palisade Basin, and then descends moderately through a moderate-to-dense forest cover of lodgepole, aspen, red fir, and some Jeffrey pine and juniper. This descent passes a packers' campsite about 1½ miles farther on, and then more campsites a short distance beyond that. Concentrations of wildflowers include Indian paintbrush, penstemon, white cinquefoil, Mariposa lily and goldenrod. The underfooting is mostly duff and sand, through alternating forest and meadow, where camping and fishing are good. Then the trail veers away from Palisade Creek, only to return, and, keeping to the north side of the creek, descends steadily over morainal debris to the Middle Fork Kings River Trail, passing a meadow signed *Stillwater Meadow*. Our route turns right, up the Middle Fork Kings River, and proceeds for a gentle uphill mile over an easy ridge to the excellent campsites at the east side of Grouse Meadows.

5th and 6th Hiking Days: Follow trip 56, 5th and 6th hiking days. 14½ miles.

Grouse Meadows on the Middle Kings River

Esther Higgins

South Lake to Courtright Reservoir   **45**

TRIP   From South Lake to Courtright Reservoir, via
Bishop Pass, Dusy Basin, John Muir Trail, Muir
Pass, Evolution Valley, Goddard Canyon, Hell-for-
Sure Pass, Rae Lake, Post Corral Meadows (shuttle
trip). Topo maps *Mt. Goddard, Blackcap Mountain.*
Best mid or late season; 58½ miles.

Grade	Trail/layover days	Total recom- mended days
Leisurely	11/5	16
Moderate	9/4	13
Strenuous	7/3	10

HILITES   So much laudatory prose has been written about the
famous Muir Trail that it seems redundant to add to
it. Suffice it to say that this section of trail tours the
essence of high country, and has the added fillip of
finishing via the elegant forest stretches found west
of Hell-for-Sure Pass.

DESCRIPTION (Moderate trip)

1st Hiking Day: Follow trip 40 to **Dusy Basin,** 7 miles.

2nd Hiking Day (**Dusy Basin** to **Little Pete Meadow,** 6 miles): The
trail from the northernmost lake of the Dusy Basin descends over
smooth granite ledges and tundra sections. Occasional clumps of
the flaky-barked, five-needled whitebark pine dot the glacially
scoured basin, and impressive views of Mts. Agassiz and Winchell
and Thunderbolt Peak background Isosceles Peak to the east. To
the south the heavily fractured and less well defined summits of
Columbine and Giraud peaks occupy the skyline. This moderate
descent swings westward above the lowest lakes of the Dusy
Basin, and begins a series of steady switchbacks along the north
side of Dusy Branch Creek. Wildflowers along this descent include Indian paintbrush, pennyroyal, lupine, white cinquefoil,
penstemon, shooting star and some yellow columbine. Views of

the U-shaped Middle Fork Kings River are seen constantly during the zigzagging downgrade, and on the far side of the valley one can see the major peaks of the Black Divide, flanked, in the foreground, by The Citadel and Langille Peak. As the trail descends, the very sparse forest cover of stunted whitebark seen in most of Dusy Basin gives way to the trees of lower altitudes, including silver pine, juniper, lodgepole, aspen and some red fir near the foot of the switchbacks. Naturalists will be interested in the record girth of the old juniper marking the "elbow" of the final switchback before a bridge crossing of Dusy Branch Creek.

The chutes and cascades of Dusy Branch Creek are dramatic examples of High Sierra streams, and are time-honored favorites of the photographer. The trail recrosses Dusy Branch Creek at the head of a stepladdering bench, and then makes the final switchbacking descent to the junction with the John Muir Trail in LeConte Canyon. Emergency services are available from the ranger station just a few yards northwest of the junction. Our route turns right, onto the famous Muir Trail, and ascends moderately over a duff trail through moderate-to-dense stands of lodgepole. Langille Peak dominates the views to the left, and its striking white, fractured granite face is a constant reminder of the massive forces expended by the river of ice that once filled this canyon. Abundant fields of wildflowers color the trailside, including corn lily, white mariposa, tiger lily, buckwheat, fireweed, larkspur, red heather, shooting star, paintbrush, cinquefoil, monkey flower, pennyroyal, penstemon, aster, gooseberry, currant, goldenrod and wallflower. As the trail approaches the south end of Little Pete Meadow, occasional hemlock will be found mixed with the lodgepole, and the view north at the edge of the meadow includes Mts. Powell and Thompson. There are good but heavily used campsites at Little Pete Meadow, and fishing for rainbow, golden and brook is good (to 13″).

3rd Hiking Day (**Little Pete Meadow** to **Upper Middle Fork Kings River,** 3½ miles): The trail from Little Pete to Big Pete Meadow is a moderate ascent on rock and sand through a sparse-to-moderate forest cover of lodgepole and occasional hemlock. Looking back over one's shoulder rewards the traveler with fine views of LeConte Canyon, while ahead the granite walls where the canyon veers west show glacially smoothed, unfractured faces. Some quaking aspen can be seen as the trail ascends through Big Pete Meadow and passes the large area of campsites. As the trail turns westward, one has his first, excellent views of the darker rock of Black Giant, and a few yards beyond the turn the trail fords the tributary stream draining the slopes of Mts. Johnson and Gilbert. Passing more campsites, the trail continues west on an easy-to-moderate ascent through grassy extensions of Big Pete Meadow. Most of the rock underfooting encountered to this point has been of the rounded morainal variety, but as soon as the trail leaves the westernmost fringes of Big Pete Meadow, the rock's sharp, fractured edges reflect its weathering origins. Over this talus, the trail ascends more steeply through a moderate forest cover of silver, lodgepole and whitebark pine and some hemlock.

Canyon ecologies, such as the one encountered in LeConte Canyon, are of scientific interest to the naturalist, but they hold an equal fascination for laymen who simply appreciate natural beauty. The two natural features that usually claim the traveler's attention are the canyon walls and the watercourse. In LeConte Canyon both are worthy of study because they are dramatic and exciting, but equally deserving of scrutiny is the geologic history of the meadowed and forested flats encountered on the trail. On the canyon floor, accumulations of sand—usually of granitic origin, weathered or chemically eroded from the canyon walls—combine with silt to make an environment suitable for dense stands of evergreens and wildflowers. These alluvial deposits occur as a result of both glacial and subsequent river erosion. Canyon flats, frequently meadowed, that owe their birth to glacial cutting, occur where the glacier "ground down on its heel." After the ice had melted, what was left was a stepladdering canyon. The flats, which were first covered by lakes, later filled with sediment, and the sediment provided a foothold for grasses and trees. As one ascends to timberline above Big Pete Meadow, he becomes increasingly aware of this evolutionary process, and of the complicating factors of the harsher climatic environment affecting the process at higher elevations. The meadowed flat where the trail jogs north toward the tiny, unnamed lake east of Helen Lake is an earlier stage of the process, and supports a sparse forest fringe of lodgepole, silver and some whitebark pine. This hiking day ends at the fair-to-good campsites just above the 10,350-foot meadow.

4th Hiking Day (**Upper Middle Fork Kings River** to **Wanda Lake,** 6 miles): An early start for crossing Muir Pass is both expedient and rewarding. Steep climbs, even over snow, are best done in the cool of the morning. But arriving at the summit of Muir Pass in the early hours has compensations greater than those of physical comfort, for, with early light, one is treated to a rare and beautiful panorama unmatched anywhere. The ascent to the pass starts with a steady climb over sand and rock through a sparse timber cover of whitebark pine. That timber cover soon disappears, giving way to low-lying heather. At the talus-bound, round, unnamed lake east of Helen Lake, the trail veers west, crossing and recrossing the trickling headwaters of the Middle Fork Kings River. Excellent views to the southeast of the Palisades and Langille, Giraud and Columbine peaks make the breather stops welcome occasions. The trail becomes rocky and the slope more moderate as it passes the next unnamed lake and winds over the terminal shoulder of the Black Divide to Helen Lake. Rocks in colorful reds, yellows, blacks and whites that characterize this metamorphic divide are on every hand. The trail rounds the loose-rocked south end of this barren lake, and ascends steadily over a rocky slope that is often covered with snow throughout the summer. Looking back, one can see the striking meeting of the black metamorphic rock of the Black Divide and the white granite just east of Helen Lake.

Muir Pass (11,955') is marked by a sign and a unique stone shelter. This hut, erected by the Sierra Club in memoriam to John Muir, the Sierra's best-known and most-loved mountaineer, stands as a shelter for stormbound travelers. In a sense, it is a wilderness monument, and should be treated as such—leave nothing but your boottracks and firewood for those who follow. From this pass the views are magnificent. In the morning light, the somber crags to the north and south relieve the intense whites of the lighter granite to the east. Situated in a gigantic rock bowl, Wanda Lake's emerald blue waters contrast sharply with its lower white sides, which, on the south side, disappear into the darker rock of the Goddard Divide. The descent from the pass is moderate and then steady over crushed rock, and then it levels out, passing the south end of Lake McDermand. Skirting the east side of Wanda Lake, the trail affords excellent views of snow-and-ice-necklaced Mt. Goddard, and then arrives at the fair-to-good campsites near the lake's outlet. The expansive views from these campsites include Mt. Goddard and the Goddard Divide to the south, and Mts. Huxley, Spencer, Darwin and Mendel to the north.

5th Hiking Day (**Wanda Lake** to **Colby Meadow**, 6½ miles): Occasional wildflowers, including heather, wallflower and penstemon, can be seen as the trail descends over rock and sand. The trail crosses Evolution Creek and stays on the west bank on a moderate descent that becomes switchbacks above Sapphire Lake. Fine views of the Sierra crest to the east make watching one's footing a difficult task. Sapphire Lake is indeed a high-country gem, fringed with green, marshy grass, and situated on a large glacial step, with some very large trout. Our route traverses its steeper west side, and, after a steady descent, refords Evolution Creek just above Evolution Lake (difficult ford in any season). The trail crosses a meadowy section before winding the length of the lake's east shore. Glacial smoothing and some polish can be seen in the granite surrounding the lake, and on the abrupt walls on either side of the lake. Passing several campsites at the lower end of the lake, the trail makes a brief northward swing before switchbacking down to Evolution Valley. This northward swing passes the unsigned, ducked trail ascending to Darwin Canyon, and the route to the Darwin Glacier. The zigzagging downgrade over morainal debris re-enters forest cover and passes clumps of wildflowers that include penstemon, paintbrush, swamp onion, lupine, forget-me-not, cinquefoil, buckwheat and tiger lily. At the foot of the grade, where the trail fords the stream emptying Darwin Canyon, our route passes more campsites, and then continues on a relatively level course through moderate stands of lodgepole to the good campsites at Colby Meadow. Fishing for golden is fair (to 9″) in nearby Evolution Creek.

6th Hiking Day (**Colby Meadow** to **Lower Goddard Canyon**, 5½ miles): From Colby Meadow the trail continues westward, passing the McClure and Evolution meadows. The trail joining these meadows is a pathway that winds through moderate and dense stands of lodgepole, and, in the midst of McClure Meadow, passes a ranger station (emergency services available here). The friendly intimacy of the meadows has, over the past sixty years, made this valley a favorite camping site for backcountry travelers, and one which, with the subsequent establishment of the John Muir Trail, has subjected these delicate wild pastures to serious overuse. As our route winds past the campsites in McClure Meadow, the largest of the Evolution group, the traveler can see for himself the toll taken by the heavy traffic, both human and stock. Before controls were exerted upon grazing stock of large pack-train parties, the foraging animals trampled tender, young spring shoots of grass in such quantities as to change the meadow to a patchwork of barren hillocks. In the absence of grasses to hold back the water, serious erosion became a matter of concern, and today, to preserve these meadows, stock forage is necessarily limited, and the trail has been rerouted to skirt the meadows on the north side.

The duff trail passes the drift fence below McClure Meadow on a moderate-to-steady descent that fords several tributaries draining the Glacier Divide. These fords are usually accomplished via footlogs or easy rock-hopping. At Evolution Meadow the trail crosses Evolution Creek (on a log—difficult at high water) for the last time, and then continues west to the head of the switchbacks that drop down to the South Fork San Joaquin River. Views before the descent are excellent of the cascades of the stream draining Emerald Peak, the falls and cascades of Evolution Creek below the ford, and the South Fork San Joaquin River drainage. Midway down the switchbacks, one has impressive views of Goddard Canyon, part of the route for the 7th hiking day. The forest cover along the zigzags is sparse-to-moderate lodgepole, juniper and some aspen, and flowers seen along the trail include pennyroyal, larkspur, penstemon, cinquefoil, currant, monkey flower, buckwheat and paintbrush. The switchbacking trail crosses glacial polish exhibiting some striations, and, at the bottom, passes a packer campsite and several good primitive sites as it passes through a heavy stand of lodgepole. Just beyone these campsites, our trail crosses the footbridge, meets the Goddard Canyon/Hell-for-Sure Pass Trail, and branches left. The forest cover of lodgepole, with large concentrations of quaking aspen, continues as the trail ascends moderately past a drift fence. About ½ mile above the drift fence, near a small meadow, the trail reaches several good-to-excellent campsites. Fishing on nearby South Fork San Joaquin is fair for rainbow, some golden and brook (to 10″).

7th, 8th and 9th Hiking Days: Reverse the 3rd hiking day, trip 30, the 2nd hiking day, trip 25, and the 1st hiking day, trip 23, 24 miles.

Wanda Lake, Mt. Goddard (aerial view)

E. P. Pister

South Lake to Bear Dam Junction

46

TRIP

From South Lake to Bear Dam Junction via Bishop Pass, Dusy Basin, John Muir Trail, Muir Pass, Evolution Valley, Sandpiper Lake, (shuttle trip). Topo maps *Mt. Goddard, Blackcap Mountain, Mt. Abbot.* Best mid or late season; 67 miles.

Grade	Trail/layover days	Total recommended days
Leisurely	12/4	16
Moderate	10/4	14
Strenuous	8/3	11

HILITES

Best traveled in midsummer, this long, choice route tours high alpine country and winds through dramatic, glacially scoured canyons. The renowned Muir Trail, over which most of this route passes, retains its primitive appeal despite its heavy use, and anyone who would "know" the Sierra surely should travel it.

DESCRIPTION (Moderate trip)

1st 5 Hiking Days: Follow trip 45 to **Colby Meadow**, 29 miles.

6th Hiking Day (**Colby Meadow** to **Piute Canyon Trail Junction**, 9 miles): Proceed to the Goddard Canyon/Hell-for-Sure Pass Trail junction as described in the 6th hiking day, trip 45, where our route continues right on the John Muir Trail. After the bridge crossing of the South Fork San Joaquin River, the trail passes more packer and primitive campsites situated in aspen groves, and descends steadily past a drift fence. This stretch boasts many wildflowers, including penstemon, Bigelow sneezeweed, yellow cinquefoil, groundsel and Indian paintbrush. Just beyond the drift fence, the trail crosses another bridge (steel suspension) over the river, and then it continues to descend steadily over morainal underfooting. The narrow canyon walls open briefly at Aspen

Flat, where the forest cover thickens. Several good campsites in the flats make this a good alternative camping site for this hiking day. The duff footing of Aspen Flat gives way to rock and dust as the trail becomes steeper and the forest cover thinner. Then the trail crosses Piute Creek via a footbridge, and arrives at the good campsites near the Piute Canyon Trail junction. Fishing for rainbow, some golden and brook is fair (to 10″).

7th Hiking Day (**Piute Canyon Trail Junction** to **Sally Keyes Lakes**, 7½ miles): Reverse the first part of the 5th hiking day, trip 15.

8th Hiking Day (**Sally Keyes Lakes** to **Sandpiper Lake**, 5 miles part cross country): Reverse the first part of the 3rd hiking day, trip 8.

9th and 10th Hiking Days: Reverse the steps of trip 6, 16½ miles.

Sierra crest near Independence   *Jason Winnett*

Taboose Creek Roadend to Bench Lake **47**

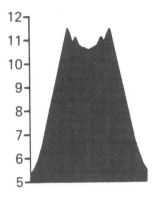

TRIP   From Taboose Creek Roadend to Bench Lake (round trip). Topo maps *Big Pine, Mt. Pinchot*. Best mid or late season; 25 miles.

Grade	Trail/layover days	Total recom- mended days
Leisurely	....	....
Moderate	....	....
Strenuous	4/0	4

HILITES   The expansive views, the delightful flower-bedecked basin just over the pass, and the direct access via this route to the sparkling gem of Bench Lake make the great effort worthwhile *if* you are in top shape.

DESCRIPTION (Strenuous trip)

1st Hiking Day (**Taboose Creek Roadend** to **Upper Taboose Creek,** 6½ miles): From the trailhead we cross a low lateral moraine and ascend gently westward over a sandy, sage-covered desert plain, with the awesome rampart of the Sierra just ahead. As we enter the broad portal of Taboose Creek canyon, the path veers left and gradually rises, staying above the rushing creek. Then we drop momentarily alongside the willow-and-birch-lined creek, before climbing steeply up-canyon on footing alternately gravel and rock. The trail zigzags up a steep slope, passing a handful of lonely Jeffrey pines, then contours over to the creek, which we cross by boulder-hopping, taking extreme care not to slip.

From the ford, the trail switchbacks up through a mini-forest of white fir and a few Jeffrey pines, crosses a bench, and climbs steadily west, once again in the open, through thickets of chinquapin, willow and other greenery. Looming high on the left are the yellowish-brown spurs of Goodale Mountain. The trail crosses Taboose Creek twice more and then climbs to a picturesque bench valley, shaded around the edges by gnarled whitebark pines and hemmed in between rust-colored cliffs, where there are several excellent campsites on the left (south) side of the bench.

2nd Hiking Day (**Upper Taboose Creek** to **Bench Lake**, 6 miles): After the trail crosses the creek for the fifth time, it switchbacks steeply up through very rocky terrain to a last bench just east of Taboose Pass. Though well above timberline, lush grasses and colorful wildflowers make the scene delightful. We wind up and between granite outcroppings, passing several limpid tarns, and finally reach Taboose Pass, marked by a large sign announcing one's entry into Kings Canyon National Park. The scene that abruptly unfolds is breathtaking. Directly ahead is the deep crease of the Kings River's South Fork. Slightly to the left is beautiful Bench Lake, with the symmetrical spire of Arrow Peak as a backdrop. To the right is the ragged citadel of Mt. Ruskin.

From the pass, the trail drops southwest down a gradual slope, passing through sky gardens of buttercup, shooting star and senecio, carpeted with velvet green. We ford a rivulet, pass just north of a rockbound tarn, and reach a hard-to-spot junction. After turning left here, we climb and then contour along a rocky slope, staying above the U-shaped bowl of the South Fork, to a junction with the John Muir Trail. Just 100 yards south on the Muir Trail is the lateral trail to Bench Lake, and we turn west onto this high, easy trail. Hikers will appreciate the short side trip to this sublime mountain lake, less than an hour's walk off the Muir Trail. The pathway leads west across a flower-bedecked meadow, descends a short distance, and then contours southwest along a granite bench under a canopy of lodgepole pines. We ford a shallow stream, pass two limpid tarns, and in 1½ miles from the John Muir Trail reach the northeast shore of Bench Lake. In the clarity of its waters and in its splendid setting amid granite peaks and spurs, this sparkling jewel has few peers in the High Sierra. The whitish pyramid of Arrow Peak, reflected in the lake's mirrorlike waters, is one of the classic views in the Sierra. Many fine campsites are among the lodgepoles along the north shore. (Halazone tablets are recommended.)

3rd and 4th Hiking Days: Retrace your steps, 12½ miles.

Taboose Creek Roadend to Twin Lakes   48

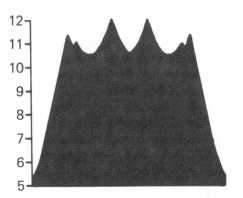

TRIP From Taboose Creek Roadend to Twin Lakes (round trip). Topo maps *Big Pine*, *Mt. Pinchot*. Best mid or late season; 43 miles.

Grade	Trail/layover days	Total recom- mended days
Leisurely	....	....
Moderate	....	....
Strenuous	6/0	6

HILITES In addition to the attractions of the previous trip, this route offers the alpine beauties of Lake Marjorie, which has one of the most colorful settings in the High Sierra. Off-the-beaten-path camping at Twin Lakes is ample reward for the long hike in.

DESCRIPTION (Strenuous trip)

1st and 2nd Hiking Days: Follow trip 47 to **Bench Lake**, 12½ miles.

3rd Hiking Day (**Bench Lake** to **Twin Lakes**, 9 miles): After retracing the path to the John Muir Trail, this day's route turns south and climbs through rocky meadows and clumps of lodgepole and whitebark pine, passing above a shimmering lakelet on the left, then another one on the right. Gnarled whitebark pines, harbingers of approaching timberline, begin to replace the lodgepoles as the forest thins to scattered groves. After skirting another rockbound lake, the granite-paved trail climbs to the north shore of magnificent Lake Marjorie. The setting here is as richly colorful as any in the Sierra: to the right, ramparts of steel-gray granite rise abruptly from the lake. South, above the lake's head, are slopes of black and ruddy brown. Just visible on the southeastern skyline is the dark notch of Pinchot Pass. To the left, rising above all, are the broken, multihued cliffs of Mt. Pinchot.

The Muir Trail passes above the east shore of Lake Marjorie and climbs above the last, stunted whitebarks into the world of snow and bare rock. On it, we ascend steadily over granite benches and through boulder fields, passing above two stark lakelets. After fording an icy rivulet, the path traverses upward and then switchbacks steeply up over rocky terrain to 12,110-foot Pinchot Pass, on the divide that separates the waters of the Kings' South Fork from its tributary, Woods Creek. The views in both directions are inspiring. Far to the north, over Mather Pass, loom the black sentinels of the Palisades. South, beyond the serrated face of Mt. Cedric Wright, ridge after ridge fades into the distance.

From Pinchot Pass the pathway descends a steep talus slope, crosses a slight rise and drops into a high, open basin lush with grass and wildflowers. Particularly abundant are clusters of red heather and shooting star. We veer east, passing several placid tarns and fording the twin headwaters of Woods Creek, then turn south again and parallel the vibrant stream through alpine meadow country. As the trail descends toward 11,000 feet, clumps of whitebark pine welcome us back to timberline. The dominating round bulk of Mt. Cedric Wright looms up close by in the south, and the knifelike peak on the southern skyline is Mt. Clarence King, monarch of the Sixty Lake Basin. The trail drops steadily southward, passing a marshy lakelet on the right. Occasionally visible down to the left are Twin Lakes, nestled close under the spines of Mt. Cedric Wright. A quarter mile below the lower lake we meet the Twin Lakes Trail and turn northeast onto it for 1/3 mile to the good campsites along the west shore of the lower lake.
4th, 5th and 6th Hiking Days: Retrace your steps, 21½ miles.

Sawmill Creek Roadend to Sawmill Lake **49**

TRIP   From Sawmill Creek Roadend to Sawmill Lake (round trip). Topo map *Mt. Pinchot.* Best early season; 16 miles.

Grade	Trail/layover days	Total recommended days
Leisurely	....	....
Moderate	....	....
Strenuous	2/0	2

HILITES   This strenuous trip up from hot Owens Valley to a lovely, cool lake at 10,000 feet gives one the satisfaction of getting high on his own sweat, and the thrill of strolling back down with next to no effort.

DESCRIPTION (Strenuous trip)

1st Hiking Day (**Sawmill Creek Roadend** to **Sawmill Lake,** 8 miles): To avoid the precipitous gorge of lower Sawmill Creek, the route up from Sawmill Creek roadend climbs the steep, sage-covered slope north of the creek. In early summer, this desert slope is splashed with flowering shrubs and blossoms of bright blue woolly gilia and yellow and white buckwheat. From the trail you look down on the Big Pine volcanic field, spotted with reddish cinder cones and black lava flows that erupted from the west side of Owens Valley. After a lengthy switchback, the trail rounds Sawmill Point high above the waters of Sawmill Creek, visible as a white ribbon far below. The pathway descends slightly, then contours, and finally climbs along the precipitous north wall of Sawmill Creek canyon. As we near the sloping ridge known, appropriately, as The Hogsback, Jeffrey pines and white firs make a most welcome appearance. If one looks carefully at the lower end of The Hogsback, one can spot the remains of the Blackrock sawmill and flume, dating from the 1860s, after which Sawmill Creek and Sawmill Pass are named. For some distance above The Hogsback, one can occasionally see stumps, felled trees and logs used as "gliders" in this century-old operation to supply Owens Valley miners with lumber.

The trail climbs to meet a tributary stream north of The Hogsback, the first water on this hot climb. Beyond the ford, the trail zigzags steeply up the north slope of The Hogsback. Once over the top of this long, rounded ridge, the path veers south, contouring and climbing on a moderate grade back into the main canyon, and reaches Sawmill Meadow, boggy and lush green in early summer, but drying considerably as the summer months progress. Beyond, the trail follows the creek, then zigzags steeply upward through Jeffrey pine and red fir to swampy Mule Lake, perched on a small bench high up the canyon. After fording the creek, we climb through a jumbled mass of metamorphic rocks that are home for a large colony of conies. After recrossing the creek, we finally arrive at the northeast shore of beautiful Sawmill Lake. Good campsites under clumps of foxtail pine are located here and fishing for rainbow trout is fair to good.

Second Hiking Day: Retrace your steps, 8 miles.

Lake 11599, Upper Basin

Jason Winnett

Sawmill Creek Roadend to Twin Lakes   **50**

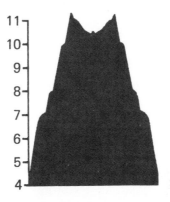

TRIP   From Sawmill Creek Roadend to Twin Lakes (round trip). Topo map *Mt. Pinchot*. Best mid or late season; 28 miles.

Grade	Trail/layover days	Total recommended days
Leisurely	....	....
Moderate	....	....
Strenuous	4/0	4

HILITES   This trip proceeds by way of a horrendous ascent to Sawmill Pass and then takes you through the headwaters of Woods Creek, in a high basin clothed with whitebark pine, verdant meadows and multihued alpine flowers.

DESCRIPTION (Strenuous trip)

1st Hiking Day: Follow trip 49 to **Sawmill Lake,** 8 miles.

2nd Hiking Day (**Sawmill Lake** to **Twin Lakes,** 6 miles): Above Sawmill Lake the trail winds up through a thinning forest of foxtail and whitebark pine, crosses a small timberline basin, and climbs steeply upward to Sawmill Pass (11,347′), on the border of Kings Canyon National Park. From the pass you walk northwest across nearly level talus and sand, then drop into a resplendent lake-dotted alpine basin, the headwaters of Woods Creek. The trail winds westward, gradually descending as it passes just north of two small, nameless lakes. The largest body of water in the basin—Woods Lake—is a short cross-country jaunt south of the trail. Our route descends to the lower end of the basin, then turns abruptly north to climb and contour along the lower slopes of Mt. Cedric Wright. Finally, the trail drops to the North Fork of Woods Creek, goes north along its east bank a short distance, and then fords the creek to a junction with the John Muir Trail. A short half mile up this arterial route the Twin Lakes Trail turns off and leads northeast to the good campsites on the west shore of Lower Twin Lake.

3rd and 4th Hiking Days: Retrace your steps, 14 miles.

Shooting stars

Ron Felzer

Sawmill Creek Roadend to Oak Creek   **51**

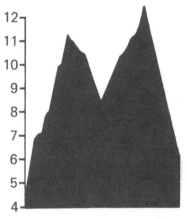

TRIP   From Sawmill Creek Roadend to Oak Creek Roadend (shuttle trip): Topo map *Mt. Pinchot.* Best mid deason; 33½ miles.

Grade	Trail/layover days	Total recom-mended days
Leisurely	....	....
Moderate	....	....
Strenuous	4/1	5

HILITES   Another trip for those in top condition, this strenuous jaunt uses a small piece of the John Muir Trail to permit passage between two out-of-the way, lake-dotted alpine basins—the headwaters of Woods Creek and the Baxter Lakes basin.

DESCRIPTION (Strenuous trip)

1st Hiking Day: Follow trip 49 to **Sawmill Lake,** 8 miles.

2nd Hiking Day (**Sawmill Lake** to **Woods Creek Crossing,** 8½ miles): Follow the 2nd hiking day, trip 50, to the John Muir Trail and turn left (south) on it.

Your path veers southwest, ever dropping, following the U-shaped canyon cut by the glacier that flowed down Woods Creek. You pass another fine campsite on the left, and when you abruptly emerge from the forest,, the great trough of Woods Creek opens in full grandeur ahead. For the next 3 miles, the trail descends through the gorge, sometimes alongside the joyous creek but more often well above it, through tangled thickets of dwarf aspen, willow and other greenery. Wildflowers add an abundant splash of color, and you may see paintbrush, larkspur, purple aster, mountain violet, Bigelow sneezeweed, Labrador tea and yarrow. A ribbon of white water plunges from the dark cliffs high on the left. We cross several benches shaded by isolated clusters of lodgepole, then ford the White Fork of Woods Creek, sometimes difficult in early season when the water runs high. Ahead is the great bend of Woods Creek, with the stupendous ramparts of King Spur as a backdrop. A descent over rocky terrain brings us back into the forest, now consisting of Jeffrey pine and gnarled junipers. The trail fords another side stream and drops alongside Woods Creek, its white froth spilling wildly over huge, inclined granite slabs. On the final descent to the canyon floor, manzanita provides a thick and thorny ground cover, with scattered Jeffreys for shade. At a major trail junction, the fork to the right is the Woods Creek Trail down to Paradise Valley; the Muir Trail goes left. Where we re-reach Woods Creek, it is swollen to river proportions by the addition of its South Fork's waters. There are fair campsites, shaded by tall aspens and white alders, on both sides of the creek. Fishing for brook and rainbow trout to 10 inches is fair to good.

3rd Hiking Day (**Woods Creek Crossing** to **Baxter Lakes**, 7 miles): After crossing the creek via a log with railing, we turn southeast and begin the long climb up the South Fork. Juniper and red fir provide forest cover as we pass several adequate campsites on the left, along the creek. Also to the left, half-hidden by foliage, is one of Shorty Lovelace's pigmy log cabins. Shorty ran a trap line through this country during the years before Kings Canyon National Park was established. Remains of his other miniature cabins are located in Gardiner Basin and along Bubbs Creek.

The trail rounds the base of King Spur and climbs well above the stream, through alternating stretches of lush greenery and wildflowers, and sparse forest of aspen, red fir and lodgepole pine. We jump the rivulet that hurries down from Lake 10296 and enter an open, rocky area. Beyond, a wooden span provides an easy crossing of a boggy meadow. From the meadow, the trail climbs over a rocky ridge and fords the major creek descending from Sixty Lake Basin, passing through a gate in a drift fence. There are several small campsites here, under scattered pines. Across the canyon, Baxter Creek stitches a ribbon of white down the rock-ribbed slope. The trail climbs through rocky terrain, then approaches the main creek, passing a lodgepole-sheltered campsite on the left, before again breaking into the open and ascending bouldery terrain. Ahead looms the peaked monolith of

Fin Dome, heralding your approach to the beautiful Rae Lakes. To your right are the impressive steel-gray ramparts of King Spur. In contrast, the massive, sloping Sierra crest in the east is made up of darkish metamorphic rocks. The long black striations that cross the face of Diamond Peak and the ridge north of it are metamorphosed lava, visual evidence of ancient volcanic activity.

Finally this long ascent climbs over a low, rounded spur and abruptly reaches the northernmost of the Rae Lakes chain, jewel-like Dollar Lake. The setting here is magnificent: lodgepoles crowd the shore amid granite outcroppings, and Fin Dome, along with some blackish spires beyond, provides a jagged backdrop for the mirroring blue waters of the lake. Good, though overused, campsites lie on the north and northwest shores. The unmarked Baxter Pass Trail takes off northeast from the north side of Dollar Lake. From this junction follow most of the 4th hiking day, trip 62.

4th Hiking Day: Follow the 5th hiking day, trip 62, 10 miles.

Rae Lakes, Painted Lady *Tom Ross*

52   Cedar Grove to Kennedy Lakes

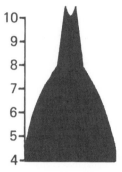

TRIP
From Cedar Grove to Kennedy Lakes (round trip. Topo map *Marion Peak*. Best mid or late season; 20 miles.

Grade	Trail/layover days	Total recom- mended days
Leisurely	....	....
Moderate	5/1	6
Strenuous	4/0	4

HILITES
By going north instead of east out of Cedar Grove, this trip avoids the hordes of hikers bound for the John Muir Trail and instead brings the traveler to secluded, charming East Kennedy Lake, which lies in a private cirque virtually on top of the Monarch Divide.

DESCRIPTION (Strenuous trip)

1st Hiking Day (**Cedar Grove** to **Frypan Meadow**, 6 miles): The trail starts 1½ miles down-canyon (west) from the Cedar Grove Ranger Station, across from a fair-sized parking lot on the river side of the road.

The trail starts climbing at once, rising quite steeply up the large eastern lateral moraine of Lewis Creek under a sparse forest cover of incense-cedar, ponderosa pine, black oak and canyon live oak, with manzanita and kit kit dizze growing underneath. About ¾ mile up the trail, a few open areas offer fine views across the Kings River Canyon to Sentinel Ridge, and up and down the canyon. One-half mile farther the grade levels off, and we meet the Hotel Creek Trail. Our route descends slightly to cross an unnamed stream which may be dry in late summer, but supports an exquisite flower garden in late spring and early summer. The trail now climbs moderately again, to stay high ulnder an open forest of large trees. Occasional views of the peaks on the Monarch Divide in the north are seen from the open areas. Then the trail decends for a short distance to cross Comb Creek, near a small campsite. When the stream is high, look for a footlog crossing downstream. As the trail clilmbs steeply up the opposite bank, it passes through a forest of young Jeffrey pines.

Less than a mile past Comb Creek the trail crosses the East Fork of Lewis Creek. (If needed there is a good footlog upstream.) We then climb moderately up to a junction with the first Wildman Meadow Trail, and continue climbing to the second trail to Wildman Meadow. Just beyond, we drop slightly and cross the lower end of Frypan Meadow, which is quite boggy until late summer. About 200 yards up the meadow is a large camp spot on a lovely stream, where fishing can be surprisingly good for small trout. The flowers in the meadow bloom from early spring until fall, changing with the seasons but always making a large and beautiful garden.

2nd Hiking Day (**Frypan Meadow** to **East Kennedy Lake**, 4 miles): The sign at the top of the meadow reads *Kennedy Pass 4 mi.* but one should remember that it goes from about 7800 to 10,800 feet in elevation, strenuous for anyone not in top physical condition. From a junction at the top of the meadow, the trail goes east over a moderate-to-steep grade, crossing three streams in the first ½ mile. The forest is largely white fir, but there is a large grove of aspens in this section, and the degree of difficulty in pushing through this grove depends on the avalanche conditions of the winter before. Beyond the aspen thickets we cross several more small streams, and from open areas we can look south to the immense cirques of the Kings-Kaweah and Great Western divides.

The route now climbs the last, steep, switchbacked grade to Kennedy Pass (10,800′). From the top, the scene to the north is outstanding. In the distance are the canyons of Goddard Creek and its large tributary, Disappearing Creek, topped by the great peaks near Muir Pass. In the foreground, just below Kennedy Pass, are several small tarns surrounded by brilliant green, grassy meadows. Camps can be made in these meadows but there are much better ones at West Kennedy Lake, reached by a short cross-country hike east from a point midway down the east-trending leg of the descent from Kennedy Pass to Kennedy Canyon.

3rd and 4th Hiking Days: Retrace your steps, 10 miles.

53   Cedar Grove to Volcanic Lakes

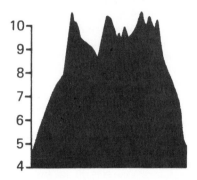

TRIP   From Cedar Grove to Kennedy Canyon, Volcanic
              Lakes, Granite Lakes (shuttle trip). Topo map
              Marion Peak. Best mid or late season; 33 miles.

Grade	Trail/layover days	Total recom-mended days
Leisurely	....	....
Moderate	5/1	6
Strenuous	4/0	4

HILITES   The little-traveled divide that separates the gigantic
              gashes of the south and middle forks of the Kings
              River, the Monarch Divide, is the setting for this
              loop trip through high, wild, dramatic country dotted
              with dozens of lakes, named and unnamed, on-trail
              and off-trail.

DESCRIPTION (Strenuous trip)

1st 2 Hiking Days: Follow trip 52 to **East Kennedy Lake**, 10 miles.

3rd Hiking Day (**East Kennedy Lake** to **Granite Lake**, 14½ miles):
The trail down Kennedy Canyon is delightful to walk, crossing
the stream several times and passing several campsites, the last
ones being at the lower end, where the trail turns back to begin
the climb up Dead Pine Ridge. The trail is quite steep and there is
water in only one place, about two thirds of the way up this climb,
where we find a good spring and a lush flower garden.

On the climb we see Jeffrey pine, Sierra juniper, white and red
fir, silver pine, and, at the top, a forest of lodgepole pine. As we
drop down the east side, the slope is at first gradual and then
more steep. Only one of the many Volcanic Lakes is visible from

the trail, but the basins in which they lie can be seen. The trail drops over a series of rocky benches and arrives at a stream, a large tarn and a sign *Volcanic Lakes*. The lakes are in several basins up this stream, the first one about ½ mile up. Most of the lakes have campsites—and excellent fishing for rainbow and golden trout (to 16″).

The trail crosses the stream, skirts the lower end of a tarn, and climbs on slab rock and thin soil cover, passing the lowest Volcanic Lake, to cross the saddle between the West and Middle forks of Dougherty Creek. At the top is a small grassy lake, and from here the trail descends to the Middle Fork of Dougherty Creek and the Granite Pass Trail. Turning right (south), our route ascends beside sparkling Middle Fork Kennedy Creek, fords the stream and climbs steeply to a meadow which has fair campsites and one of Shorty Lovelace's old trapline cabins. The trail then leads south over glacier-polished bedrock through another meadow and up a narrow canyon to Granite Pass (10,673′). Views from the pass are limited only by the far divides: Kings-Kaweah and Great Western on the south and the Sierra crest on the north.

From the pass, the rocky-sandy trail descends, steeply at times, to a small meadow filled with lavender shooting stars in early season, where there are several good campsites. Our trail then descends moderately through lodgepole forest to a junction with the spur trail to Granite Lake (10,100′). Here we turn right (west) and skirt the north side of a meadow to the good campsites on that lake, where fishing is fair-to-good for brook trout (to 10″).

4th Hiking Day (**Granite Lake** to **Cedar Grove Roadend**, 8½ miles): Reverse the steps of the 1st hiking day, trip 54.

54   Cedar Grove to Granite Lake

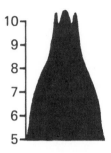

TRIP   From Cedar Grove Roadend to Granite Lake (round trip). Topo map *Marion Peak*. Best early or late season; 17 miles.

Grade	Trail/layover days	Total recommended days
Leisurely	....	....
Moderate	....	....
Strenuous	2/0	2

HILITES   "The first day is always the toughest" is an old adage to the backpacker. And this old saw added to the 5000-foot-plus elevation gain should warn the hiker that this "weekender" is one to be undertaken only after some conditioning. However, it should also be noted that the fine views and the good alpine campsite at the end of the trek compensate for the effort.

DESCRIPTION (Strenuous trip)

1st Hiking Day (**Cedar Grove Roadend** to **Granite Lake,** 8½ miles): The extreme elevation change encountered in the course of this trip (over 5000 feet), necessarily removes it from the "Leisurely" grade, but it makes a fine weekender for the person who has one or two warm-up trips already under his belt. Starting at the north side of the parking loop (5035'), the Copper Creek Trail winds through a mature stand of ponderosa, incense-cedar, sugar pine and black oak. As the traveler begins this trip, he might contemplate the historic usage of this trailhead. Evidence from archeological excavations nearby indicate that Zumwalt Meadows was a permanent base camp for Indian hunting parties for a period of time ranging from (in the white man's terms) Magna Carta to the Declaration of Independence. Mortar rocks, pestles and manos found in the yard-deep midden piles in this vicinity indicate that the acorn of the plentiful black oak was one of the main staples of the Indian's diet. It is also possible that these grinding implements were used to grind the pine nut (occasional pinon trees are found in the canyon). But also found in the excavation sites were bones of deer and various rodents, indicating that foraging parties took to the higher country—and arrowheads found in the country of the Monarch Divide indicate that these parties frequently used this same trail.

The flats of Zumwalt Meadows soon fall behind, and the trail ascends above the dense forest cover to a moderate forest cover of scrub oak. Turning northward, the trail begins steadily rising switchbacks through dense thickets of oak and manzanita. Views of glacially smoothed Grand Sentinel dominate the scenery of the canyon's south wall. The first set of switchbacks terminates just east of North Dome, and the grade abates to a moderate-to-steady ascent through a mixed forest cover of sugar pine, ponderosa, incense-cedar and black oak. Looking back over one's right shoulder, to the southeast, one has a fine view of two beautifully formed avalanche chutes on the northeast face of The Sphinx. The trail then fords several trickling tributaries of Copper Creek, and passes several campsites sheltered in a grove of white fir at Lower Tent Meadow. Rising steeply, the trail leaves Lower Tent Meadow and ascends a rocky slope to Upper Tent Meadow.

The switchbacks above Upper Tent Meadow are steep, and they bring the traveler into the red-fir belt. However, the acquaintance with this belt is brief as the trail soon climbs to an area mostly covered with lodgepole, silver pine and quaking aspen (along the creek). If it is of consolation, today's traveler can rest assured that the red man who preceded him up this climb also paused to pant and wonder. Leveling out, the trail fluctuates up and down through properly named Granite Basin. Near the head of the basin, the trail skirts a small, alpine meadow and strikes the Granite Lake Trail lateral. Our route turns left on it and ascends an easy slope to the north side of scenic Granite Lake (10,100'). Good campsites dot the outlet and east side of the lake. Views of the Comb Spur are excellent, and the camper will soon establish a vocal relationship with the many noisy marmots that share this private cirque. Fishing for brook trout is fair-to-good (to 10").

2nd Hiking Day: Retrace your steps, 8½ miles.

55 Cedar Grove to State Lakes

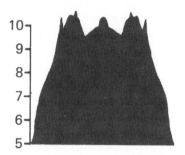

TRIP

From Cedar Grove Roadend to State Lakes via Granite Basin, Granite Pass (round trip). Topo map *Marion Peak*. Best early or late season; 31 miles.

Grade	Trail/layover days	Total recommended days
Leisurely	....	....
Moderate	....	....
Strenuous	4/2	6

HILITES

Once past the initial, tough 5000-foot climb, this exciting route has all the aspects of a glorious fishing trip. Beneath the peaks of the Monarch Divide, this trail visits the excellent fishing lakes of the State Lakes chain, and offers fine side trips for those who would linger.

DESCRIPTION (Strenuous trip)

1st Hiking Day: Follow trip 54 to **Granite Lake,** 8½ miles).

2nd Hiking Day (**Granite Lake** to **State Lakes,** 7 miles): This hiking day begins by a retracing of one's steps to the Granite Pass Trail, where our route turns left toward Granite Pass. The ascent starts moderately, but soon steepens over rocky underfooting. Passing a tiny meadow with several campsites, the trail climbs again, and arrives at Granite Pass (10,673'). This summit marks the divide between the immense canyons of the Middle and South Forks of the Kings River. Views from the pass are fair of jumbled Goat Crest and the unnamed granite divide to the northwest. From the pass, the trail descends moderately through a granite-walled ravine. Probably following a fault line, the ravine is deep-cut, and exhibits fine examples of mirrorlike glacial polish. Through a sparse cover of lodgepole, the trail passes over some marshy sections that in late season of a normal year dry up, and then passes a drift fence. There are several excellent campsites just south of the drift fence, in an alpine meadow setting. This descent then resolves into steep switchbacks that drop down over a granite face to leveler going through a denser forest cover of lodgepole. Our route then passes by the Volcanic Lakes Trail, and about ½ mile farther passes the unmarked and unmaintained spur to Lake of the Fallen Moon. As our trail begins the general descent toward the East Fork of Dougherty Creek, it turns east and passes a trail to Simpson Meadow. From the junction we continue over undulating terrain to ford the outlet stream of Glacier Lakes. Although not abundant, the wildflowers along the trail are of many species. One is sure to encounter wallflower, shooting star, penstemon, currant and cinquefoil. In the vicinity of the ford there are excellent views up Glacier Valley to the Glacier Lakes cirque, and the sheer face of Goat Crest. After the ford, the trail ascends moderately to the excellent campsites on the north and northwest sides of the westernmost lake (10,300') of the State Lakes complex. Here, fishing for golden (to 17") is excellent; and excursionary side-trip possibilities are magnificent. Anglers will want to try the waters of Glacier Lakes, the three other lakes in the State Lakes chain, and Horseshoe Lakes. Climbers looking for challenge will find the Cirque Crest peaks more than adequate.

3rd and 4th Hiking Days: Retrace your steps, 15½ miles.

Onion Valley roadend

Thomas Winnett

56   **Cedar Grove to South Lake**

TRIP   From Cedar Grove Roadend to South Lake via Granite Basin, Granite Pass, State Lakes, Simpson Meadow, Middle Fork Kings River, Dusy Basin, Bishop Pass (shuttle trip). Topo maps *Marion Peak, Mt. Goddard*. Best mid or late season; 48 miles.

Grade	Trail/layover days	Total recommended days
Leisurely	....	....
Moderate	7/3	10
Strenuous	6/3	9

HILITES   This trans-Sierra route is relatively little used from Cedar Grove Roadend to the junction with the Muir Trail, and the hiker can count on a measure of solitude. Fine angling and magnificent panoramas are expectations to be realized, and the sweeping variety of flora and fauna encountered on this trail knows no equal in Sierra trips.

DESCRIPTION (Strenuous trip)

1st and 2nd Hiking Days: Follow trip 55 to **State Lakes,** 15½ miles.

3rd Hiking Day (**State Lakes** to **Simpson Meadow,** 8 miles): Our ducked trail starts northward on the north side of the meadow at the northwest end of the lake. Wildflower fanciers will find the area around the State Lakes visited by the trail a plethora of color. Rank fields of false solomon's seal cover the open flats, and lush-foliaged shooting stars wave above dense mats of moss and low-lying fern in the damp grottos along the streams. In the drier stretches along the trail that continues northward to the next of the State Lakes group, one will find the supine pussy paws, prim Douglas phlox, taller lupine, and the tall, stately bluebell. The grassy fringes of this next lake offer good campsites on the west side where the trail fords the outlet stream. (A warning note: this stream marks the last reliable water until the Middle Fork Kings River.) Beyond State Lakes the trail turns west, going moderately down and then up, past the lateral to enchanting Horseshoe Lakes and then past the sandy junction with the Dougherty Meadow Trail. Beyond the divide ridge, our route descends moderately and then steeply. Across the canyon of the Middle Fork Kings River, the heights of Tunemah Peak and the White Divide come into view, and, from several vantage points, one can see up rocky Goddard Creek and Enchanted Gorge to the Black Divide.

The rapidly descending route continues down via steep, eroded switchbacks through three life zones. Lodgepole, the predominant tree of the higher elevations, shows growing inclusions of juniper, silver pine, sugar pine and incense-cedar. The mixed forest cover drops behind as the trail zigzags its final drop to the canyon floor. There the trail passes a drift fence and, winding through lush vegetation, meets the Middle Fork Trail. At this junction, our route turns right into Simpson Meadow. Used first by the Yokuts Indians, and then by sheepmen and cattlemen, this meadow is presently nearly forgotten. Its remoteness and difficulty of access have made it one of the least-visited meadows in this part of the Sierra, and today it is usually visited only by the wilderness traveler who seeks solitude and is not alarmed by the sight of an occasional rattlesnake around the area of Simpson Meadow.

Our route passes a sometimes-manned ranger station about 200 yards above the junction on a gently ascending, very rough trail, and arrives at the fair packer and primitive campsites on nearby Horseshoe Creek (5910'). Alternative primitive sites can be found along the river upstream. Travelers with two layover days and an inclination to a lengthy side trip may wish to visit Tehipite Valley 12 miles downstream, there to see the magnificently polished granite facade of Tehipite Dome, and the adjacent impressive falls. Rattlesnakes are commonly encountered en route and at Tehipite Valley. Fishing on the Middle Fork Kings River is good-to-excellent for rainbow and golden (to 14").

4th Hiking Day (**Simpson Meadow** to **Grouse Meadows,** 10 miles): Ascending gently, the poorly maintained trail continues northeast through alternating meadow and moderate forest of white fir, incense-cedar, Jeffrey pine and quaking aspen. Sagebrush frequently overhangs the trail, making footing sometimes difficult, and in the wetter sections the eroded trail is obliterated. As the trail rounds the talus-ridden slopes of Windy Peak, it offers good views of Goddard Creek canyon, and the evidence of a fire that swept unchecked up Middle Fork Kings River and Goddard Creek canyons is painfully evident in their brush-choked, black-stumped slopes. Still ascending gently, the sandy trail swings somewhat more eastward as it fords multibranched Windy Canyon Creek. To the northeast, the east canyon wall shows the break carved there by the feeder glacier emanating from the upper reaches of Cartridge Creek.

Just beyond the ford of Windy Canyon Creek, the trail turns north, and the canyon walls narrow dramatically. The trail then crosses Cartridge Creek by a substantial bridge, and passes the Cartridge Creek Trail, branching right from the packer's campsite. Ascending more steeply now, the trail crosses rocky stretches broken by pockets of timber cover, and the visible waters of the Middle Fork are white with rapids and cascades. The trail keeps to the canyon walls, usually 50 to 100 feet above the stream, and the drop to the river's waters is frequently a sheer face of polished granite. Flowers seen along this stretch are generally of the dry-country variety, including paintbrush, penstemon, Collinsia, forget-me-not, lupine and fleabane. The trail climbs steeply to the flats just below Devils Washbowl. To the right, the east canyon walls provide a fascinating study in convoluted glacial polish, and the views to the west and northwest of the Great Cliffs and the heavily fractured rock of Devils Crags portend later, equally exciting views of the Black Divide. The trail touches the river briefly near some sandy campsites, and then switchbacks up to awesome Devils Washbowl, a wild, spectacular falls and cataract in a granite gorge setting. Leaving the tumult of the water behind, the trail continues to ascend over rock to the innocuous-looking but treacherous ford of the unnamed creek draining Windy Cliff to the southeast. The flora around these tributary fords deserves the traveler's attention because of both its lushness and the presence of the very rare copper birch. Among the wildflowers one is sure to find at stream crossings are paintbrush, penstemon, pennyroyal, white Mariposa, cinquefoil, tiger lily, lupine, columbine and elderberry.

Ascending and descending steeply, the vacillating trail is sometimes at river's edge, and other times 200 feet above. The underfooting is very rocky and treacherous until we near the Palisade Creek crossing. This crossing is preceded by a reacquaintance with a timber cover of Jeffrey, lodgepole and silver pine and white fir. Just after the steel bridge crossing of Palisade Creek, our route meets and turns left onto the John Muir Trail and passes

Lake Reflection

from Lone Pine

Two views of Mt. Whitney

from the summit trail

Tarn below Bullfrog Lake

Pond at Mono Pass

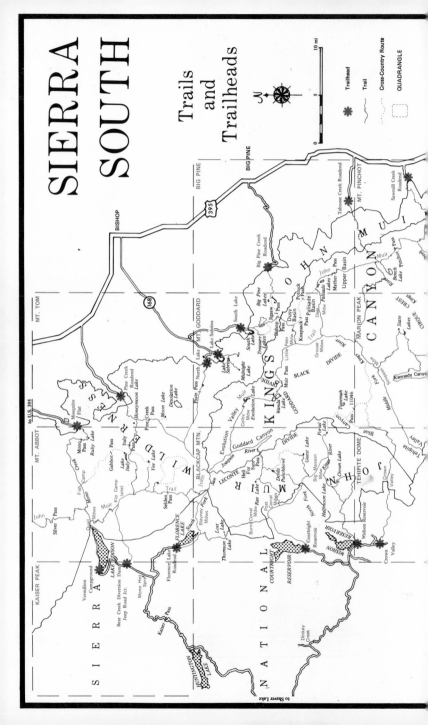

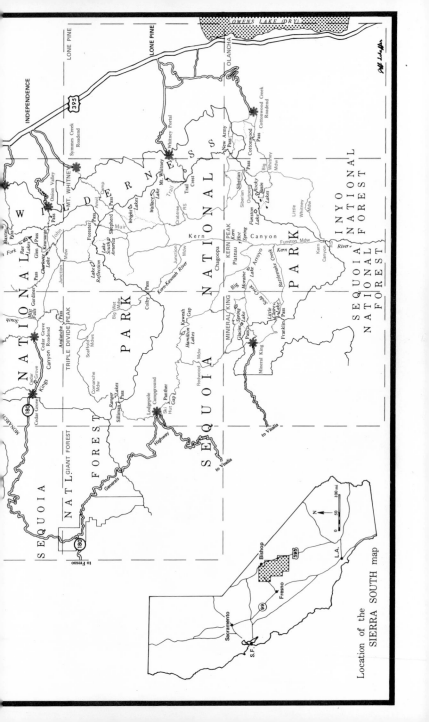

Location of the SIERRA SOUTH map

Evolution Lake, Mt. Spencer, Mt. Huxley

Little Lakes Valley, Sierra crest

Autumn in Cloud Canyon

Headwaters of the Kern—looking south

The Sierra crest from Lower 60 Lake Basin

several excellent campsites. Continuing north, the trail crosses an easy ridge, fords the unnamed tributary draining the west slopes of Giraud Peak, and arrives at the excellent campsites at the east side of Grouse Meadows. The intimate views are excellent of the lush meadows, and the quiet waters of the meandering river. Fishing for rainbow, some golden and brook (to 13″) is good.

5th Hiking Day (**Grouse Meadows** to **Dusy Basin,** 7½ miles): Leaving the pleasant grasslands of Grouse Meadows behind, the trail continues its gentle but steady ascent. On the left, the river foregoes the placid temperament of its winding meadow course and resumes its mad, white-water plunge. Beyond the river to the west, The Citadel's granite face stands guard over the south side of an obvious hanging valley, and the early-morning traveler is often treated to a burst of reflected sunlight from glacially polished surfaces high on the canyon's west wall north of that valley. The trail undulates up and down the east wall, sometimes 80 to 100 feet above the river, sometimes right alongside it. The thin lodgepole forest cover occurs mostly in stands, with intermittent stretches of grassy pockets, and the underfooting is mostly rocky. Ahead, the canyon narrows, and the trail crosses Dusy Branch via a substantial steel footbridge, and meets the Dusy Basin Trail. A few yards north of this junction is the LeConte Ranger Station, where emergency services are available.

Our route turns right (east) and begins the steep, switchbacking ascent of the east canyon wall. This ascent is broken into two distinct steps that gain 2000 feet in about 2 miles, but the steepness of the slope is tamed by the well-graded switchbacks. Touching the creek at strategic intervals (a cold drink on this climb is always welcome), the trail offers magnificent views of the monolithic granite structures on the far side of the canyon. Near the creek, the wildflower lover will find lush shooting star, fireweed, penstemon, pennyroyal and some yellow columbine nestling next to damp, moss-covered, rocky grottos. Along the switchbacks, occasional lodgepole and juniper break the monotony of the slab granite, and one particular juniper stands out with a near-record girth. Like a bettle-browed sentinel this ancient specimen guards the north end of one of the switchbacks near the top of the first climb. Views of the chutes and cascades of Dusy Branch reward the dusty trail-pounder as he finishes the first climb and enters the cooling bower of a mixed stand of lodgepole and aspen. The trail crosses the creek on a bridge and then returns over another to continue the switchbacking up through a sparse forest cover of aspen. This ascent levels out near the lowest of the Dusy Basin lake chain, and emerges to open, breathtaking views of Mt. Winchell, Mt. Agassiz and Columbine Peak. Rounding the north side of the lower Dusy Basin lake chain, the trail turns north and climbs a series of grass-topped ledges. A short, well-worn spur trail branches right, leading to alternative campsites situated both alongside Dusy Branch and on the middle lakes of the Dusy Basin chain (11,300′).

Our route veers away from the creek, climbing above it, and where it rejoins the creek while on an eastward jog, our route turns right a short cross-country distance and descends through an alpine fell field to the good campsites near the west side of the northernmost large lake in the basin. Fishing for golden and golden hybrids is good (to 8″). This campsite offers the camper a fine base for further explorations of Dusy and Palisades basins, and a granite outcropping just east of the lake provides the finest panoramic viewpoint in the entire basin. Those with a bent for angling will find the fishing on the outlet of the large lake to the east rewarding (golden and golden hybrids to 23″).

6th Hiking Day (**Dusy Basin** to **South Lake,** 7 miles): Reverse the 1st hiking day, trip 40.

Bishop Pass Trail   *Thomas Winnett*

Cedar Grove to Vidette Meadow   **57**

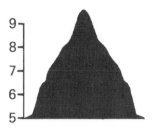

TRIP   From Cedar Grove Roadend to Vidette Meadow (round trip). Topo maps *Marion Peak, Mt. Pinchot.* Best early-to-mid season; 26 miles.

Grade	Trail/layover days	Total recom- mended days
Leisurely	4/1	5
Moderate	3/0	3
Strenuous	2/0	2

HILITES   Climbing 4000 feet, this trip follows an old Indian trade route paralleling Bubbs Creek. Beyond the realm of the Park's dayhiker, the trail climbs the path of an old glacier to beautiful Vidette Meadow, a "high country crossroads." Here in the shadow of the spectacular Kearsarge Pinnacles this route meets the famous John Muir Trail.

DESCRIPTION (Moderate trip)

1st Hiking Day (**Cedar Grove Roadend** to **Sphinx Creek Trail Junction,** 4 miles): From the paved roadend loop (5035′) the wide, sandy trail ascends gently through a mixed forest cover of ponderosa, incense-cedar, black oak, sugar pine and white fir. The balmy climate usually characteristic of the gently sloping canyon floor made this area a favorite of the Indians, who had their summer hunting camps here. Foraging parties of Indians made their "spur" camps along Bubbs Creek at many of the same spots chosen by today's backcountry traveler.

The murmur of the South Fork Kings River, sometimes near, sometimes far, accompanies the traveler as he winds up the gentle ascent and passes the Paradise Valley/Woods Creek Trail (branching north) just before crossing a steel bridge over the South Fork and a series of wooden bridges over the branches of Bubbs Creek. The last bridge crossing marks the beginning of a series of steady switchbacks. Along them we find some rare (for this side of the Sierra) pinon pines. This tree, whose fruit provides the delicious pine nut, is of the single-needle group, and may be identified by either its single needle or its distinctive spherical cone. Most noticeable about the cone is its very thick, blunt, four-sided scale. This ascent offers fine views back into the dramatic U-shaped South Fork Kings River canyon. On the south side of the Bubbs Creek canyon the dominating landmark is the pronounced granite point known as The Sphinx. To the east its namesake stream cuts a sharp-lipped defile on the peak's east shoulder. Above the switchbacks, at the Sphinx Creek Trail junction (6280') are several fair campsites with ample firewood. Evidence of Indian camps in this vicinity was found just upstream. Fishing for rainbow and brown trout (fry) is poor. Camping here and on the entire Rae Lakes loop is limited to one night in any campsite. Hikers bound for East Lake and Lake Reflection who wish to get there in one more day would do well to choose a campsite 1 or 2 miles upstream from the Sphinx Creek Trail junction.

2nd Hiking Day (**Sphinx Creek Trail Junction** to **Vidette Meadow,** 9 miles): Keeping to the north side of Bubbs Creek, the trail ascends steadily up the canyon, passing a number of fair campsites. The trail fords several unnamed tributaries and then Charlotte Creek. The sparse-to-moderate forest cover reflects the altitude gain, with inclusions of lodgepole and fir and some Jeffrey pine. Beautiful stands of these trees offer those who would come to know the trees a splendid opportunity to study and identify them. The lodgepole, the most common, is usually identified by its straight, slender trunk, although in higher elevations the tree is frequently stunted, twisted and weathered. The tree's normal shape gave it its name, for it caused the Indians of the Great Plains to journey far into the Rocky Mountains in search of poles for their skin lodges, or tepees. Even more distinctive are the two needles to a bunch and the grayish, thin-scaled bark. Those with discriminating noses will discern an odor from the bark which very much resembles that of a newly opened bottle of gin.

Continuing up Bubbs Creek canyon, we can see, on the north wall of the canyon, the cleft of the Charlotte Creek drainage, guarded on the west by Charlotte Dome (Point 10690 on the topo map). The south wall presents several avalanche chutes, which are responsible for the patch of bent and broken trees on the near side of the canyon—they all lean north, away from the onslaught of the snow masses. After a short, steep stretch of rocky going, the trail travels through fine stands of quaking aspen and black cottonwood to beautiful Junction Meadow. Views through the trees of Mt. Bago to the north reveal two interesting septa of metavolcanic rock in black stripes.

Beyond the west end of the meadow, our route passes the East Lake/Lake Reflection Trail. This meadow is closed to grazing because of serious deterioration brought on by past use. At the end of the meadow the trail switchbacks up a dry manzanita slope, sometimes distant from the creek and sometimes right alongside. The steepest part of the climb ends at the conclusion of the switchbacks, and the trail then proceeds on a moderate ascent to the junction with the John Muir Trail. Looking back, one has fine views of the avalanche-scarred north face of West Vidette. Our route turns right, fords the tiny outlet creek from Bullfrog Lake and arrives at the good campsites (9600′) at beautiful Vidette Meadow, scattered along Bubbs Creek. Fishing for brook, rainbow and some brown (to 8″) is fair, and emergency services are available from a summer ranger.

3rd Hiking Day: Retrace your steps, 13 miles.

East Lake *Thomas Winnett*

58   Cedar Grove to Charlotte Lake

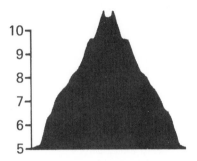

TRIP

From Cedar Grove Roadend to Charlotte Lake (round trip). Topo maps *Marion Peak, Mt. Pinchot.* Best mid or late season; 33 miles.

Grade	Trail/layover days	Total recom- mended days
Leisurely	5/1	6
Moderate	4/1	5
Strenuous	2/1	3

HILITES

Striking right into the heart of the high country, this route ascends a lengthy stretch of the Bubbs Creek drainage to the charming meadows at the foot of the Kearsarge Pinnacles and the Videttes. The terminus of this trip, Charlotte Lake, is an exciting base camp location for trips to four major lake basins.

DESCRIPTION (Leisurely trip)

1st and 2nd Hiking Days: Follow trip 57 to **Vidette Meadow,** 13 miles.

3rd Hiking Day (**Vidette Meadow** to **Charlotte Lake,** 3½ miles): First, retrace your steps to the junction of the John Muir Trail and the Bubbs Creek Trail. Following the Muir Trail as it switchbacks up the steep north side of the canyon, the traveler is treated to breathtaking views of the Kearsarge Pinnacles to the east, and the Videttes and snow-necklaced Deerhorn Mountain to the south. It is easy, while viewing this spectacle, to understand the popularity of the Muir Trail, and it is with a sense of loss that one leaves the Bubbs Creek valley and crosses the lip of the Bullfrog Lake basin. Our route bypasses Bullfrog Lake, continuing northwest on a series of switchbacks to the Charlotte Lake Trail. This trail leaves the Muir Trail at an "X" junction in a sandy saddle after providing one last look back to the Bubbs Creek drainage and far south into Center Basin, with the Kings-Kern Divide in the background, and zigzags down to Charlotte Lake. High on the left of the switchbacks tower the several summits of red-rocked Mt. Bago. Good campsites may be found along the north side of the lake (10370'). Emergency services are available from the resident summer ranger. Fishing for rainbow and brook trout (to 10") is good. The meadows around and above the lake are closed to grazing.

4th Hiking Day (**Charlotte Lake** to **Junction Meadow,** 5 miles): Retrace the steps of the 3rd and part of the 2nd hiking day.

5th Hiking Day (**Junction Meadow** to **Cedar Grove Roadend,** 11½ miles): Retrace the steps of part of the 2nd and all of the 1st hiking day.

East Vidette over Bullfrog Lake   *Thomas Winnett*

59   Cedar Grove to Gardiner Basin

TRIP From Cedar Grove Roadend to Gardiner Basin (round trip). Topo maps *Marion Peak*, *Mt. Pinchot*. Best mid or late season; 50 miles.

Grade	Trail/layover days	Total recom- mended days
Leisurely	7/2	9
Moderate	6/1	7
Strenuous	5/0	5

HILITES The hiker who values serenity and relative seclusion amid true alpine surroundings, and is tired of encountering the swarms of hikers and campers who crowd the Muir Trail and other popular routes in the Sierra, will appreciate Gardiner Basin. This hidden sanctuary, forested in its lower reaches and spotted with sparkling lakes, ringed on three sides by granite ridges and sharp peaks, will satisfy a longing for a genuine wilderness experience.

DESCRIPTION (Leisurely trip)

1st 3 Hiking Days: Follow trip 58 to **Charlotte Lake**, 16½ miles.

4th Hiking Day (**Charlotte Lake** to **Gardiner Basin**, 8½ miles): From the west end of Charlotte Lake, the trail fords Charlotte Creek, skirts the south edge of a grassy clearing, and crosses again to the north side of the creek. Beyond here, the trail is infrequently maintained. We cross a maze of avalanche-downed trees and descend westward, above the stream, through a mixed forest of aspen, lodgepole and some juniper, punctuated with clumps of manzanita. The trail drops gradually along the south slope of Gardiner Ridge, leaving the rapidly descending creek far below.

Ahead is the Yosemitelike monolith of Charlotte Dome, unnamed on the map but strikingly prominent. Finally we begin climbing through an open forest, cross a low rocky spur, and reach the bubbling North Fork of Charlotte Creek. The trail recrosses the creek twice, traverses a small meadow, and commences the long climb to Gardiner Pass. On this lengthy ascent, the trail makes numerous switchbacks through a fine forest of lodgepole pine, until tall foxtail pines become predominant near 11,000 feet. From the 11,200-foot pass—one of the few forested passes higher than 11,000 feet in the Sierra—one has breathtaking panoramas. To the south, the high, rugged summits of the Kings-Kern Divide lace the sky. Northward, one can look over the deep trench of Gardiner Basin to peaks as far north as Mt. Goddard.

From Gardiner Pass the trail zigzags steeply down into the glaciated head of Gardiner Creek's South Fork, fords the icy creek, and reaches an unnamed lake. For the next 2 miles, we descend from granite bench to granite bench, arranged like progressive stepping-stones, several of them harboring tarns or marshy lakes. The forest cover becomes exclusively lodgepole, interspaced with verdant clearings laced with colorful wildflowers. The trail passes 50 feet above the east edge of the large lower lake, then drops to a superb campsite along the northeast shore. From here, you cross a low rise, them abruptly drop in unbelievably steep zigzags to the floor of Gardiner Creek's main basin. To your left, hidden in forest and brush on a small flat 200 yards south of the creek, is the remains of one of Shorty Lovelace's pigmy cabins, built in the years when Shorty ran a trap line before the establishment of King Canyon National Park. Beyond this point, the topo map shows a footpath ascending east into upper Gardiner Basin. It is nothing but a ducked route, with occasional semblances of trail.

5th Hiking Day: Reverse the 4th hiking day, 8½ miles.

6th and 7th Hiking Days: Reverse the 5th and 4th hiking days, trip 58, 16½ miles.

60   **Cedar Grove to Rae Lakes**

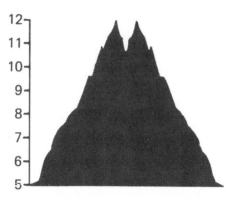

TRIP   From Cedar Grove Roadend to Rae Lakes via Vidette Meadow, Glen Pass (round trip). Topo maps
Marion Peak, *Mt. Pinchot*. Best late season; 42 miles.

Grade	Trail/layover days	Total recom- mended days
Leisurely	6/2	8
Moderate	5/2	7
Strenuous	4/1	5

HILITES   Rae Lakes have long been a favorite of the high-
country hiker and photographer—and with good
cause. Situated beyond Glen Pass, and between the
Sierra crest and the King Spur, these lakes are a
scenic paradise. Because of this, and because of the
central location, anyone contemplating this trip
should plan on spending some days exploring the
Sixty Lake Basin.

DESCRIPTION (Moderate trip)

1st 2 Hiking Days: Follow trip 57 to **Vidette Meadow**, 13 miles.

3rd Hiking Day (**Vidette Meadow** to **Rae Lakes**, 8 miles): From
Vidette Meadow our route follows the John Muir Trail north as it
climbs out of Bubbs Creek canyon. This climb parallels and sometimes crosses a tributary stream in a series of switchbacks. Excellent views of the Kearsarge Pinnacles to the east complement the
view of the Videttes to the south. Beyond the Videttes tower the
peaks of the Kings-Kern Divide, foregrounded by the barren
granite of Center Basin. The peaks of the main Sierra crest ap-

pear to the northeast, and although mostly white granite, some of the higher peaks reveal more ancient sedimentary and metamorphic rocks. Our route, on the John Muir Trail, passes a trail lateral to Bullfrog Lake and, at the top of the climb, a lateral to Charlotte Lake and a trail to Kearsarge Pass (most of which is not on the topo map). Because of the heavy traffic and camping impact from the Muir Trail and the Kearsarge Pass lateral, Bullfrog Lake is closed to camping. From the Charlotte Lake Trail, our route turns north on a long, steady ascent that rounds a granite promontory; then it descends slightly, veers east, and passes another trail to Charlotte Lake. As the headwall of Glen Pass comes into view, it is hard to see where a passable trail could go up it. And indeed the last 500 feet up to the top are steeply switchbacking, but never on the edge of a cliff. This trail section offers good views of Charlotte Lake, the Charlotte Creek canyon, Charlotte Dome and Mt. Brewer. At the pass (11,978'), one can look north down on the unnamed glacier lakes immediately to the north, and several of the Rae Lakes below. Beyond them in the north are Mt. Cotter, Mt. Clarence King, Mt. Pinchot, Dragon Peak, Black Mountain, and, far north, the 14,000-foot Palisades.

The descent from the pass is by zigzagging, rocky switchbacks down to the granite bench holding the unnamed lakes seen from the pass. (The bad underfooting requires care in placing one's feet.) After crossing the outlet stream of these lakes, the trail resumes its switchbacking descent, re-enters a pine forest cover and skirts the west shore of upper Rae Lake. Just before the trail crosses the narrow isthmus separating the upper lake from the rest of the chain, we pass a spur trail branching west to Sixty Lake Basin. After crossing the sparsely timbered isthmus, the route swings north, passes the short lateral to Dragon Lake, and arrives at the many good campsites near the east shores of middle and lower Rae Lakes (10,560'). Fishing is good for brook trout and some rainbow (to 16"). Views from the campsites across the beryl-green lake waters to the dramatically exfoliating Fin Dome and the King Spur beyond are among the best and longest remembered of the trip. A summer ranger is stationed on the east shore of the middle lake.

4th and 5th Hiking Days: Retrace your steps, 21 miles.

61 Cedar Grove to Rae Lakes

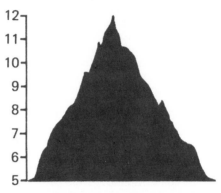

TRIP   From Cedar Grove Roadend to Rae Lakes, return via
            South Fork Woods Creek, Paradise Valley (loop trip).
            Topo maps *Marion Peak, Mt. Pinchot.* Best late sea-
            son; 41½ miles.

Grade	Trail/layover days	Total recom-mended days
Leisurely	8/2	10
Moderate	6/2	8
Strenuous	4/1	5

HILITES Known as the "Rae Lakes Loop," this fine trip circles
             the King Spur. The landscape viewed en route is
             dramatic enough to challenge the most accomplished
             photographer or artist as the route circles beneath
             the Videttes and the Kearsarge Pinnacles and tra-
             verses a lengthy stretch of the Sierra crest.

DESCRIPTION (Moderate trip)

1st 3 Hiking Days: Follow trip 60 to **Rae Lakes,** 21 miles.

4th Hiking Day (**Rae Lakes** to **Woods Creek Crossing,** 6½ miles): The
trail covered in this hiking day is an easy downhill stretch that
traces the length of the South Fork Woods Creek. Beginning from
the campsites along the east side of Rae Lakes, the trail continues
along the east side of the lake chain and the intervening stream
on a moderate descent. Fin Dome drops behind, and the outstanding landmark is Diamond Peak to the east. The long black striations seen along the face of Diamond Peak and the continuing
ridge to the north are metamorphosed lava, one of the few remaining bits of volcanic evidence to be found in this area. Just

west of Diamond Peak the trail fords the South Fork Woods Creek and skirts the west side of the lowest lake of the Rae Lakes chain. At the outlet our route passes the turnoff to Baxter Pass, and then descends more sharply over rocky stretches that are interrupted by pockets of alluvial sand. The moderate forest cover is mostly clumps of lodgepole that show evidence of the lodgepole needle-miner, a tree-killing insect. The valley floor is relatively open as the trail descends and crosses the stream draining the Sixty Lake Basin (difficult ford in early season) and the stream draining Lake 10296.

Rounding the northernmost prominence of the King Spur, the trail swings west, and its moderate descent levels off as it approaches the Woods Creek Crossing. A few yards above this crossing the traveler should keep an eye peeled for one of this region's most interesting historic landmarks, one of Shorty Lovelace's unusual line cabins, which still stands on the west side of the creek. Those who take time out to examine this structure will soon discern its unique character. Appearing to be almost a miniature replica of the real article, it was erected to suit the needs of its builder, and it would scarcely accommodate the average person—standing or sleeping. It was from this cabin and several others in this general area that Shorty worked his trap line before it was included within the Park's boundaries. The trail fords just below the confluence of the South and North forks of Woods Creek via a footlog (8492'). Fair campsites may be found near the crossing. Fishing in the creek is good for brook and rainbow (to 10").

5th Hiking Day (**Woods Creek Crossing** to **Paradise Valley,** 7 miles): Leaving the John Muir Trail our route turns west, staying on the north side of Woods Creek. The underfooting is alternately sandy and rocky as the trail descends gently between the narrowing canyon walls. The forest cover, still predominantly lodgepole, shows inclusions of red fir as the altitude lessens, and clumps of the water-loving quaking aspen dot the stream banks. This smooth-barked, whispering tree is the most conspicuous member of the deciduous group found in the high country. Always found near running water or at the edge of porous seepage areas (lava, talus, gravel), it acts as a native water locator, and its ghostly white trunk can be seen for great distances. Hikers who have camped in a grove of aspen will always remember the tree's gentle rustling sound as the leaves, responding to the slightest breeze, tremble against one another.

The trail passes a burn scar (caused by a careless camper's campfire), and winds through Castle Domes Meadow, named for the obvious landmarks to the north. Undulating up and down the north canyon wall, the trail descends on a moderate grade, fords two unnamed right-bank tributaries, and then descends more steeply to the ford of South Fork Kings River (difficult in early season). In contrast to the manzanita-covered slopes to the south, the steep walls up the South Fork canyon to the north are barren and forbidding. Known as Muro Blanco ("white wall"), they are part of the largest untrailed area in Kings Canyon National Park. After the ford, the trail turns southwest and descends gently past a drift fence to the open expanses of Paradise Valley (6640'). Good campsites are near the stream, and fishing for rainbow and some brown is fair (to 8").

6th Hiking Day (**Paradise Valley** to **Cedar Grove Roadend**, 7 miles): On a gentle descent through a mixed forest cover of lodgepole, red fir, white fir, Jeffrey pine and some juniper and aspen, the trail continues southwest. At the lower end of Paradise Valley, the descent steepens, and the smooth, serpentining South Fork Kings River straightens out and dashes down the canyon. Views during this descent include the already familiar landmark, The Sphinx. Midway down this stretch the trail pauses in its descent near Mist Falls, a cascade that deserves its name only during times of high water, because by midsummer this white-water tumble becomes sedate and subdued. Beyond Mist Falls the trail dips steeply over a rocky surface, and zigzags before leveling out on the wide valley floor. A short distance farther on, our route meets and joins the Bubbs Creek Trail, and returns over the short 2-mile stretch described in the 1st hiking day.

On the Bubbs Creek Trail

Thomas Winnett

Cedar Grove to Oak Creek Roadend **62**

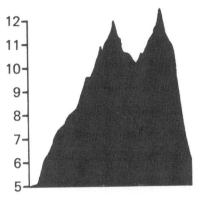

TRIP		From Cedar Grove Roadend to Oak Creek Roadend via Bubbs Creek, Glen Pass, Rae Lakes, Baxter Pass (shuttle trip). Topo maps *Marion Peak, Mt. Pinchot.* Best late season; 36½ miles.

Grade	Trail/layover days	Total recommended days
Leisurely	7/2	9
Moderate	5/2	7
Strenuous	4/1	5

HILITES This trans-Sierra crossing makes a delightful S-curve as it journeys from the Bubbs Creek drainage to Rae Lakes and emerges on the east side via little-used Baxter Pass. The scenic lakes and towering, alp-like peaks of this route make this a fine route for photography.

DESCRIPTION (Moderate trip)

1st 3 Hiking Days: Follow trip 60 to **Rae Lakes,** 21 miles.

4th Hiking Day (**Rae Lakes** to **Baxter Lakes,** 5½ miles): The first 2½ miles of this day's hike follow the gentle-to-moderate descent of the South Fork Woods Creek. From Rae Lakes the trail passes through granite slab areas broken by stands of dwarfed lodgepole as it skirts the east side of the lower lakes of the Rae Lakes chain. Anglers will want to try their luck for the good brook trout fishing on some of these lakes and the stream flowing between them. The route fords the stream between the lowest and next-to-lowest lakes, and circles the west side of the lowest lake before leaving

the John Muir Trail at the outlet of this lake, locally called Dollar
Lake. We cross the outlet on logs and pick up a faint, unsigned,
sometimes ducked trail that diagonals up the east wall of the
valley. This ascent makes a long northward traverse, and from it
we have fine views down the canyon of the South Fork Woods
Creek. On the far side, a very evident line is the John Muir Trail,
and most likely we will see a number of hikers on this wilderness
boulevard. After a mile of ascent, the trail descends down into the
Baxter Creek drainage, into a handsome grove of foxtail pines
that give welcome shade. Then it swings east to continue the
steep ascent to the Baxter Lakes. The trail here is ducked but
sometimes hard to see as it follows the course shown on the topo
map. The sparse forest cover thins as the route fords Baxter
Creek and passes several tiny lakelets. Fair campsites may be
found in a grove of whitebark pines below the highest lake
(11,150'), where fishing for brook trout (to 12") is good.

5th Hiking Day (**Baxter Lakes** to **Oak Creek Roadend,** 10 miles):
After rounding the north side of the highest and largest lake of
the basin, the trail turns south as it ascends the steep granite
scoop above the lake. Excellent views of Mt. Baxter and Ac-
rodectes Peak to the north accompany the climb, and rockhounds
can marvel at the dramatic striping on some of the peaks, known
as mafic diking. These dikes, glaciated remnants of ancient
magma intrusions, are evidence of the substantial igneous action
that played a part in the petrology of the area. The rocky footpath
ascends southwest, mostly on a moderate grade, and then descends momentarily across a snowfield. Even in this high, mineral world the vegetable kingdom stays alive, in the form of small
specimens of alpine sorrel, Davidson's penstemon and Sierra
primrose. Finally, the trail switchbacks up to scree-laden Baxter
Pass (12,320'), where one has fine views of the Sierra crest, including multistriped Diamond Peak to the southwest, the North
Fork Oak Creek canyon to the south, looking like a vertical-sided,
giant gash, and even the town of Independence, far below in
Owens Valley. The trail is over loose rock as it descends to Summit Meadow, where one can enjoy the russet and copper colors of
the nearby rocks. The trail stays mostly well above the tumbling
waters of the North Fork Oak Creek, undulating down through
many fields of very colorful wildflowers that include monkey
flower, arnica, milfoil, cinquefoil, pennyroyal, buckwheat,
spiraea, gilia, penstemon, Queen Anne's Lace, shooting star,
paintbrush and buttercup.

The trail follows the sharply cut defile of the stream, and one
can see the heavy concentrations of metavolcanic rock which was
vented nearby and which characterizes the remaining descent

onto the alluvial apron below. Midway down this long, flowery descent we ford the creek (difficult at high water) in the middle of a mixed forest cover, and soon embark on another long set of zigzags. These are succeeded by a gentle, sandy descent to end with a few more quick switchbacks down to the last crossing of the creek. As the trail drops to the creek, one encounters a good sampling of typical east-side Sierra flora including rabbit brush, bitter brush, sagebrush, juniper, and mountain mahogany. Beyond a log over the North Fork Oak Creek we leave the John Muir Wilderness, boulder-hop a side stream, and arrive at a dirt road (6000') west of Oak Creek Campground.

Fin Dome close up

Thomas Winnett

63 **Cedar Grove to Lake Reflection**

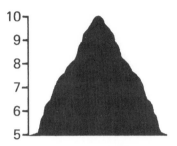

TRIP   From Cedar Grove Roadend to Lake Reflection (round trip). Topo maps *Marion Peak, Mt. Pinchot, Mt. Whitney*. Best mid or late season; 30 miles.

Grade	Trail/layover days	Total recom- mended days
Leisurely	6/1	7
Moderate	4/1	5
Strenuous	3/1	4

HILITES   Those who appreciate the serenity of high, alpine lake basins will find this trip to the upper reaches of East Creek a rewarding choice. Excellent fishing amidst spellbinding surroundings makes this a fine angling trip, and if one doesn't fish, it is time well spent just "soaking up the country."

DESCRIPTION (Moderate trip)

1st Hiking Day (**Cedar Grove Roadend** to **Junction Meadow,** 10 miles): Proceed to Junction Meadow as described in the 1st and part of the 2nd hiking day, trip 57.

2nd Hiking Day (**Junction Meadow** to **Lake Reflection,** 5 miles): At Junction Meadow our trail branches right, fords Bubbs Creek, and ascends East Creek canyon. This ascent is accomplished via rocky switchbacks that zigzag through a sparse-to-moderate forest cover of lodgepole, fir, silver pine, Jeffrey pine and some aspen. The view back to the north is dominated by the red metamorphic rocks of Mt. Bago, with Mt. Gardiner coming into view beyond it. As one tops the first rise of the ascent, peaks of the Kings-Kern Divide come into view. Anglers trying their luck along East Creek will find rainbow and brook trout (to 8″), and the trout are somewhat larger in East Lake.

After a brief stretch of moderate uphill going and a ford of East

Creek, the trail again steepens for one more climb before leveling off at East Lake. One's first view of these picturesque waters with their grassy fringes may be accompanied by a sighting of one of the many mule deer that frequent the canyon. The barren, unjointed granite walls that rise on either side—especially Mt. Brewer on the west—are an impressive backdrop for leisure moments spent on the shores of this mountain gem, and it is always with some reluctance that visitors move on. Beyond the head of East Lake the trail climbs steadily through rock-broken stands of lodgepole, red fir and foxtail pine. The right canyon wall breaks, and one can clearly spy the cirque in which Lake Reflection lies. Just before crossing a 50-yard-wide rockslide, we pass the unmarked junction of the Harrison Pass Trail. Beyond the rockslide it is an easy grade to the excellent campsites at the northeast end of Lake Reflection (10,005'), where the angler will find good fishing for golden, rainbow and hybrids (to 16"). When a breeze is not stirring the waters of this lake, the tableau of peaks reflected in their depths is a memorable scene of a scope seldom matched in the Sierra. At the head of the cirque basin, all side excursions are up, but the expenditure of sweat and effort required to explore the surrounding lakes and lakelets is repaid by great views and a sense of achievement that has been shared by many mountaineers since the Brewer Party first ascended these heights.

3rd Hiking Day (**Lake Reflection** to **Charlotte Creek,** 8 miles): Retrace the steps of the 2nd and part of the 1st hiking day to the fair campsites where Charlotte Creek joins Bubbs Creek.

4th Hiking Day (**Charlotte Creek** to **Cedar Grove Roadend,** 7 miles): Retrace the steps of part of the 1st hiking day.

Lake Reflection swimmers

Thomas Winnett

64   Cedar Grove to Upper Kern River

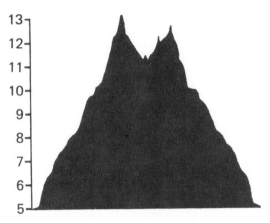

TRIP From Cedar Grove Roadend to Upper Kern River via Bubbs Creek, Forester Pass, return by Harrison Pass, East Lake (semiloop trip). Topo maps *Marion Peak, Mt. Pinchot, Mt. Whitney.* Best late season; 49 miles.

Grade	Trail/layover days	Total recom- mended days
Leisurely	9/3	12
Moderate	7/3	10
Strenuous	6/2	8

HILITES Crossing two high passes, this trip explores the glaciated upper reaches of the Kern Trench and circumnavigates a good piece of the Kings-Kern and Great Western divides. This is a long and rugged route that is recommended for the hearty backcountry traveler possessed of a sense of adventure and a liking for high, barren surroundings.

DESCRIPTION (Strenuous trip)

1st Hiking Day: (**Cedar Grove Roadend** to **Junction Meadow**, 10 miles): Proceed to Junction Meadow as described in the 1st and part of the 2nd hiking day, trip 57.

2nd Hiking Day (**Junction Meadow** to **Upper East Fork Bubbs Creek**, 5 miles): Follow the 2nd hiking day, trip 57, to Vidette Meadow, where our route joins the John Muir Trail and turns southeast, ascending the East Fork Bubbs Creek. About ½ mile above Vidette Meadow our route passes an old trapper's cabin. Shorty Lovelace trapped this country until it was made into a national park, and a network of his cabins remains to remind today's travelers of an era of the not-too-distant past. After the initial steep ascent above Vidette Meadow, the trail levels out to a moderate but steady ascent along the east bank of the creek through a moderate forest cover of lodgepole and occasional hemlock. Several campsites line the East Fork Bubbs Creek, and those at 10,200 feet offer fine campsite views of University Peak to the east, Center Peak to the southeast, and East Vidette and East Spur to the west. Fishing for brook trout (to 7″) is good. Side excursions for golden-trout fishing or mere pleasure can be made via the old Muir Trail route to Center Basin.

3rd Hiking Day (**Upper East Fork Bubbs Creek** to **Outlet Stream of Lake 11440**, 10½ miles, part cross country): From these campsites the gradually ascending trail fords two tributaries and arrives at the Junction Pass Trail junction. Our route (the "new" John Muir Trail) keeps to the right, ascending steeply over the barren granite west of Center Peak. This climb takes one above timberline as it winds back and forth over the tributary that drains Lake 12248, and over one's shoulder the peaks of the Sierra crest march away on the northern horizon. Rounding the steep west shore of Lake 12248, the trail hugs the west wall of the canyon, and then switchbacks steeply up to the narrow notch in the Kings-Kern Divide which is Forester Pass (13,200′). Views from the pass to the north and east include Mt. Pinchot, Junction Peak, Mt. Keith, Center Peak, Mt. Bradley and University (once University of California) Peak, Mt. Stanford and Caltech Peak are to the west. To the south are Mt. Kaweah and the Kaweah Peaks Ridge, the Red Spur, Picket Guard Peak and Kern Point.

Leaving this windy orientation point behind, the trail descends steeply by numerous, short switchbacks, some of which are barely more than shelves carved into the steep face of the Junction Peak ridge. A few hardy polemonium and some yellow hulsea share the high slope with scurrying conies, and the traveler who lifts his eyes is sometimes treated to a sighting of a golden eagle soaring high above the granite steeples. After the trail levels off somewhat, the rocky route winds among a number of unnamed lakes that make up the headwaters of Tyndall Creek. To the east the unusual formation called Diamond Mesa appears as a sheer-walled, flat-topped ridge dangling from the jumbled heights of Junction Peak. Here, the trail passes through "marmot land," and the traveling human intruder is looked upon indulgently as a seasonal part of the scenery—accepted, at a respectful distance.

Near timberline, our route intersects the signed Lake South
America/Milestone Creek Trail and turns right onto it. This trail
soon turns west, and then ascends gently at timberline for ½ mile
to another signed junction, where the Lake South America Trail
turns north and our route veers southwest. At the outlet stream
of Lake 11440, the hiker should turn left and descend cross country to the good campsite (11,200') in foxtail pines at the edge of
the meadow ¼ mile south.

4th Hiking Day (**Outlet Stream of Lake 11440** to **East Lake,** 10
miles, part cross country): Retrace the steps of the previous hiking
day to the Lake South America/Milestone Creek Trail junction,
where this day's route turns north and ascends gently up the east
side of a long, boulder-strewn meadow. At the head of this ascent,
the trail becomes steeper, and switchbacks up 500 feet of barren,
broken granite to a saddle which gives access to the large cirque
basin at the head of the Kern River. Beside a charming little lake
that feeds the Kern River our route meets the trail coming up
from the river and turns right, toward Lake South America (so
called from its shape), where the angler may wish to try the good
fishing for golden to 12″. From here the trail is ducked (inade-
quately) as it climbs toward Harrison Pass. Ahead, locating the
pass by visual sighting is difficult, as the lowest point on the
headwall of the canyon is nearer Mt. Ericsson than the actual
pass is. Our ducked route veers eastward, toward Mt. Stanford,
where the best descent on the north side may be had. This descent
is often snow-choked until late summer, and should not be at-
tempted with stock (despite the record of precedent). Views from
Harrison Pass to the south include Mt. Kaweah, Kaweah Peaks
Ridge, Milestone Mountain and Mt. Guyot. Looking north,
Deerhorn Mountain with its avalanche chutes and talus fans
stands athwart the view, but Mt. Goddard can be seen far in the
distance to the left of it, and Middle Palisade in the distance to its
right. From the pass, the route leads down the talus (sometimes
over snow) to the lakes visible from the summit.

Keeping to the east side of the bowl, we carefully pick our way
downward, toward the first lake visible on the cirque floor. We
cross its outlet and veer west to ford the stream connecting the
second and third lakes in the cirque. From here the ducked route
ascends a few hundred feet and then drops to the outlet of the
third lake, passing close under the buff-and-tan granite cliffs of
soaring Ericsson Crags. In the canyon below the third lake we
encounter timber, and also achieve our first view of Mt. Brewer,
due west across the canyon of East Creek. The route then levels
off briefly in a meadow and fords the crystal stream to the north
side. The white color of the trumpet-shaped flowers of alpine gen-

tian in this meadow tells us we are still quite high; blue gentians lie below. After passing several lovely tarns not shown on the topo map, the ducked and sometimes blazed trail easily crosses a little divide on a southbound course and traverses down to Golden Lake (not named on the map), where there is one excellent campsite. From the lake we have a direct view of Lucys Foot Pass, on the Kings-Kern Divide. This pass is Class 3 in places and it is not advised for ordinary backpacking or for inexperienced mountaineers. Due to all the loose "garbage" on the north side, the best passage is south-to-north.

From Golden Lake the route has a short level segment and then it descends steeply on a rocky-dusty, ill-maintained trail down poorly built switchbacks to the East Creek Trail, meeting it at an unsigned junction a few yards north of a talus rockslide. Here we turn right (north) and descend gently, sometimes moderately, for 1 mile to the good campsites at the north and south ends of East Lake, described in the 2nd hiking day, trip 63.

5th Hiking Day (**East Lake** to **Charlotte Creek,** 6½ miles): Descend to Junction Meadow, then retrace your steps to Charlotte Creek.

6th Hiking Day (**Charlotte Creek** to **Cedar Grove Roadend,** 7 miles): Reverse part of the 2nd hiking day and all of the 1st hiking day, trip 57.

Ridge east of Lake South America *Thomas Winnett*

65   Cedar Grove to East Lake

TRIP   From Cedar Grove Roadend to Upper Kern River and East Lake via Colby Pass and Harrison Pass (semiloop trip). Topo maps *Marion Peak, Mt. Pinchot, Mt. Whitney, Triple Divide Peak.* Best mid to late season; 69½ miles.

Grade	Trail/layover days	Total recom- mended days
Leisurely	....	....
Moderate	9/4	13
Strenuous	7/2	9

HILITES   Few trips that do not involve shuttling cars offer the variety of this loop around the major portion of the Great Western Divide. This is a trip for experienced backpackers, whose rewards for much effort will include almost continuous views of the highest High Sierra and great stretches of wilderness solitude.

DESCRIPTION (Moderate trip)

1st through 4th Hiking Days: Reverse the 8th through the 5th hiking days, trip 71, 30 miles.

5th Hiking Day (**Kern-Kaweah River** to **Upper Kern River,** 7 miles): Reverse the 4th and part of the 3rd hiking day, trip 76 to the junction of the Kern River Trail and the High Sierra Trail. One half mile up the canyon from the junction is a roofless cabin that was a powder magazine used by crews constructing trails in this region. Beginning here there are several good campsites along the river, where fishing is good for rainbow and golden trout (to 10″).

6th Hiking Day (**Upper Kern River** to **Outlet Stream of Lake 11440,** 9 miles): Reverse most of the 3rd hiking day, trip 70. At Lake 10650 our route turns right up a short, steep ascent through a cover of moderate lodgepole and foxtail. After half a mile the trail passes a picturebook lake. This lake is fast (geologically speaking) becoming a meadow. The trail continues eastward up a moderate ascent through alternating rocky and meadowy sections, where the Oregon junco is likely to be seen flitting among the willows. Careful study of the ground as one walks along may discover a junco nest under the overhang of a boulder, a fallen log or a tree bole. This route climbs above timberline and crosses the ridge coming down from Point 12223, where there are good views back to the west of Mt. Jordan, Thunder Mountain, Milestone Mountain, Midway Mountain, Kern Ridge and the Red Spur. Beyond this point the trail descends slightly and skirts the north side of a small, unnamed lake. Just beyond this lake the trail meets the outlet stream of Lake 11440. Here the hiker should turn right and descend cross country to the good campsite at the edge of the meadow ¼ mile south.

7th, 8th and 9th Hiking Days: Follow the 4th through the 6th hiking days, trip 64, 23½ miles.

Milestone Mountain

Thomas Winnett

66 Onion Valley to Flower Lake

TRIP   From Onion Valley to Flower Lake (round trip). Topo
           Map *Mt. Pinchot*. Best early or mid season; 5 miles.

Grade	Trail/layover days	Total recom-mended days
Leisurely	2/0	2
Moderate	....	....
Strenuous	....	....

HILITES Employing one of the "easiest" east-side entries, this
            trip climbs to the friendly lakes making up the
            headwaters of Independence Creek. The ample op-
            portunities for good angling, and the exciting alpine
            scenery occupy one's weekend time in grand style.

DESCRIPTION (Leisurely trip)

1st Hiking Day (**Onion Valley** to **Flower Lake,** 2½ miles): The trail
leaves the road a few yards north of the campground and switchbacks up over a dry, manzanita-covered slope. Switchbacks always seem to come in bunches, and this ascent is no exception.
The first set of switchbacks is relatively open and exposed, offering fine views back on Onion Valley and south to the heavily
diked summit of Independence Peak. After about one-third of a
mile there is a short level stretch where one may study the distinctive shapes of the large foxtail pines nearby. The trail enters
the John Muir Wilderness and switchbacks steadily again, until
after a mile it comes close to enough tumbling Independence
Creek, that only a few steps are needed to reach the wildflower-
lined stream bank and slake one's thirst.

On a more gradual slope our path crosses many runoff rills in
early and mid season, where a neophyte botanist may identify
specimens of Queen Anne's lace, paintbrush, wallflower, tiger
lily, columbine, shooting star and whorled penstemon. At the top
of this gentle grade is Little Pothole Lake, not much for camping,
but boasting two beautiful, willow-lined cascades pouring into its
south and west bays. After another set of rocky switchbacks, the
trail levels off in a slightly ascending groove across a glacial
moraine and then reaches small, round Gilbert Lake (10,930′).
Poor-from-overuse campsites dot the shores of this fine swimming

lake, and fishing for rainbow and brook trout is good in early season. This small lake absorbs much of the day-hiking impact from people camping at Onion Valley, as does Flower Lake, at the top of the next set of switchbacks. Less used and more scenic are Matlock and Slim lakes, the first reached by a trail that leads south from the east side of Flower Lake, the second, cross country west from the first. There are many highly used campsites along the north and east sides of this shallow lake (10, 450'). Fishing for rainbow and some brook trout is fair on this small lake, but serious anglers would hike to the more distant lakes in the timbered cirque basin to the south.

2nd Hiking Day: Retrace your steps, 2½ miles.

Gilbert Lake   *Jeff Schaffer*

67 **Onion Valley to Cedar Grove**

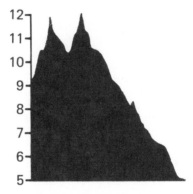

TRIP   From Onion Valley to Cedar Grove Roadend via
               Kearsarge Pass, Charlotte Lake, Glen Pass, Rae
               Lakes, South Fork Woods Creek, Paradise Valley
               (shuttle trip). Topo maps *Mt. Pinchot, Marion Peak.*
               Best mid or late season; 34 miles.

Grade	Trail/layover days	Total recommended days
Leisurely	6/2	8
Moderate	5/2	7
Strenuous	4/2	6

HILITES   Kearsarge Pass, because of its relative low elevation
               and proximity to an east-side roadend, is a popular
               way to reach the John Muir Trail. Because of this
               popularity, many of the lakes and meadows en route
               have been overrun, and Park officials have felt it
               necessary to close these "impacted" areas to grazing
               and camping. Despite these restrictions, the country
               retains its popularity, and anyone planning to tramp
               the Muir Trail in the vicinity of this pass should
               expect company.

DESCRIPTION (Leisurely trip)

1st Hiking Day: Follow trip 66 to **Flower Lake**, 2½ miles.

2nd Hiking Day (**Flower Lake** to **Charlotte Lake**, 5½ miles): The
Kearsarge Pass Trail turns north and ascends steeply to a viewpoint overlooking Heart Lake. From this point the trail switchbacks up to another overlook—this time the lake is the nearly

perfect blue oval of Big Pothole Lake. In the course of this climb, one can look back across the Owens Valley to the White Mountains. From the trail high above the water, the lake, with its backgrounding granite finger, is particularly photogenic. From the switchbacks on, the trail rises above timber (excepting a few hardy whitebark specimens) and then makes two long-legged traverses across an exposed shaley slope to the low saddle of Kearsarge Pass (11,823'). To the west, the view is impressive, as it includes the Kearsarge Lakes, Bullfrog Lake and the serrated spires of the Kearsarge Pinnacles.

Our route drops down on the west side of the pass on a traverse that later resolves into the inevitable switchbacks. Passing a spur trail branching left to the Kearsarge Lakes and Bullfrog Lake (no camping), the route continues westward on a gentle descent into sparse timber. About ½ mile from the junction is the wood frame of a ranger station that is not manned most summers. Crossing several small runoff streams in early season, the rocky-sandy trail contours high on the slopes above Bullfrog Lake. The multibranched trails in the meadow above this lake are evidence of the overuse that led Park authorities to prohibit camping on the lake so that the shores might recover.

Now descending steadily through sparse-to-moderate whitebark and foxtail pine, the trail offers fine views south to Center Peak and Junction Peak. We meet the topo-map trail that leads northwest from Bullfrog Lake and follow it past a junction where a shortcut trail leads right to the Muir Trail. Our route descends gently onto a sandy flat in a broad saddle overlooking Charlotte Lake, where at an "X" junction we take a signed trail that switchbacks down moderately-to-steeply for a short mile to Charlotte Lake (10,370'). Good campsites line the north shore, and fishing for rainbow and brook trout (to 10″) is fair. Emergency services are available from the resident summer ranger on the north shore.

3rd Hiking Day (**Charlotte Lake** to **Rae Lakes**, 5½ miles): Retrace your steps to the John Muir Trail and then proceed as in the 3rd hiking day, trip 60.

4th, 5th and 6th Hiking Days: Follow the 4th, 5th and 6th hiking days, trip 61, 20½ miles

Bubbs Creek to Lower Kern

This stretch of country composes the least visited, least known, and least trampled region in the southern Sierra. It owes its integrity not to its lack of scenic or recreational potential, but rather to the presence of a fortuitously placed series of natural barriers—Great Western Divide, Kings-Kern Divide, and the Sierra crest. Joined together in an upside-down U, they protect the first 24 miles of the Kern River watershed with a wall of mountains crossed only by 1) people who have business here (rangers, packers, etc.), 2) people who have a love for the high country, and 3) people who fly over in airplanes. There are those among us who would restrict the third category because of the objectionable sonic booms.*

The one area described in this section that sits outside this protective cup of divides and ranges is the Roaring River Country. Remoteness from roads and a convoluted terrain guarantee its sanctuary. And sanctuary it is, for in the remote headwaters of Roaring River a hiker can walk for one, two, or even three days without seeing a soul.

With the notable exceptions of Mineral King and Horseshoe Meadow, this section is protected from commercial exploitation by national-park status and a wilderness-area title. At this writing, private business concerns are at work to establish large ski resorts at these vulnerable spots, over the objections of Park officials, conservation organizations, mountaineers and others sympathetic to the maintenance of primitive Sierra country. The establishment of major roads, and the breach of the "buffer" zone, cannot help but affect the peace, serenity and pristine wilderness quality of this hitherto remote section. With these road intrusions and the resulting concentrations of people, there cannot help but be a consequent, devastating impact upon this region's fragile ecology.

The delicate balance between plant and animal life is nowhere more manifest than in the alpine fell fields over Cottonwood Pass just west of Horseshoe Meadow, or around the subalpine meadows just south of Little Claire Lake over the crest from Mineral King. Here, in an incredibly brief 6-7 week span, some 40 varieties of hardy-yet-vulnerable grasses, sedges and flowering plants grow, bud, blossom, seed, and are harvested, running their

*Should the reader and the writers ever meet and share a backcountry campfire,remind us to recount the hairy tale of the mountain climber who was hanging by his fingertips beneath an overhanging snow cornice when one of these supersonic jets went by.

appointed course under the daily threat of killing frost, and before the juggernaut deadline of the first winter snows. Caught in the complex "web of life," year-round resident animals like the cony, marmot and pocket gopher stake their very existence on the plants' explosively short summer tenure. Inexorably linked in the ecological chain, the migrating and hibernating carnivores, such as the coyote, mountain lion, black bear, red fox, marten, weasel and wolverine, would perish without their dependable rodent and squirrel food supply. So fragile and tenuous is this balance that the trampling by man and his livestock of a high, grassy meadow—particularly during the early, wet days of spring—can have and has had catastrophic effects upon the food chain.

This is not to argue that man does not have a place in this setting. His trails, within strict practical and esthetic limitations, are as legitimate as those of the deer. He has the right to share the fish of the streams and the berries of the hillside with the bear. Like the marmot, he has his place in the sun—preferably a big flat rock where he too can laze away a warm afternoon. Man's propensity for mountaintops and places of quiet solitude is as valid as the bighorn sheep's. And, like the Hermit thrush at nesting time, or the Brewer blackbird at sundown, he has the right to sing of his exultation at being alive and here.

But, because he knows the devastation wrought by large, concentrated numbers of his species upon this country, he owes it to his co-habiters, and to himself, to expand rather than constrict the size of primitive country, and to disperse his impact upon the country. Implicit within both of these obligations should be a profound respect for the ecological chain, of which man is a part, for this respect will give birth to a deeper knowledge and appreciation of the re-creating benefits of a region such as this. Apart from sharing their appreciation of and passion for this grand part of the Sierra, it was the hope of the authors that they might, with this modest guide, call the attention of the prospective traveler to the less traveled byways and thereby contribute, in small measure, to the distribution of human impact. Because many of the routes described here are the lesser traveled, they are therefore sometimes faint, but that is as it should be. The passes are sometimes steeper than those used on the more traveled routes, but the rewards of scenery and solitude are commensurate.

As the quality of the wilderness experience is important, so is the quantity. For it is only through public support that requisite public legislation and administrative decisions will reflect man's desire and need for wild areas. The more people that are introduced to basic wilderness values, perhaps through guides like this, the greater will be the demand for more and better wilderness areas and national parks. If pieces of untrammeled country like that between the Kings-Kern Divide and the lower Kern River will remain bastions of peace and solitude, it will be not so much because government officials discourage and restrict wilderness travel as because more wilderness alternates are created for people to use. The sooner people recognize this fact, the sooner the trend to wilderness attrition will be reversed.

There are seven trailheads cited in the text that give access to this region—three on the west side, and four on the east.

Lodgepole Campground. Go 50 miles east from Fresno on State Highway 180 to a junction with State Highway 198, then 26 miles southeast on 198 to a 1-mile spur road that leads east to a parking area. This spur road is 54 miles northeast from Visalia on Highway 198.

Crescent Meadow. Go about 2 miles south and east of Giant Forest Village on a road running past Moro Rock to the road's end.

Mineral King. Go 37 miles east from Visalia on State Highway 198, turn east, and go 25 miles on a partly paved but mostly dirt road. This narrow, winding 25 miles takes several hours to drive.

Symmes Creek Trailhead. Go 4½ miles west from Independence on the Onion Valley Road, turn left and go 1.3 miles to a fork, take the right-hand fork, and follow the *Shepherd Pass Trail* signs to the backpackers' trailhead (different from the horsepackers' trailhead).

Whitney Portal. Go 13 miles west from Lone Pine on the Whitney Portal road.

Cottonwood Creek Trailhead. From U.S. 395 at a point 4 miles south of Lone Pine, turn west on Lubken Canyon Road. This junction is just south of Diaz Lake, and very hard to spot at night. Go 3 miles on this road, then turn south on Horseshoe Meadow Road and go 13.2 miles to the Cottonwood Creek Trailhead.

Horseshoe Meadow. Go 0.7 mile past the Cottonwood Creek Trailhead, to the end of the road.

Symmes Creek Trailhead to Wright Lakes **68**

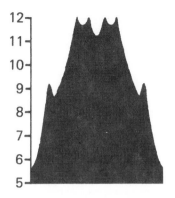

TRIP   From Symmes Creek Trailhead to Wright Lakes via Anvil Camp and Shepherd Pass (round trip). Topo map *Mt. Whitney*. Best mid or late season; 28 miles.

Grade	Trail/layover days	Total recom- mended days
Leisurely	....	....
Moderate	......	....
Strenuous	3/0	3

HILITES   This trip provides the great satisfaction of reaching the high, remote backcountry via a tough climb up the canyon of Shepherd Creek, one of the immense gashes that typify the eastern Sierra escarpment. The great elevation gain makes it a trip only for those in excellent physical condition.

DESCRIPTION *1st Hiking Day* (**Symmes Creek Trailhead** to **Anvil Camp**, 7½ miles): Leaving the Symmes Creek trailhead, the sandy trail winds through sagebrush on a gentle desert ascent. As it enters the Symmes Creek canyon, pinon pine appears, and, at streamside, alders. Our trail fords the creek several times (fill your canteen), passing clumps of showy early and midseason columbine, and then begins a long, gruelling series of rocky switchbacks that climb a whopping 2300 feet to the saddle straddling the Shepherd and Symmes Creek watersheds. Above 8000 feet red fir and then silver pine form a moderate forest cover, and the entire hot slope supports sagebrush, mountain mahogany and creamberry. From the saddle at the head of this slope, one may take a rest while inspecting the great peak to the south, Mt. Williamson, second highest in California—though, surprisingly, it is not on the Sierra crest. The deep, steep gash that contains Shepherd Creek falls away at one's feet, and it is an impressive introduction to the immense canyons of the eastern escarpment.

From the saddle, the sandy trail leads to another saddle and then veers down around the headwaters of an intermittent stream. Still descending, it then crosses an unnamed creek which sometimes is the only water between Symmes Creek and Anvil Camp. From here the trail approaches Shepherd Creek, but turns away before reaching it and switchbacks up to Mahogany Flat, which is a gently sloping hillside where a fire killed all the mountain mahogany. At the upper end of this flat, the trail enters a region of sparse lodgepole, Jeffrey, silver and foxtail pine, and then switchbacks up a rocky slope to gain the elevation of the cascade visible to the southwest on Shepherd Creek. As the route passes a large talus slope, the entire surroundings change dramatically within a few hundred feet. The trail has been largely on decomposed granite, and the vegetation generally sparse and desertlike. But as the trail reaches Anvil Camp (10,000') the experienced Sierra traveler suddenly recognizes that he is in the *High* Sierra: there is duff, a burbling stream, a campsite, willows, grass, and young lodgepole pines.

2nd Hiking Day (**Anvil Camp** to **Wright Lakes,** 6½ miles, part cross country): From Anvil Camp the trail ascends moderately over rocky slopes on the south side of Shepherd Creek. After a mile the ill-defined trail to Junction Pass turns off to the right. (Until Forester Pass was opened in 1931 the John Muir Trail, in passing from the Kings River to the Kern River drainage, detoured to the east side of the Sierra crest over Junction Pass, down to this trail junction, and recrossed westward over Shepherd Pass.) The route crosses the area labeled "The Pothole" on the topo map, and ascends past great boulders to the giant declivity, below the pass, for which that label should have been reserved. Here is a gargantuan jumble of great jagged rocks that have been weathered out of the headwall of the cirque. The last 500-foot ascent to Shepherd Pass (12,050') is on switchbacks up a steep scree slope where the snow is thick in early July and may last all summer.

At the summit the route enters Sequoia National Park and begins a descent down a broad boulder-strewn field to alpine meadows and stands of foxtail pine. Immediately to the south is the northern flank of Mt. Tyndall (14,018'), which the famous mountaineer Clarence King climbed in 1864 believing it to be the highest Sierra peak. He did not realize his error until he reached the summit.

At the 11,600-foot level the hiker should leave the trail and traverse southwest cross-country to the saddle between Peak 13540 and Peak 12345. The panoramic view from this saddle includes the noble series of summits of the Great Western Divide, Junction Peak, Mts. Keith, Brewer, Kaweah, Guyot and Young, and the top of Mt. Whitney, as well as the Kern River trench. Even in this high, rocky saddle there are flowers, including the prostrate purple-flowered pussypaws. Our route traverses down the east wall of the cirque that lies south of the saddle, to the fair campsites in a grove of foxtails where the outlet stream of Lake 11952 meets the other two draining the upper basin. Fishing is good for golden (to 8″). The hiker who is willing to forego a wood supply may camp on Lake 11952, a classic cirque lake under the south slope of Mt. Tyndall which boasts good fishing for rainbow (to 14″).

3rd Hiking Day: Retrace your steps, 14 miles.

Rock glacier below Shepherd Pass   *Thomas Winnett*

69 Symmes Creek Trailhead to Milestone Basin

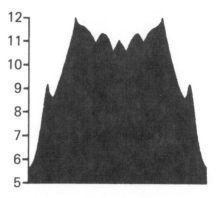

TRIP   From Symmes Creek Trailhead to Milestone Basin
             via Anvil Camp and Shepherd Pass (round trip).
             Topo map *Mt. Whitney*. Best mid or late season; 38
             miles

Grade	Trail/layover days	Total recommended days
Leisurely	....	....
Moderate	....	....
Strenuous	4/0	4

HILITES   Milestone Basin is a fine choice for the lover of high
             country who wants to be alone. Many fish-filled lakes
             lie under the prepossessing heights of the Great
             Western Divide, where the delicate quality of the
             light and the air work their magic on all who come.

DESCRIPTION (Strenuous trip)

1st Hiking Day: Follow trip 68 to **Anvil Camp**, 7½ miles.

2nd Hiking Day (**Anvil Camp** to **Milestone Basin**, 11½ miles): Follow the 2nd hiking day, trip 68, from Anvil Camp to where that day's route leaves the Shepherd Pass Trail. Our route continues down the trail beside Tyndall Creek, through a huge, boulder-strewn, sloping meadow, with the 13,000-foot peaks of the Great Western Divide filling the western horizon. After fording Tyndall Creek, the trail diverges from the stream and enters a sparse cover of lodgepole and foxtail pine, meeting the stream again at the John Muir Trail. Our route turns right (north) onto the Muir Trail, fords Tyndall Creek (difficult in early season) and ascends a moderate slope to timberline. Three fourths of a mile from the last ford we turn left onto the Lake South America Trail. Then, a half mile farther on across alpine fell fields, we turn left again, onto the Milestone Basin Trail. Views in this upper Kern basin are at all times panoramic, and the traveler will mentally record pictures of the skyline he will not soon forget.

At the outlet stream of Lake 11440 the angler may wish to veer north and sample that lake's waters for the good fishing for golden (to 12″). The trail then skirts along the north side of a small lake, and makes a short, rocky climb to a ridge where the descent to the Kern River begins. From the ridge the traveler has closer views of Mt. Jordan, Thunder Mountain, Milestone Mountain, Midway Mountain—all on the Great Western Divide—and Kern Ridge and Red Spur in the west. The trail descends moderately through rocky and meadowy sections with a moderate cover of foxtail, lodgepole and some whitebark pine, and arrives at a picturebook lake that is fast (geologically speaking) turning to meadow. One may regret that all these high lakes are doomed, but one may enjoy the blend of meadows and lakes existing in the time to which he was born.

After climbing slightly, our route begins the last, steep descent to the Kern River, where it emerges at an unnamed lake at 10,650 feet elevation (good fishing for golden and rainbow-golden hybrids to 10″). Our route turns left at the east side of this lake and descends gently beside the infant Kern River for about 200 yards to the signed trail turning west to Milestone Basin. Fording the river, the trail contours to meet Milestone Creek and then veers west up a rocky slope away from the creek. After another ½ mile it rejoins the creek at a bench where, beside a waterfall, there is a good campsite (11,100′). Fishing in Milestone Creek is good for rainbow (to 10″). Those who wish to camp as high as possible may climb to the high lake (11,900′) just to the right of *Midway Mtn* on the topo map. The trail shown on the topo map beside Milestone Creek above the confluence of the north fork does not exist, and the hiker should follow the ducked route that turns right up the north fork, passes through a defile, skirts a small lake barren of fish, and traverses up to the high lake, where fishing is good for golden (to 12″). There are fair campsites below this lake on the outlet stream.

3rd and 4th Hiking Days: Retrace your steps, 19 miles.

70 Symmes Creek Trailhead to Mineral King

TRIP From Symmes Creek Trailhead to Mineral King via Anvil Camp, Shepherd Pass, Upper Kern River, Rattlesnake Creek and Franklin Pass (shuttle trip). Topo maps *Mt. Whitney*, *Kern Peak*, *Mineral King*. Best mid-to-late season; 53½ miles.

Grade	Trail/layover days	Total recommended days
Leisurely	....	....
Moderate	....	....
Strenuous	6/0	6

HILITES This long shuttle trip provides a grand sample of everything the High Sierra has to offer: sweeping vistas, intimate groves, barren granite, streamside meadows, rainbow, golden, brook and brown trout, pages of geological history, access to the highest Sierra peaks, the marks of great glaciers, thick pine forests, alpine fell fields—and that feeling of grandeur which calls the backpacker to the Sierra again and again.

DESCRIPTION (Strenuous trip)

1st Hiking Day: Follow trip 68 to **Anvil Camp**, 7½ miles.

2nd Hiking Day (**Anvil Camp** to **Lake on Upper Kern River**, 10 miles): Follow the 2nd hiking day, trip 69, to the lake on the Kern River at 10,650 feet elevation, where the Milestone Basin Trail meets the Kern River Trail. There are good campsites at the lake inlet, and fishing is good for golden and hybrids (to 10″).

3rd Hiking Day (**Lake on Upper Kern River** to **Junction Meadow**, 6 miles): From the lakeside campsites the trail proceeds south along the east shore of the lake, where red penstemon, or mountain pride, is especially abundant in the broken granite slopes. After 200 yards the Kern River Trail leaves the Milestone Basin Trail branching right, and soon begins the steep 600-foot descent of a granite-slabbed slope down which the young river cascades and falls. In the shade of lodgepole pines, one sees yarrow milfoil, paintbrush, penstemon, fleabane, and red mountain heather. Despite the topo map indication, the trail remains on the east side of the river. As the descent begins to level off, the trail passes through a bank of shield fern among which grows the delicate, white-headed Queen Anne's lace. At the foot of the descent our route enters a dell where lodgepole pines with notably straight trunks form a thick stand. Yellow groundsel flowers dominate the ground cover under these pines, complemented by the hues of orange tiger lily, purple swamp onion and red columbine. After fording the outlet stream of Lake 11440, the trail begins a dusty section where the sagebrush is spottily shaded by a few lodgepole and foxtail pines. Shortly before the junction with the Tyndall Creek Trail there is a good packer campsite beside the river and here one begins to see red fir and aspen, indicating arrival in the Canadian life zone. The sandy, exposed trail continues its gentle descent to the Tyndall Creek ford (difficult in early season), where a stock drift fence bears a sign indicating that Junction Meadow (ahead) is closed to grazing. Beyond this ford, the canyon becomes steeper, and the trail becomes more dufflike and tree-shaded. The first Jeffrey pines of this trip appear, along with a few mountain juniper. One-half mile beyond a roofless, decaying cabin our route meets the High Sierra Trail coming down from Wallace Creek, and from here down almost to Upper Funston Meadow the Kern River Trail and the High Sierra Trail are "superimposed." From this junction it is a steep descent of 1 mile to Junction Meadow. Views on this descent are good down the Kern canyon, an immense U-trough which was given that shape by the main Kern glacier, which left the tributary valleys hanging. The forest cover on this descent is sparse lodgepole and Jeffrey, along with clumps of aspen, on a slope dominated by manzanita and currant. As the trail levels off, it enters a parklike grove of stalwart Jeffrey pines that provide a noble setting for the good campsites on the Kern River. Fishing is good for rainbow, golden and brook (to 10″).

4th Hiking Day (**Junction Meadow** to **Rattlesnake Creek/Kern River**, 11½ miles): This day's hike is entirely beside the young Kern River, but it is not lacking in contrasts and discoveries. Fording Wallace Creek (high water in early season) the trail descends gently down the U-trough of the Kern River. This trough is remarkably straight for about 25 miles, as it parallels the Kern Canyon fault. The fault, a zone of structural weakness in the Sierra batholith, is more susceptible to erosion than the surrounding rock. This deep canyon has been carved by both glacial and stream action: at least three times the glacier advanced down the canyon, shearing off spurs created by stream erosion and leaving some tributary valleys hanging above the main valley. The glacier also scooped and plucked at the granite bedrock, creating basins (like the lake at the start of the 3rd hiking day) which became lakes when the glacier melted and retreated. It is interesting to speculate that our trail probably passes over some of these ancient lake beds, now buried beneath river sediments.

The descending trail becomes a little steeper as it fords Whitney Creek, where a thirsty hiker can sample water that coursed down from the highest point in the contiguous United States. Tributaries cascading down the east face of Red Spur provide excellent views as the trail steepens again and fords the stream that drains Guyot Flat. Rounding the most salient part of Red Spur, the trail turns slightly west as it skirts the steep bluffs on the east canyon wall. The gravelly, flat canyon floor widens as the trail approaches the fords of the branchlets of Rock Creek. Just beyond the first of these is the delightful mountain spa of Kern Hot Spring—a treat for the tired, dusty hiker. To the traveler, the crude cement bathtub here becomes a regal, heated (115°) pool. Only a few feet away, the great Kern River rushes past, and its cold waters can be dipped into to cool the hot-spring water as desired. Beyond Kern Hot Spring the valley floor widens and the river bifurcates as it flows past Chagoopa Falls. Chagoopa Creek descends 1700 feet from its hanging valley on Chagoopa Plateau, but the actual waterfall drops only 150 feet.

A short distance to the south the route crosses a bridge to the west side of the Kern, and then continues its gentle descent past the Big Arroyo turnoff—thereby leaving the High Sierra Trail—to a ford of Funston Creek. Then, keeping away from the willow-infested banks of the Kern, the trail continues south past Upper Funston Meadow through a moderate-to-heavy forest cover of white fir, Jeffrey and sugar pine and some black oak, birch and aspen. Heavy patches of bracken fern inhibit the going in the wetter stretches, and the trail crosses through the site of an old burn before passing a drift fence and crossing the steel cantilever bridge spanning Big Arroyo Creek. From the bridge it is but a mile of level going to the good packer campsite at the confluence of Rattlesnake Creek and the Kern River. Fishing on the Kern is excellent for rainbow and brown (to 8″). Emergency services, should they be required, are available at the Kern Canyon Ranger Station 6 miles down-canyon. A cautionary note is warranted here: Rattlesnake Creek came by its name honestly, and one should exercise some care in hiking and climbing in the vicinity.

5th Hiking Day (**Rattlesnake Creek/Kern River** to **Upper Rattlesnake Creek**, 8 miles): Reverse the 2nd hiking day, trip 100.

6th Hiking Day (**Upper Rattlesnake Creek** to **Mineral King**, 10½ miles): Reverse the 1st hiking day, trip 96.

Kern Hot Spring *J.C. Jenkins*

71 Symmes Creek Trailhead to Cedar Grove

TRIP   From Symmes Creek Trailhead to Cedar Grove
Roadend via Shepherd Pass, Upper Kern River,
Junction Meadow, Colby Pass, Scaffold Meadows and
Avalanche Pass (shuttle trip). Topo maps *Mt.
Whitney*, *Triple Divide Peak*, *Marion Peak*. Best
mid-to-late season; 59½ miles.

Grade	Trail/layover days	Total recommended days
Leisurely	....	....
Moderate	....	....
Strenuous	8/1	9

HILITES   Staying entirely on trails sometimes limits one's experiences, but this route is diversified enough for any
taste. Visiting four life zones, the trip offers a complete sampling of High Sierra ecologies, and affords
grand views of deep canyons and serrated skylines.

DESCRIPTION (Strenuous trip)

1st 3 Hiking Days: Follow trip 70 to **Junction Meadow**, 23½ miles.

4th Hiking Day (Junction Meadow to **Kern-Kaweah River**, 6 miles):
Follow the 4th hiking day, trip 76.

5th Hiking Day (**Kern-Kaweah River** to **Big Wet Meadow**, 7 miles):
Leaving the Kern-Kaweah drainage behind, the trail ascends
steeply and quickly transcends the sparse cover of lodgepole pine.
This steep climb offers magnificent views back into the headwaters of the Kern-Kaweah drainage and the backgrounding
Kaweah Peaks Ridge. Just to the north of these distinctive summits rise the pyramidal heights of aptly named Triple Divide

Peak—this landmark peak divides the drainages of the Kern, Kings and Kaweah rivers. The steep ascent levels briefly as it crosses the tributaries draining Milestone Bowl, and then, by a faint and unreliably ducked trail, resumes its steep, steady climb to Colby Pass (12,000'). Here one has grand views down Cloud Canyon and of Glacier Ridge and the cockscomblike sentinels atop the Whaleback. This pass is often snow-covered until late in the season, but the route down to Cloud Canyon is easy to discern as it drops down past occasional foxtail and whitebark and then around the northeast side of Colby Lake (campsites). Anglers may wish to sample the sometimes good fishing for rainbow at Colby Lake before continuing.

The poorly ducked trail follows the outlet stream from the wooded area at its source, zigging and zagging back and forth across the stream in the descent. Dwarfed and twisted whitebark pines dot the slopes on either side as the route dips steeply down over the unjointed granite shoulder of the Whaleback to the Cloud Canyon floor, where it meets a trail descending from upper Cloud Canyon. Our trail turns right, crosses to the east side of Cloud Canyon Creek just north of Table Creek, and proceeds downstream through a lodgepole forest cover for about ½ mile to the good campsites located on the west side of the stream just south of Big Wet Meadow (8700').

6th Hiking Day (**Big Wet Meadow** to **Scaffold Meadows**, 7 miles): North of Big Wet Meadow the moderate-to-heavy stands of lodgepole occasionally give way to clumps of aspen as the trail passes the lower "Grand Palace Hotel Drift Fence" and a nearby packer campsite. The descent is moderate on a duff surface as it passes Cement Table Meadow (not marked on the topo map) and a nearby campsite. The gradual loss of altitude is reflected in the changing forest cover, which now shows red fir, juniper, and white fir mixed with the lodgepole. Views of the glacially smoothed granite, particularly on the west wall of the canyon, continue as the duff-and-sand trail takes the traveler down past the signed (but unmapped) turnoff to Brewer Lakes and Brewer Creek. A few yards past the upper drift fence at Scaffold Meadows, our trail arrives at the campground that is signed *Austin Camp* (7500'). Fishing in Roaring River is fair for rainbow and some golden (to 10″), and a summer ranger is stationed here.

7th Hiking Day (**Scaffold Meadows** to **Campsites, Sphinx Creek Ford**, 9 miles): Crossing the bridge by the ranger station, our route takes the Avalanche Pass Trail northward on a steady ascent over a sandy trail, through a heavy forest cover of Jeffrey pine, red and white fir, and juniper. At the Scaffold Meadows drift fence the ascent becomes moderate to steep as the trail switchbacks up a lateral moraine whose morainal nature is identified by its rounded boulders and granite sand. From the crown of this moraine, views are good up Deadman Canyon to the head of the cirque near Elizabeth Pass. Here another trail turns right to Brewer Lakes and Brewer Creek, as our route begins a short, steady descent to the easy ford of Moraine Creek. The moist sections near the creek support a variety of wildflowers, including shooting star, sneezeweed, cinquefoil, aster, groundsel and milfoil.

Beyond the ford the duff-and-sand trail ascends steadily to moderately to the tributary that drains the Avalanche Pass area. The forest cover of lodgepole, red fir and a few juniper is moderate to heavy, and some aspen thrive along the creek. Our trail remains on the east side of the creek, and has a number of switchbacks as it climbs from 8800 feet to 9200 feet. The trail becomes less steep, and finally level, as it nears Avalanche Pass (10,050'). Views from the pass are inhibited by the moderate-to-heavy forest cover of foxtail and some lodgepole. Along the moderate descent north of the pass, foxtail pines disappear and red fir and silver pine join the lodgepole to compose a heavy forest cover over the trail on granite sand. After fording the westernmost tributary of Sphinx Creek, our trail descends moderately to ford a second tributary, and then drops again on a moderate descent to Sphinx Creek and a packer campsite. An unmaintained, unmapped trail to the Sphinx Lakes leads south from here.

8th Hiking Day (**Sphinx Creek Ford** to **Cedar Grove Roadend**, 7 miles): Leaving Sphinx Creek via a short, steady descent, the trail makes a long level traverse high above the creek on the east canyon wall. Part of the Sphinx Crest is visible to the south through the trees, a moderate cover of Jeffrey pine and red fir, and at the ford of a tributary stream one can pause to enjoy not only a drink but a mountain garden of wildflowers and ferns. The traverse ends as the trail begins a series of long, well-built switchbacks that descend to the banks of Sphinx Creek in its deep, V-shaped gorge. Both the creek and the trail follow along granite slabs for much of the way from the beginning of the switchbacks to the foot of the descent, and some of the trail has been blasted across these slabs. As the trail leads out onto the north side of a granite nose, there are very good views up the Bubbs Creek drainage, down the canyon to the flats around the roadend, and northwest to the peaks of the Monarch Divide, which separates the South and Middle Forks of the Kings River. The last portion of the descent to Bubbs Creek is moderate, via many more switchbacks than are shown on the topo map. Then the forest cover thickens and our route meets the Bubbs Creek Trail, where it turns left and retraces the steps of the 1st hiking day, trip 57.

Whitney Portal to Outpost Camp   **72**

TRIP	From Whitney Portal to Outpost Camp (round trip). Topo maps *Lone Pine, Mt. Whitney*. Best mid or late season; 7 miles.

Grade	Trail/layover days	Total recom- mended days
Leisurely	2/1	3
Moderate	2/0	2
Strenuous	....	....

HILITES	This overnight trip offers an experience of the high country in the shadow of Mt. Whitney. Outpost Camp can be used as a base camp for climbing Mt. Whitney or for exploring the spectacular surrounding country.

DESCRIPTION (Leisurely trip)

1st Hiking Day (**Whitney Portal** to **Outpost Camp,** 3½ miles): At the roadend (8367′) a register stands in the shelter of a 35-foot-high granite monolith, a foretaste of the great granitic buttresses and pinnacles that lie ahead. The trail begins on a steep ascent up switchbacks through a moderate forest cover of Jeffrey pine and red fir. After ½ mile the foot trail is joined by the stock trail coming from the pack station, and the route enters the John Muir Wilderness. Soon the forest cover thins, and the slope is covered with a chaparral that includes mountain mahogany, Sierra chinquapin and sagebrush. This steep slope can get very hot in mid-morning, and the trip is best begun as early as possible. (Carry water.) Breather stops on this trail section provide a view down the canyon framing the Alabama Hills. The trail levels off through several willow-covered flats having a moderate forest cover of lodgepole and foxtail, and passes fields of corn lilies, delphinium, tall lupine and swamp whiteheads as it approaches the ford of Lone Pine Creek.

Beyond this log ford is a junction with a lateral that leads east to Lone Pine Lake. From here, our route switchbacks up another slope through a moderate lodgepole tree cover to Outpost Camp (10,365′—called "Bighorn Park" on the topo map), a willow-covered meadow that was once a lake. A very large abandoned stove near the upper end of this park is evidence of the days when a packer's wife ran a little camp here, renting tents and selling meals. The camp had to be removed when the area was made wilderness by Congress. There are many fair campsites here in Outpost Camp, but wood fires are forbidden, as they are on all of the Mt. Whitney Trail. Those bound for the summit of Whitney or for Crabtree Meadows and beyond may have enough steam left to climb on to Trail Camp, 3 miles ahead, the next legal camping place on the trail, which is above timberline.

2nd Hiking Day: Retrace your steps, 3½ miles.

Mt. Whitney over Lone Pine church   *Thomas Winnett*

Whitney Portal to Crabtree Ranger Station   **73**

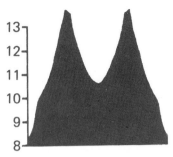

TRIP

From Whitney Portal to Crabtree Ranger Station (round trip). Topo maps *Lone Pine, Mt. Whitney*. Best mid-to-late season; 30 miles.

Grade	Trail/layover days	Total recommended days
Leisurely	....	....
Moderately	5/1	6
Strenuous	4/0	4

HILITES

Despite the elevation at the pass where this route crosses the Sierra crest, it offers the fastest way into the high country of Sequoia National Park. Just beyond the pass is the lateral trail to the top of Mt. Whitney, an easy amble from there.

DESCRIPTION (Strenuous trip)

1st Hiking Day: Follow trip 72 to **Outpost Camp,** 3½ miles.

2nd Hiking Day (**Outpost Camp** to **Crabtree Ranger Station,** 11½ miles): (This hiking day is a long one, owing to a lack of campsites short of Crabtree Ranger Station, and it involves an ascent of 3400 feet. The prudent hiker will start early.) After an easy ascent beside the outlet stream of Mirror Lake, the trail ascends the south wall of the Mirrow Lake cirque via switchbacks. At the top of the ascent the trail passes timberline, as a last foxtail pine and a broken, weathered, convoluted whitebark snag are seen, along with a few last willows. Soon Mt. Whitney comes into view, over Pinnacle Ridge. From here, the rocky trail ascends moderately alongside the gigantic boulders on the north side of the South Fork Lone Pine Creek. In the cracks in the boulders the hiker will find ivesia, cinquefoil, creambush, currant and much gooseberry, and looking across the canyon he will see the cascading outlet of Consultation Lake. Beside a rock bridge that crosses the stream are specimens of the moisture-loving shooting star. After ascending over some poured concrete steps—which unfortunately detract from the wilderness feel of this country—the trail arrives at the last campsite before the crest, Trail Camp (12,000′). Here beneath Wotan's Throne is also the last reliable water in late season. There are numerous level campsites.

As the trail begins the 100 or so switchbacks to Trail Crest Pass, Mt. Whitney disappears behind a sharp spire, and Mt. Russell, farther north, comes into view. The rocky, barren talus slope is not entirely barren, for one may see a dozen species of flowering plants, climaxed by the multiflowered, blue "sky pilot." The building of this trail section involved much blasting with dynamite, and the natural fracture planes of the granite are evident in the blasted slabs. Finally the 1700-foot ascent from Trail Camp ends at Trail Crest (13,777′), and the hiker suddenly has vistas of a great part of Sequoia National Park to the west, including the entire Great Western Divide. To the east, far below, are Consultation Lake and several smaller, unnamed lakes, lying close under the Whitney crest, which may not be free of ice the whole summer.

From Trail Crest the route descends for a short ½ mile to a junction with the 2-mile lateral to Mt. Whitney (14,495′). The highest mountain in the United States until Alaska was admitted as a state, this peak was first climbed on August 18, 1873, by three fishermen, who made the ascent up the southwest slope. The present trail between this junction and the summit lies close to the crest on the western slope.

As our switchbacking descent on the west side of the Sierra crest begins, one can make out the Hitchcock Lakes below in a cirque basin that has been changed but little since its glacier melted. The parallel avalanche chutes on the northeast wall of Mt. Hitchcock all terminate at the upper limit of glacial erosion. Along the switchbacks, the most prominent flower is the yellow, daisylike hulsea, or alpine gold. The switchbacks end and the trail follows a moderate descent on a traverse of the "back" side of Mt. Whitney, leveling off at the first possible campsites, overlooking Guitar Lake (not named on the map). From these campsites our route crosses the outlet of Arctic Lake, descends on a moderately steep, rocky trail into a sparse cover of lodgepole, and arrives at Timberline Lake (no camping or grazing, but fair fishing for golden to 7″). After skirting the shore of this lake (viewpoints for focusing the camera on Mt. Whitney and its reflection), the trail passes through a small meadow (good campsite) and descends the narrow valley of Whitney Creek to the good campsites near Crabtree Ranger Station, where emergency services are available. Fishing in Whitney Creek is fair for golden (to 7"). (During times of heavy trail traffic, the hiker who wants more solitude may choose to camp at Upper Crabtree Meadow, ½ mile southwest of the ranger station, or Lower Crabtree Meadow, 1 mile southwest. These sites are reached by taking the Rock Creek Trail at the junction west of the ranger station.)

3rd and 4th Hiking Days: Retrace your steps, 15 miles.

Mt. Whitney from the west *Thomas Winnett*

74 **Whitney Portal to Wallace Lake**

TRIP
From Whitney Portal to Wallace Lake via Trail Crest, Crabtree Ranger Station and Wallace Creek (round trip). Topo maps *Lone Pine, Mt. Whitney.* Best late season; 47 miles.

Grade	Trail/layover days	Total recommended days
Leisurely	....	....
Moderate	8/1	9
Strenuous	6/0	7

HILITES
Wallace Lake, lying in the heart of the Mt. Whitney region, is thought by many to be the finest fishing lake in the region. Well off the "beaten track" it is also a base from which to climb Mts. Barnard and Russell.

DESCRIPTION (Strenuous trip)

1st and 2nd Hiking Days: Follow trip 73 to **Crabtree Ranger Station,** 15 miles.

3rd Hiking Day (**Crabtree Ranger Station** to **Wallace Lake,** 8½ miles): From Crabtree Ranger Station our route branches right (north) onto a sandy trail and climbs the north slope of Whitney Creek canyon into a foxtail-pine forest. On an overcast day, this foxtail forest, with its dead snags, fallen trees, and lack of ground cover, has an eerie, gloomy, otherworldly quality. The trail then switchbacks up to the junction with the Lower Crabtree Meadow/Army Pass Trail. These switchbacks offer the hard-breathing hiker views of Mts. Hitchcock, Pickering and Chamberlain, and the flanks of Mt. Whitney, whose summit is over the horizon. From the ridge, the route descends gently on a sandy trail through a moderate cover of lodgepole and foxtail to a ford

(10,636') of an unnamed creek. Beginning here the trail skirts what is called "Sandy Meadow" on the topo map, but it is neither flat nor grassy. Instead, it is a bowl whose lower slopes are bare and sandy. The small meadowy sections of trail that exist in the bowl lie beside several little streams not shown on the topo map, and in season they are graced with the yellow blossoms of groundsel and monkey flower.

After these crossings the trail ascends a moderate slope with a lodgepole canopy and a heavy lupine ground cover to the saddle marked 10,964 on the topo map. From this saddle the route descends gently on a sandy trail around the west shoulder of Mt. Young. Leveling off, the trail winds among some massive boulders that make up a lateral moraine, and then leads down a rocky hillside from which the traveler has fine views of Mt. Ericsson, Tawny Point, Junction Peak, the flank of Mt. Tyndall, Mt. Williamson, Trojan Peak and, farthest right, Mt. Barnard. After the ford of a tributary of Wallace Creek the descent becomes gentle again, through a moderate cover of lodgepole, foxtail and whitebark pine. Beyond the next tributary ford the descent steepens, and the trail switchbacks ¼ mile down to Wallace Creek. Just past the ford (very difficult in early season) the High Sierra Trail and the John Muir Trail, which have been "superimposed" from the top of Mt. Whitney to here, diverge, the High Sierra Trail turning left (west) toward Giant Forest and the Muir Trail continuing north toward Yosemite.

Our route turns right (east) up Wallace Creek canyon. Under a forest cover of sparse-to-moderate lodgepole the trail ascends gently amid sprinklings of western wallflower, penstemon, groundsel, yarrow milfoil and Labrador tea. At the meadow where the outlet of Wales Lake joins Wallace Creek, the trail fords the creek and then fords the tributary, staying on the south side of Wallace Creek. Here the ascent becomes moderate for a short distance, and then reverts to a gentler grade. This route up Wallace Creek canyon is sometimes indistinct and sometimes confused by multiple trail sections and inadequate ducking. Careful negotiation of the indistinct sections will bring one to the fair campsites at timberline (11,400') about ½ mile below Wallace Lake. Those who prefer to camp at the lake will find sufficient shelter but no wood. Wallace Lake lies at the foot of the arete that connects Mt. Barnard with Tunnebora Peak. Fishing in Wallace Lake is good for golden (to 14"), and the same is true of Wales Lake, reached by cross country southwest from the inlet of Wallace Lake.

4th, 5th and 6th Hiking Days: Retrace your steps, 23½ miles.

75   Whitney Portal to Milestone Basin

13		
12		
11		
10		
9		
8		

TRIP   From Whitney Portal to Milestone Basin via Trail Crest, Crabtree Ranger Station, Wallace Creek, Junction Meadow, Upper Kern River and Tyndall Creek (semiloop trip). Topo maps *Lone Pine*, *Mt. Whitney*. Best mid-to-late season; 59½ miles.

Grade	Trail/layover days	Total recom- mended days
Leisurely	....	....
Moderate	10/2	12
Strenuous	8/1	9

HILITES   This trip samples both well-traveled trails and little-used trails, country above timberline and deep, dense forests. Milestone Basin, set under the giant finger of Milestone Mountain, is remote enough to suit the solitude-seeking hiker, and the lakes piscatorial enough to suit the most avid angler.

DESCRIPTION (Strenuous trip)

1st 2 Hiking Days: Follow trip 73 to **Crabtree Ranger Station**, 15 miles.

3rd Hiking Day (**Crabtree Ranger Station** to **Upper Kern River**, 8½ miles): Follow the 3rd hiking day, trip 74, to the junction of the John Muir Trail and the High Sierra Trail at Wallace Creek. Taking the High Sierra Trail from this junction our route proceeds down Wallace Creek canyon on sandy underfooting, with views ahead of Mt. Kaweah and the Kaweah Peaks Ridge. The trail veers away from Wallace Creek and then meets it again after a short, moderate descent on an exposed slope. Our trail passes campsites lining both sides as it winds among sparse-to-moderate lodgepole and a great variety of wildflowers (in midsummer), including fireweed, paintbrush, arnica, sulfur flower, wild buckwheat, pennyroyal, mountain pride and creamberry. After fording Wright Creek (difficult in early season), the trail descends more steeply through sparse lodgepole mixed with some foxtail pine.

As the canyon widens and the trail veers more westward, the timber cover diminishes almost to nothing, and the slope (hot in afternoon) is covered with manzanita, creambush, hollyleaf redberry, mountain mahogany and Sierra chinquapin. The main splash of color in this chaparral is the red penstemon, or mountain pride. This exposed slope offers views down the great trough of the Kern River, south to Mt. Guyot and west to Kaweah Peaks Ridge. The descent now reaches the Canadian life zone as Jeffrey pines are seen, along with mountain juniper. Our route turns northward and traverses down the Kern Canyon wall to meet the Kern River Trail, where it turns right (north), leaving the High Sierra Trail. One mile up the canyon our route passes a decaying roofless cabin. Beginning here there are several good campsites along the river, where firewood is ample and fishing is good for rainbow (to 10″). These are the Kern River rainbow, *Salmo gairdneri gilberti*, found only in the upper Kern River.

4th Hiking Day (**Upper Kern River** to **Milestone Basin**, 6 miles): Once past the cabin, the trail ascends less steeply, and soon it reaches a ford of Tyndall Creek (difficult in early season). Beyond the ford, the trail becomes sandier and drier, and the red fir and aspen gradually disappear, leaving a forest cover of lodgepole and some foxtail that is sparse on the hillsides and moderate on the river terraces. There are numerous campsites along this stretch of trail, including a packer campsite ½ mile beyond the Tyndall Creek Trail. Beyond the Tyndall Creek Trail, our route becomes more exposed, with considerable sagebrush. The trail fords the outlet stream of Lake 11440 and soon comes to a dell thick with lodgepole trunks. The excellent wildflower display in this large dell is dominated by groundsel, but also includes tiger lilies, swamp onions and red columbine. The trail ascends above the dell and passes through a bank of shield fern, Queen Anne's lace and bush chinquapin, staying on the east side of the river. Our route ascends steeply through a sparse lodgepole cover on a rocky trail over granite slabs that rise 600 feet to the upper Kern plateau. The trail levels off and soon reaches a signed junction with the Milestone Basin Trail, where our route turns left (west). From this junction, continue as in the last part of the 2nd hiking day, trip 69.

5th Hiking Day (**Milestone Basin** to **Tyndall Creek Tributary**, 6 miles): Reverse steps of the 2nd hiking day, trip 69, from Milestone Basin to the ford at the John Muir Trail/Shepherd Pass Trail junction, where our route turns right (south) on the John Muir Trail. The rocky trail ascends gently along the east flank of Tawny Point through a sparse-to-moderate cover of lodgepole and foxtail pine past many poor campsites, and then arrives at the good campsites on a tributary of Tyndall Creek (11,000'), near a small lake where swimming is good in late season.

6th Hiking Day (**Tyndall Creek Tributary** to **Crabtree Ranger Station**, 9 miles): Reverse the 3rd hiking day, trip 77.

7th and 8th Hiking Days: Retrace the 2nd and 1st hiking days, 15 miles.

Moraine south of Wallace Creek

Thomas Winnett

Whitney Portal to Kern-Kaweah River   **76**

TRIP From Whitney Portal to Kern-Kaweah River via Trail Crest, Crabtree Meadow, Wallace Creek, Junction Meadow (round trip). Topo maps *Lone Pine, Mt. Whitney*. Best mid-to-late season; 61 miles.

Grade	Trail/layover days	Total recommended days
Leisurely	....	....
Moderate	10/2	12
Strenuous	8/1	9

HILITES This route combines the high, rocky country along the Whitney crest with the alluvial meadows on the Kern River and the intimate camping on the little-visited Kern-Kaweah River canyon.

DESCRIPTION (Strenuous trip)

1st 2 Hiking Days: Follow trip 73 to **Crabtree Ranger Station**, 15 miles.

3rd Hiking Day (**Crabtree Ranger Station** to **Junction Meadow**, 9½ miles): Follow the 3rd hiking day, trip 75, to the junction of the High Sierra Trail and the Kern River Trail, and turn left (south). From here the rocky trail descends steeply to Junction Meadow through stands of aspen and past occasional Jeffrey and lodgepole pines, winding through a ground cover of manzanita and currant. As the trail levels off, it enters a parklike grove of stalwart Jeffrey pines that provide the setting for the good campsites near the Kern River. Fishing is good for rainbow and some brook trout (to 10″).

4th Hiking Day (**Junction Meadow** to **Kern-Kaweah River**, 6 miles): This day's route is unmaintained, but a knapsacker with any experience will have no trouble staying on the route. Soon after the ford of the Kern River (difficult in early season) the trail begins the steep ascent up the Kern canyon wall to the hanging valley above. Veering away from the Kern-Kaweah River, it ascends to the north side of a granite knob, or spine, and passes through what has been called "Kern-Kaweah Pass." This difficult climb is repaid by the delightful valley above it, one of the finest in the Sierra. From the "pass" the trail descends slightly to Rockslide Lake, with its crystal-clear, emerald-green water. Just beyond the lake, the canyon widens into a kind of granite amphitheater, where two tributary streams, meeting, dash into the main canyon over a rocky ledge, to meet the main river below the fall by which the river arrives at the bowl. The ascent through a sparse-to-moderate lodgepole cover is moderate as the trail threads the deep canyon lying between Kern Point and Picket Guard Peak. One more steep ascent is required to reach the bowl that contains Gallats Lake, a pond in a large, wet meadow (fishing is good for golden to 8″). Fair campsites are here, but the traveler will prefer those about 1 mile ahead where the trail turns away from the river toward Colby Pass, where fishing is excellent for golden (to 7″). These campsites are a good explorer's base for excursions into the lightly-visited headwaters of the Kern-Kaweah River and into Milestone Bowl.

5th, 6th, 7th and 8th Hiking Days: Retrace your steps, 30½ miles.

Polemonium

Whitney Portal to Symmes Creek Trailhead **77**

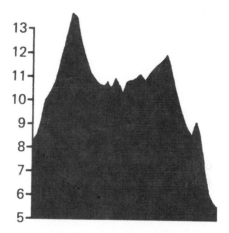

TRIP

From Whitney Portal to Symmes Creek Trailhead via Trail Crest, Crabtree Meadow, Tyndall Creek, Shepherd Pass (shuttle trip). Topo maps *Lone Pine*, *Mt. Whitney*. Best mid-to-late season; 39 miles.

Grade	Trail/layover days	Total recommended days
Leisurely	....	....
Moderate	6/2	8
Strenuous	5/0	5

HILITES

This high trip loops around "the Whitney group," the culmination of the Sierra spine, with five peaks standing over 14,000 feet. A spur trail will take the hiker to the highest point in the contiguous 48 states, 14,495 feet above sea level. The vast panoramas of the upper Kern basin along this route are unequalled in the Sierra.

DESCRIPTION (Strenuous trip)

1st and 2nd Hiking Days: Follow trip 73 to **Crabtree Ranger Station**, 15 miles.

3rd Hiking Day (**Crabtree Ranger Station** to **Tyndall Creek Tributary**, 9 miles): Follow the 3rd hiking day, trip 74, to the junction of the John Muir Trail and the High Sierra Trail. From Wallace Creek, this day's route continues north on the John Muir Trail. The sandy and rocky trail ascends moderately through a sparse-to-moderate forest cover, to an overlook that lensmen will want to utilize for photographs of the Great Western Divide. Here the trail becomes quite level as it crosses a sandy flat bearing a forest cover of lodgepole and foxtail pines. The trail crosses Wright Creek via a rocky ford (difficult in early season) and passes good campsites located east of the trail. From here, views are good up the valley of Wright Creek toward Mt. Tyndall, and the aspiring geologist will discern several terminal moraines athwart the valley.

Several short ascents separated by level stretches bring the hiker out onto Bighorn Plateau, where the panoramic view begins with Red Spur to the southwest and sweeps north along the Great Western Divide and east along the Kings-Kern Divide to Junction Peak. In addition, one can see, to the southeast, Mts. Whitney, Young and Russell. A small lake west of the trail presents great photographic possibilities in the morning, and any time of day is good for photographing the lateral moraine of the Tyndall Creek glacier, which follows a contour along the west side of the plateau. Color is provided by a large field of lupine sweeping up the slope to the east. From here a gentle descent on a rocky trail through a sparse foxtail cover leads to the good campsites (11,100') where the trail crosses the outlet of a small lake (no fish) which offers good swimming in late season.

4th Hiking Day (**Tyndall Creek Tributary** to **Anvil Camp**, 7½ miles): As this hiking day begins, the John Muir Trail descends gently on a rocky course through a forest cover of mixed lodgepole and foxtail to a junction with the Shepherd Pass Trail. Our route

The Great Western Divide from near Bighorn Plateau

turns right (east) off the Muir Trail and begins a long, steady ascent up the meadowy, boulder-strewn upper basin of Tyndall Creek. Views improve constantly as the traveler gains elevation, and the peaks of the Great Western Divide take on new aspects as they are seen from new angles. To the north, the southern escarpment of Diamond Mesa hides an upper surface that is one of the most level areas in this region. The traveler who has read the incredible first chapter of Clarence King's *Mountaineering in the Sierra Nevada* may speculate on where King and Richard Cotter crossed the Kings-Kern Divide and traversed this basin on their way to ascending Mt. Tyndall—which, in naming, they believed to be the highest Sierra peak until they were on top of it and saw other, higher ones nearby.

The appearance of Lake 12002 heralds the approach to Shepherd Pass (12,050'), which from this side of the crest is merely the end of a long, gentle ascent. The east side of the pass is a total contrast, with its steep scree and talus slopes which are often not passable to stock until August. From the pass, the trail switchbacks down a 500-foot scree slope into a gigantic, barren bowl scooped out by the plucking action of the Shepherd Creek glacier. Winding among boulders and topping a slight rise, the trail begins a moderate descent to timberline and a poor campsite near the junction with the Junction Pass Trail. The rocky trail continues to descend moderately through a cover of sparse lodgepole to a ford of Shepherd Creek and the good campsites at Anvil Camp (10,000'), where fishing for rainbow (to 9") is fair.
5th Hiking Day (**Anvil Camp** to **Symmes Creek Trailhead**, 7½ miles): Reverse the 1st hiking day, trip 68.

Thomas Winnett

78 Lodgepole Campground to Ranger Lakes

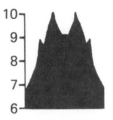

TRIP   From Lodgepole Campground to Ranger Lakes via
             Silliman Pass (round trip). Topo map *Triple Divide
             Peak*. Best mid-to-late season; 17 miles.

Grade	Trail/layover days	Total recommended days
Leisurely	....	....
Moderate	2/1	3
Strenuous	2/0	2

HILITES   Crossing the Silliman Crest on the boundary of Se-
             quoia and Kings Canyon parks, this trip terminates
             at picturesque Ranger Lakes. En route, the trail pas-
             ses through sedate fir forests, traces rambling
             brooks, and circles crystal-clear lakes.

DESCRIPTION (Moderate trip)

1st Hiking Day (**Lodgepole Campground** to **Ranger Lakes,** 8½ miles):
The trail first crosses the Marble Fork Kaweah River via a bridge
(6800'), and after a few yards of northward travel turns west on a
moderate ascent through a dense forest cover of fir and cedar.
This ascent, over alternating rocky and sandy stretches, then
turns north and levels to a ford of Silliman Creek. These woods
teem with wildlife, and the traveler is very apt to see a few mule
deer, many squirrels, and a host of birds that will include Steller
jay, pygmy nuthatch, Hammond flycatcher (until late summer),
Williamson sapsucker, Brewer blackbird, fox sparrow and Lincoln sparrow. After two more fords of Silliman Creek, the trail
continues the moderate ascent over duff and sand underfooting
through patchy, dense stands of red and white fir and some
meadow sections to Cahoon Gap. The trail then descends moderately to a ford of the unnamed tributary just south of the East
Fork Clover Creek. One fourth mile beyond this ford the trail
fords the East Fork Clover Creek, and then turns east, passing
the JO Pass Trail.

The sometimes gentle, sometimes moderate ascent up the East Fork Clover Creek witnesses the inclusion of lodgepole and silver pine in the forest cover, and as the trail approaches Twin Lakes, open ground stretches between the trees are a tide of colors. In season, one will find rank, knee-high corn lily, blue and white lupine, white mariposa lily, orange wallflower, purple larkspur, lavender shooting star, white cinquefoil, violet aster and golden groundsel. The last mile to the heavily timbered flats around Twin Lakes is a steep ascent, and the traveler may well contemplate a quick swim in the largest lake, whose shallow waters quickly warm to a midsummer's sun. This same lake has several campsites that are frequently utilized by contingents of Boy Scouts from nearby Wolverton Boy Scout Camp. Fishing at these lakes is poor.

Continuing toward Silliman Pass, the view of the two large boulder stands of exfoliating granite (Twin Peaks) dominates the horizon during the steep progress to the pass' saddle. This ascent sees the end of the fir, and the almost exclusive domination of the lodgepole pine. At the pass (10,165') one has a good view of flat-topped Mt. Silliman to the south, the heavily wooded Sugarloaf Creek drainage to the northeast, Glacier Ridge to the east, and the barren flats of the Tableland to the southeast. The descent from the pass drops steeply and then turns north to the nose of a granite ridge before switchbacking down. From the switchbacks one has fine views of Ball Dome. At the foot of the switchbacks a level duff trail leads off to the larger of the Ranger Lakes, and to the excellent campsites on the southwest side of the lake. Anglers working their way around the shallow lake plying their art on the fair-to-good fishing for brook trout (to 8″) will also enjoy the carpet of shooting stars and the rose-purple blossom of the heather. A layover day spent in this pleasant environment will allow the traveler to visit the nearby scenic settings of Beville (rainbow and brook), Lost (brook) and Seville (brook) lakes.

2nd Hiking Day: Retrace your steps, 8½ miles.

79 Lodgepole Campground to Scaffold Meadows

TRIP   From Lodgepole Campground to Scaffold Meadows via Silliman Pass, Ranger Lakes, Sugarloaf Valley (round trip). Topo map *Triple Divide Peak*. Best mid or late season; 43 miles.

Grade	Trail/layover days	Total recommended days
Leisurely	6/2	8
Moderate	5/2	7
Strenuous	4/2	6

HILITES   Scaffold Meadows, the terminus of this long trip, makes a superb location for a base camp. From here, one can explore the upper reaches of several remote drainages, and in the course of these explorations enjoy some of the finest fishing of the Roaring River country.

DESCRIPTION (Leisurely trip)

1st Hiking Day: Follow trip 78 to **Ranger Lakes**, 8½ miles.

2nd Hiking Day (**Ranger Lakes** to **Comanche Meadow**, 5½ miles): Rounding the east side of a rocky prominence on the east side of the larger Ranger Lake, the faintly ducked trail undulates northward and circles Ball Dome past the turnoff to Lost Lake. Passing through a moderate-to-heavy forest cover the trail emerges at a meadowed crossing of the outlet stream from Seville Lake. Beyond this crossing, the junctions of the Seville Lake and the Marvin Pass trails are poorly marked, but the trails are clear. Keeping right, on the northwest side of Sugarloaf Creek, our route descends sometimes steadily and sometimes moderately over duff-and-sand underfooting. This descent crosses an unnamed tributary, and a short distance beyond passes another trail lateral to Marvin Pass. About ¼ mile farther on, the trail passes the South Fork Sugarloaf Creek Trail and then fords the rocky creek emptying Comanche Meadow (7680'). Good campsites will be found on Sugarloaf Creek before and after this ford, and fishing for brook trout (to 8″) is fair.

3rd Hiking Day (**Comanche Meadow** to **Scaffold Meadows**, 7½ miles): Beginning ¼ mile after the ford, the trail drops moderately on sandy underfooting over a heavily forested slope. Then, as the trail levels out on the floor of Sugarloaf Valley, the dome from which the name is derived can be seen through the trees. More resistant than the surrounding rock, this granite island withstood the onslaught of the ice, and today it stands as a round, smooth 1000-foot-high reminder of the ice river that carved the valley. Following the course of this old glacier through sporadic meadows, the trail veers north away from Sugarloaf Creek, and at the ford of its northernmost tributary passes another trail to Marvin Pass.

On the east side of this wide, shallow ford, the trail passes more campsites before crossing a series of sharp wrinkles in the terrain to Ferguson Creek and still more campsites. After fording this creek via rocks, the trail rounds a long, dry, timbered ridge nose before dropping down a steady slope to the drift fence just below Scaffold Meadows. Living up to its name, Roaring River can be heard a few yards to the left, and with this pleasant accompaniment the trail ascends the last, gentle ½ mile to the good campsites (7360′). Fishing for rainbow and some golden trout (to 10″) is fair to good. Emergency services are available from the resident summer ranger, whose cabin is nearby. These campsites make a fine base camp for further explorations of the surrounding headwaters of Deadman Canyon Creek, Roaring River and Brewer Creek.

4th, 5th and 6th Hiking Days: Retrace your steps, 21½ miles.

Roaring River Ranger Station *National Park Service*

80 Lodgepole Campground to Ranger Meadow

TRIP   From Lodgepole Campground to Ranger Meadow via
                  Silliman Pass, Ranger Lakes, Sugarloaf Valley, Scaf-
                  fold Meadows, Deadman Canyon, return via
                  Elizabeth Pass, High Sierra Trail, Panther Gap to
                  Crescent Meadow (shuttle trip). Topo map *Triple Di-
                  vide Peak*. Best late season; 50½ miles.

Grade	Trail/layover days	Total recom- mended days
Leisurely	7/2	9
Moderate	6/2	8
Strenuous	5/2	7

HILITES   The climax of this trip is the high, wildflower-filled
                  meadows at the head of Deadman Canyon. Seldom
                  visited because of its remoteness, this glaciated
                  canyon nestles against the craggy summits of
                  Glacier Ridge in solitary splendor.

DESCRIPTION (Moderate trip)

1st 3 Hiking Days: Follow trip 79 to **Scaffold Meadows**, 21½ miles.

4th Hiking Day (**Scaffold Meadows** to **Upper Ranger Meadow**, 7
miles): Our route passes the Avalanche Pass/Cedar Grove Trail
and the Cloud Canyon/Colby Pass Trail, and, leaving Scaffold
Meadows, continues south while veering away from the river on a
gentle-to-moderate ascent. Views back over one's left shoulder include a fine example of a lateral moraine in the form of Moraine
Ridge, the northeast wall of the canyon. About 1½ miles beyond
the junctions mentioned above, our route ascends past the upper
drift fence and several more campsites. At the right time of summer, flowers seen during this short stretch include buckwheat,
sagebrush, Indian paintbrush, white Mariposa, pennyroyal, penstemon and shooting star. Continuing past the drift fence, the

trail fords Deadman Canyon Creek, passes a packer campsite, and then comes to a gravesite. Located at the north end of a large, wet meadow, about 50 yards southeast of the campsite cited above, the grave marks the derivation of the name Deadman Canyon. The citation on the grave reads: "Here reposes Alfred Moniere, sheepherder, mountain man, 18-- to 1887."

The ascent continues along the east bank of the creek, offering good views up the canyon of the spectacularly smoothed, un-jointed, barren walls. Crossing another long, wet meadow, the trail then refords the creek and climbs alongside a dramatic, green-water, granite-slab chute. At the end of this ascent, the trail levels out as it passes through a dense stand of lodgepole and fir, and, passing a campsite, emerges at the north end of the open grasslands of Ranger Meadow. The precipitous canyon walls dominate the views from the meadow, and the cirque holding Big Bird Lake is clear on the west wall. By midsummer, the meadow is a colorful carpet of wildflowers including shooting star, pen-stemon, Labrador tea and red heather. From Ranger Meadow the trail resumes its steady ascent over duff and sand through stands of lodgepole and clumps of aspen. As the trail reaches the Upper Ranger Meadow flat, one has awesome glimpses of the headwall of the Deadman Canyon cirque, and this view continues to rule the skyline from the good campsites just beyond the drift fence at the north end of Upper Ranger Meadow. Fishing for rainbow, brook and hybrids is good (to 10″). One should not miss visiting scenic, deep, sheer-walled Big Bird Lake just a short climb to the southwest.

5th Hiking Day (**Upper Ranger Meadow** to **Bearpaw Meadow**, 11 miles, part cross country): Just south of the campsites cited above, the trail passes a spur trail leading to Big Bird Lake and ascends gently across grassy Upper Ranger Meadow. Low-lying willows line the stream, and clumps of wildflowers dot the green expanse. The trail turns somewhat southeast as the ascent steepens to a moderate grade; then, as it begins the steep ascent of the head-wall, it parallels a dramatic series of cascades and falls. Near the top of the falls, the trail fords the stream below a long, dashing granite chute, and then we climb steeply by a faint, infrequently ducked route up the southwest wall of the cirque. This barren, rocky climb over light-colored granite slabs contrasts with the darker metamorphic rocks (around an old copper-mine site) seen to the east, and this contrast is even more marked from the tiny saddle of Elizabeth Pass (11,380′). Views to the southwest from the pass include parts of the Middle Fork Kaweah River watershed, and the jumbled peaks of the southernmost promi-nences of the Tableland divide.

From the pass, the ducked trail descends steeply via a long, smooth granite trough to a ford of an unnamed tributary that cascades and plunges down into River Valley. After a moderately descending traverse, the trail descends the steep northern wall of River Valley via a series of rock switchbacks. At the foot of these zigzags, our route passes a spur trail to Lonepine Meadow and Tamarack Lake, and then swings southwest across the sparsely timbered nose of the ridge above Bearpaw Meadow. The descent from this ridge is steep, rocky and dry as it passes through stands of lodgepole and red fir and joins the High Sierra Trail ¼ mile north of Bearpaw Meadow. Our route turns right onto the High Sierra Trail for about 100 yards, and then branches left (south) on a 200-yard descent to the good campsites at the signed campground overlooking the Middle Fork Kaweah River canyon. Emergency services are available from the ranger station at Bearpaw Meadow, ½ mile east.

6th Hiking Day (**Bearpaw Meadow** to **Crescent Meadow**, 11 miles): Reverse the 1st hiking day, trip 81.

Snowplant

Thomas Winnett

Crescent Meadow to Whitney Portal   **81**

TRIP   From Crescent Meadow to Whitney Portal via
            Hamilton Lakes, Kaweah Gap, Junction Meadow,
            Wallace Creek, Crabtree Meadow and Trail Crest
            (shuttle trip). Topo maps *Triple Divide Peak*, *Kern
            Peak*, *Mt. Whitney*. Best mid-to-late season; 68½
            miles.

Grade	Trail/layover days	Total recommended days
Leisurely	11/4	15
Moderate	9/3	12
Strenuous	7/2	9

HILITES   Most of this dramatic trans-Sierra route follows the
            High Sierra Trail—a trail that is, in its early stages,
            literally carved out of the rock. Crossing the Great
            Western Divide, it descends to the Kern Trench, and
            emerges on the east side at Whitney Portal. The
            scenic terrain it visits, and the fine trout waters it
            crosses or camps near, make it a justly famous and
            popular route.

DESCRIPTION (Moderate trip)

1st Hiking Day (**Crescent Meadow** to **Bearpaw Meadow**, 11 miles):
Beginning from some restrooms near Crescent Meadow, we cir-
cumvent the meadow on pavement and begin climbing through a
grove of giant sequoias. Soon after passing a trail leading to Giant
Forest, we break out into the open above the Middle Fork of the

Kaweah at Eagle View Overlook, and the view is indeed awesome. Moro Rock pokes up in the west, far below is the river, and to the east is the high country. Soon one is far enough from the road and its crowds to begin saying "hello" to people along the trail. One of the best things about wilderness is that many of the citified psychological barriers between a person and his fellows are fast discarded.

The trail erratically rises and falls as we move up-canyon in a forest of ponderosa and sugar pine, black oak, bigleaf maple and even some bay trees, mixed with manzanita and whitethorn scrub. Across the canyon, those impressive sentinels of the valley, Castle Rocks, fall slowly behind as we march on. Soon we pass by a cutoff to Wolverton Corral in the north. Innumerable spring-fed streams cross the trail here late into the season, and even a hot afternoon start on this hike is not too bad. Yellow-throated gilia is abundant along the trail until rather late in the year. Beyond Seven-mile Hill, a prominent ridge jutting out in the canyon below, we pass a junction with trails that lead down to the Middle Fork and up to the Alta Trail 1300 feet above. Our trail does not follow a "natural" route, but instead stays high on the north wall of the Middle Fork Kaweah River canyon. It is not a level traverse. Frequently, the trail undulates over 400-foot rises, only to drop down into a secondary tributary canyon, and then emerge to climb again. From the above junction, the trail descends to ford an unnamed tributary and then climb steeply. Views are all to the south and southeast, where the spectacular granite dome formations of Sugarbowl Dome and Castle Rocks rise above the timbered floor. With each ford of the unnamed tributaries flowing from the slopes of Alta Peak, the trail passes precariously perched campsites, and then as it rounds a hot, dry, sparsely timbered slope to the Buck Creek ford, it passes the Moose Lake Trail. The route ascends through a dense fir forest cover to the signed turnoff to the campground 200 yards south. Here, fair campsites (7700′) enjoy fine views of the canyon to the south and southwest. Emergency services are available from the ranger station at Bearpaw Meadow, ½ mile east, and there are some concessioner's wood-frame tents, and a "restaurant."

2nd Hiking Day (**Bearpaw Meadow** to **Hamilton Lakes**, 4 miles): Returning to the High Sierra Trail, our route turns right (east), and 100 yards farther passes the Elizabeth Pass Trail. A short distance beyond this junction, the trail passes by Bearpaw Meadow, said to have been named by early stockmen who found a bear's paw nailed to a tree. Today, most of the meadow is devoted to the outbuildings of Bearpaw Lodge (advance reservations for beds and board are advisable). Just across the trail from the lodge is the ranger's cabin. The magnificent views from the meadow and the subsequent trail include Mt. Stewart and Eagle Scout Peak on the Great Western Divide, Black Kaweah beyond, the Yosemite-like depths of Hamilton Creek and Middle Fork Kaweah River and the Cliff Creek drainage below. Continuing past Bearpaw Ranger Station, the trail descends moderately through mixed, sparse forest stands. As the trail rounds the slope and descends toward River Valley, it traverses a section blasted from an immense, exfoliating granite slab. Educational views of clearcut avalanche chutes on the south wall of the canyon accompany the descent to the culvert fording wild, turbulent Lone Pine Creek. This stream cascades and plunges down a narrow granite chasm below the culvert, and the force of the torrent is clear evidence of the cutting power of the water. From the creek, the trail ascends an exposed slope, passing a side trail to Tamarack Lake. Continuing the steady ascent, the traveler is overwhelmed with the gigantic scale of the rock sculpting by ice, rock and snow to the east and southeast. The trail surface, while mostly rocky passes occasional clumps of brightly colored wildflowers, including scarlet gilia, Douglas phlox, fleabane, Indian paintbrush, penstemon, mountain bluebell, red columbine and larkspur. Overhead, the mixed forest cover, mostly in sparse stands, includes black oak. juniper, Jeffrey and sugar pine. Overshadowing the final climb to the ford of Hamilton Creek, the sheer granite wall to the north, called Angels Wing, or Valhalla, the sharply pointed granite sentinels atop the south wall, and the wall's avalanche-chuted sides are a constant source of wonderment and awe. The trail climbs alongside the stream and then boulder-hops across just below the lowest lake of the Hamilton Lakes chain. From this ford the trail climbs steeply over shattered rock to the good improved campsites at the northwest end of Lake 8235. Views from the campsites, including the silver waterfall ribbon at the east end, are superlative, but firewood is scarce owing to the heavy and concentrated camper impact. Fishing for brook, rainbow and golden (to 10′) is fair to good.

3rd Hiking Day (**Hamilton Lakes** to **Big Arroyo Trail Junction**, 7 miles): The steep climb to Kaweah Gap is an engineering marvel of trail construction, which has literally blasted the way along vertical cliff sections. Beginning at the northwest end of the lake, the trail ascends steadily through an open forest cover of juniper and red fir with constant views of the lake and its dramatic walls. Despite the rocky terrain, many wildflowers line this ascent and among the manzanita and chinquapin one will find lush lupine, yellow columbine, penstemon, Indian paintbrush, white cinquefoil, false Solomon's seal and Douglas phlox. After some doubling back the trail turns south on a steep ascent to a point just above the north shore of Precipice Lake, at the foot of the near-vertical north face of Eagle Scout Peak. The jagged summits of the peaks of the Great Western Divide dominate the skyline to the east during the final, tarn-dotted ascent to U-shaped Kaweah Gap, but as one approaches the gap one can see the equally spectacular summits of the Kaweah Peaks Ridge beyond. This colorful ridge dominates the views from Kaweah Gap (10,700'), and one can see the Nine Lakes Basin watershed to the north. Those with a bent for exploring barren high country, or interested in the good brook-trout fishing, may elect to detour across granite slab and ledge routes north to the Nine Lake Basin.

Our trail continues its steady-to-moderate southward descent along the west side of the headwaters of Big Arroyo Creek, fording over to the east side midway down. This descent crosses unjointed granite broken by substantial pockets of grass and numerous runoff streams even in late season, and the open stretches afford fine views of the U-shaped, glacially wrought Big Arroyo below, and the white, red and black rocks of Black Kaweah and Red Kaweah peaks to the east. The trail then re-enters timber cover and arrives at some good campsites along the stream (9800'). These campsites are about ¼ mile above the Little Five Lakes/Black Rock Pass Trail junction. Fishing for brook trout to 7" is fair to good. For those anglers with extra time, the short 2-mile side trip to Little Five Lakes offers fine angling for golden trout.

4th Hiking Day (**Big Arroyo Trail Junction** to **Moraine Lake**, 8 miles): Continuing past the Little Five Lakes Trail junction, the trail there begins a long, steady traverse of the north side of Big Arroyo which culminates at the Chagoopa Plateau. This route parallels the course of a trunk glacier that once filled Big Arroyo, overflowed the benches on either side, and contributed to the main glacier of Kern Canyon. Our route climbs the wall of this trough, and the timber cover of this ascent is sparse, but there is no shortage of wildflowers tucked among the sage, manzanita and chinquapin. Most colorful are yellow columbine, Indian paintbrush and lupine. The sparse forest cover thickens near the Chagoopa Plateau, and one will find lodgepole and foxtail, and an occasional juniper.

The ascent levels off near a small, mirror-faced tarn, and, swinging away north from the lip of Big Arroyo, it begins a gradual descent through alternating timber and meadow stretches. Tree-interrupted views of the jagged Great Western Divide skyline accompany the descent to a meadowed trail junction on the south side of a tributary of Chagoopa Creek. At this junction our route leaves the High Sierra Trail, branching right (south) through meadowed clumps of shooting stars. This descent becomes steeper over coarse granite sand, through dense stands of lodgepole and foxtail pine. It is time well spent during this descent to step a hundred yards west of the trail for the superlative views down into Big Arroyo and across the Arroyo to the drainages of Soda and Lost Canyon creeks. This steady down-winding trail brings one to the wooded shores of Moraine Lake. Good campsites on the south side of the lake (9290′) provide lake-fronted views back to the Kaweah Peaks, and gardens of wild azalea in season.

5th Hiking Day (**Moraine Lake** to **Kern Hot Spring**, 7 miles): After traversing a moraine just east of Moraine Lake, the trail turns north through a long, beautiful meadow, and passes an old stockman's cabin before rejoining the High Sierra Trail at Sky Parlor Meadow. Views back across this lupine-filled grassland, particularly of the Kaweahs and Red Spur, are excellent. Turning right (east) onto the High Sierra Trail, one begins the first moderate and then steep descent into the Kern trench. The initial descent sees the lodgepole being replaced by the lower-altitude white fir and Jeffrey pine; and still lower down, the trail descends steeply through manzanita and snowbrush that are over-shadowed by an occasional juniper and oak. Views of the unmistakably U-shaped Kern trench, typical of glacially carved valleys, are instructive—particularly to the south. The final climb down to the valley floor is accomplished via a series of steep, rocky switchbacks generally paralleling the plunging drop of Funston Creek. At the Kern Canyon floor our route turns north, upstream, on the Kern River Trail, drops into a marshy area, and then crosses the river on a wood bridge. Then the trail leads gently up through a forest of Jeffrey pine and incense-cedar. High on the western rim of the canyon one catches glimpses of Chagoopa Falls, a fury of plunging white water. Past a manzanita-carpeted open area the trail arrives at the southern fork of Rock Creek, which may be crossed on a log a few yards downstream. Around a point we arrive at the delightful mountain spa of Kern Hot Spring—a treat for the tired, dusty hiker. To the traveler, the crude, cemented bathtub here becomes a regal, heated (115°) pool. Only a few feet away, the great Kern River rushes past, and its cold waters can be dipped into to cool the hot-spring water as desired. In the river near the campsites, fishing is good for brown, rainbow and golden trout (to 10″).

6th Hiking Day (**Kern Hot Spring** to **Junction Meadow,** 8 miles): Continuing north, we ford the upper fork of Rock Creek and traverse the gravelly canyon floor below the immense granite cliffs of the canyon's east wall. Past the confluence of Red Spur Creek this route ascends gently, sometimes a bit stiffly, beside the Kern River, heading almost due north. The U-shaped trough of the Kern River, called the Kern Trench, is remarkably straight for about 25 miles as it traces the Kern Canyon fault. The fault, a zone of structural weakness in the Sierra batholith, is more susceptible to erosion than the surrounding rock, and this deep canyon has been carved by both glacial and stream action. Three times the glacier advanced down the canyon, shearing off spurs created by stream erosion and leaving some tributary valleys hanging above the main valley. The glacier also scooped and plucked at the bedrock, creating basins in the granite which became lakes when the glacier melted and retreated.

The walls of this deep canyon, from 2000 to 5000 feet high, are quite spectacular, and a number of streams cascade and fall down these walls. (The fords of the stream draining Guyot Flat, of Whitney Creek and of Wallace Creek can be difficult in early season.) Beyond the ford of Wallace Creek the trail enters a parklike grove of stalwart Jeffrey pines that provide a noble setting for the good campsites on the Kern River, where fishing is good for rainbow and some brook trout (to 10″).

7th Hiking Day (**Junction Meadow** to **Crabtree Ranger Station**, 8½ miles): The trail leaves the parklike Jeffrey pines of Junction Meadow and ascends steeply on rocky underfooting over a slope covered by manzanita and currant. Views down the Kern trench improve constantly, as the occasional Jeffrey, lodgepole and aspen offer frames for the lenseman who would compose a "shot" of the great cleft. After one mile we arrive at the junction of the Kern River Trail and the High Sierra Trail, where our route turns right (southeast), back toward Wallace Creek canyon. From here, reverse most of the 3rd hiking day, trip 75.

8th and 9th Hiking Days: Reverse the 2nd and 1st hiking days, trip 73, 15 miles.

Mt. Hale over Wallace Lake

Crescent Meadow to Mt. Whitney   **82**

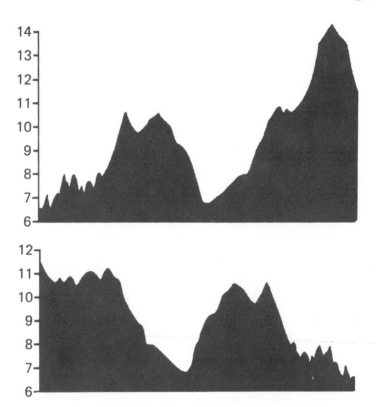

TRIP   From Crescent Meadow to Mt. Whitney via Hamilton Lake, Kaweah Gap, Big Arroyo, Junction Meadow, Wallace Creek, Crabtree Ranger Station, return via Tyndall Creek, Upper Kern River to Junction Meadow (semiloop trip). Topo maps *Giant Forest, Triple Divide Peak, Kern Peak, Mt. Whitney*. Best mid to late season; 136 miles.

Grade	Trail/layover days	Total recommended days
Leisurely	....	....
Moderate	16/3	19
Strenuous	12/1	13

HILITES   Many people plan for years to climb Mt. Whitney
                 from Giant Forest, via the well-named High Sierra
                 Trail. This trip repays the planning, and adds the
                 dividend of getting off the main track during a loop-
                 ing return from the great peak.

DESCRIPTION (Moderate trip)

1st, 2nd, 3rd, 4th, 5th, 6th and 7th Hiking Days: Follow trip 81 to
Crabtree Ranger Station, 53½ miles.

Layover Day, 18 miles: This "layover" day is the most strenuous of
the trip. The hiker should begin as early as possible. He might
camp on the Mt. Whitney Trail ½ mile above Crabtree Ranger
Station in a small meadow on Whitney Creek, or hike after din-
ner to Guitar Lake and sleep there. Those with stoves can of
course cook as high as they choose to.

From Crabtree Ranger Station our route ascends the narrow
canyon of Whitney Creek. Past a small meadow we arrive at
Timberline Lake (no camping, but fair fishing for golden trout.
Then the trail ascends somewhat steeply past the last pine trees,
crosses the outlet of Arctic Lake, and traverses above Guitar
Lake to a wet meadow where the "fun" begins. Switchback is
piled upon steep switchback until the panting hiker has to stop
for breath, only to confront another series of switchbacks. Little
windbreaks at the few flat places tell of westbound hikers who
were too tired to make it down to Crabtree Meadows. Finally,
after more than 1500 feet of climbing, we reach the side trail that
leads to the summit. If, while on top, you should wonder how
John Muir felt the first time he climbed Mt. Whitney, be it noted
that he later wrote, "I reached the summit needles about 11
o'clock that night and danced most of the time until morning, as
the night was bitterly cold and I was in my shirtsleeves."

8th Hiking Day (**Crabtree Ranger Station** to **Tyndall Creek Tributary,**
9 miles): Follow the 3rd hiking day, trip 77.

9th Hiking Day (**Tyndall Creek Tributary** to **Lake on Upper Kern
River,** 4½ miles): As the hiking day begins, we descend gently on a
rocky trail through a forest cover of mixed lodgepole and foxtail
pine to a junction with the Shepherd Pass Trail. From here, our
route northwest follows part of the 2nd hiking day, trip 69, to the
unnamed lake with elevation 10,650 feet. This natural im-
poundment on the Kern River has good campsites and good fishing for golden and rainbow-golden hybrids (to 10″).

10th Hiking Day (**Lake on Upper Kern River** to **Junction Meadow,** 6
miles): Follow the 3rd hiking day, trip 70.

11th-16th Hiking Days (**Junction Meadow** to **Crescent Meadow,** 45
miles): Retrace the steps of the first 6 hiking days.

Cottonwood Creek Trailhead to South Fork Lakes

83

TRIP   From Cottonwood Creek Trailhead to South Fork
Lakes, return via cross country down South Fork
Cottonwood Creek (loop trip). Topo map *Olancha*.
Best mid or late season; 12½ miles.

Grade	Trail/layover days	Total recom- mended days
Leisurely	2/1	3
Moderate	....	....
Strenuous	....	....

HILITES   A fine weekend loop trip, this route affords grand
scenery, and a good exposure to east-side ecology that
will benefit both beginner and old hand.

DESCRIPTION (Leisurely trip)

1st Hiking Day (**Cottonwood Creek Trailhead** to **South Fork Lakes,**
6½ miles): From the trailhead (9640') west of the pack station,
the trail leaves the road on a gentle ascent through a dense stand
of lodgepole and foxtail pine. Along the way, the traveler will find
patches of sweet-smelling lupine, delicate penstemon, low-lying,
pink pussypaws, ochre-red Indian paintbrush, yellow monkey
flower, and isolated representatives of the showy columbine. Underfoot, the sand-and-duff trail of the densely forested trailhead
area gives way to rock and sand as the trail climbs. Then, leveling
out on the east fringes of open meadowland, the footing reverts to
duff and sand. Cottonwood Creek, now close on the left, is frequently willow-choked, but the more open stretches reveal it to be
a placid, clear-running stream—ideal for fly-rod action. Beaver
reintroduced in this region in the 1940s have flooded many of
these meadows with their penchant for damming running water.
As a consequence, government officials of the Forest Service and
the DF&G differ as to their continued value on this drainage.
Rarely seen during daylight hours, these rodents still inhabit
these waters, and a little scouting around should reveal some of
their latest handiwork.

The trail swings northward, and then passes a trail leading south to Horseshoe Meadow. This steadily ascending route follows close along the east side of Cottonwood Creek, traverses a long meadow, and then passes Golden Trout Camp, a private resort. Here, our route passes the Little Cottonwood Creek Trail branching east, and then swings west, passing through meadow clearings and moderate-to-dense stands of lodgepole and foxtail pine. The ascent levels during these meadow stretches, and then the route begins a steady ascent that passes a trail, the route forking right, which parallels our route up the creek drainage. Our route fords Cottonwood Creek midway between Golden Trout Camp and Cottonwood Lakes, and continues up a steep slope covered with willow and foxtail pine to the South Fork Lakes Trail junction. Keeping to the right, our route ascends the steep morainal switchbacks, climbing westward to the meadowed foot of the lowest Cottonwood Lake (Lake 11005). After passing another trail that rounds the north side of the lake, our route follows the well-defined south-shore route across rolling fell fields. (Note: All the Cottonwood Lakes are closed to fishing.) These lakes were used at one time for research and breeding of golden trout. Beyond this lake the trail touches the south shore of a lake just to the west, and then turns southwest on an undulating ascent through and across a "rock garden." From the point where the trail turns west-northwest, a short spur trail descends a few yards to the good campsites at the west end of the westernmost South Fork Lake (11,000'). These campsites are located in a grove of sparse foxtail pines with fine views of Cirque Peak to the southwest. Fishing for golden is poor (fry). Anglers will fare better at nearby Cirque Lake and the easternmost of the South Fork Lakes.

2nd Hiking Day (**South Fork Lakes** to **Cottonwood Creek Trailhead,** 6 miles, part cross country): Within the raucous call of the Clark nutcracker echoing around the rocks, the traveler works his way across the rocky, tarn-dotted terrain to the east of the lake. Intermittent seepage leads the way to the easternmost of the South Fork Lakes, where anglers can try for the lake's golden trout (to 7"). Keeping on the north and then the east side of the outlet stream, this route descends east over heavily fractured granite to a timbered (foxtail) saddle where the stream cascades and falls from one rocky grotto to another. Clumps of shooting star topped by showy yellow columbine and orange tiger lily line the stream, and, as the route descends the rocky draw, it meets a faint fisherman's trail just north of the large meadow section at the foot of the first descent. Old blazes mark the way when the trail disappears in the duff sections, but when in doubt one should keep to the north side of the stream. This route, following the creek's course, swings east, and enters another meadow with an old notched-log cabin at its head. From the east end of this meadow, the trail drops down to Cottonwood Creek on a clearly used northeastward traverse. This traverse joins a trail from Horseshoe Meadow just before it fords Cottonwood Creek to effect a junction with the trail described in the 1st hiking day. Our route then turns south and retraces the steps of the 1st hiking day.

Cottonwood Lake and Mt. Langley *Kurt Rademacher*

84 Cottonwood Creek Trailhead to Upper Rock Creek Lake

TRIP   From Cottonwood Creek Trailhead to Upper Rock Creek Lake via New Army Pass (round trip). Topo maps *Olancha*, *Kern Peak*. Best mid or late season; 26 miles.

Grade	Trail/layover days	Total recommended days
Leisurely	4/3	7
Moderate	3/2	5
Strenuous	2/1	3

HILITES   Beautiful Rock Creek and its spectacular headwaters are the goal of this high-country trip. The tiny, unnamed lake at the end of this trip makes a fine base camp for further exploration of Miter Basin and the Soldier Lake chain.

DESCRIPTION (Leisurely trip)

1st Hiking Day: Follow trip 83 to **South Fork Lakes,** 6½ miles.

2nd Hiking Day: (**South Fork Lakes** to **Upper Rock Creek Lake**, 6½ miles): From the westernmost South Fork Lake, the trail ascends through thinning timber to Long Lake. At the east end of this lake our route passes a lateral branching east to the upper Cottonwood Lakes, and then begins a long, steadily rising traverse that takes the traveler above the campsites at the west end of Long Lake. Views of the lake from this traverse are favorites of photographers, but it is wise to save some film for the panoramic shots farther up. This traverse brings one above timberline, and the remainder of the climb is accomplished over granite slopes covered only with grass, willows and wildflowers. The first step of the climb tops a series of glacially smoothed granite ledges, and touches the south edge of High Lake. A pause for a drink of the icy water at High Lake's outlet will brace one for the forthcoming rocky switchbacks. The higher one climbs up this cirque wall, the better the views to the east of the lakes immediately below and of the Cottonwood Creek drainage. One frequently sights a scurrying marmot on the cirque floor, and marmots' piping accompanies the hiker all the way to New Army Pass. At the pass (12,340') one should walk southwest on the knifelike crest for the majestic views across the Kern Trench to the Kaweah Peaks and the Great Western Divide. Back to the east, one can see across the Owens Valley to the White Mountains, and, on a clear day, make out Saline Valley beyond. To the north towers the Mt. Whitney complex, and nearer one can make out the cirques of upper Miter Basin.

Descending from New Army Pass into Sequoia National Park, the trail crosses a long, barren slope of coarse granite sand sprinkled with exfoliating granite boulders. Seepages with attendant grassy strips appear like creeping tendrils below, and up closer they are seen to be dotted with clumps of lupine. A few yards down this steady descent, our trail passes a trail that branches right to the old Army Pass. This pass, about ½ mile northeast, was the original pass constructed by an Army troop stationed in Owens Valley in the 1890s. Beyond this junction the route swings west and descends steadily over rocky trail and then across runoff-eroded meadow sections. The trail then re-enters a sparse-to-moderate forest cover and shortly thereafter passes a signed trail to Siberian Pass. There are excellent campsites on the south side of the stream just east of this junction.

Our route keeps to the right, continuing to descend through denser forest cover that includes lodgepole pine, and when the forest cover gives way to the open spaces of a lovely meadow, our trail meets and turns left onto the Rock Creek Trail. This trail descends steeply alongside a willow-infested tributary of Rock Creek until the rocky slope gives way to the meadow just above Upper Rock Creek Lake. (This name is not employed on the topo map, but is generally used by mountaineers who frequent this country.) Around these meadows one may sight the relatively rare white-tailed jackrabbit. There are good campsites at the head of this meadow, but better ones are located at the lake outlet. These campsites are reached by fording Rock Creek and rounding the north edge of the lake. Fishing for golden (to 10″) in the lake and adjoining stream is good to excellent. Several marmot families live in the granite to the north.

This meadowed lake site makes a grand base camp for side trips to the rugged Miter Basin and the adjoining "Soldier Lakes" (just south of The Major General). Fishing for golden in most of the lakes below the Miter and The Major General is good, but the season is usually very short because of late ice melt. Other fine

side trips include a looping cross-country exploration of the
Boreal Plateau via Siberian Outpost; or the hardy and experienced knapsacker with a yen for adventure may wish to take the
Guyot Flat Trail to Crabtree Meadow and then take the scrambling cross-country route up the Crabtree Lakes chain which
rounds Mt. Chamberlin, Mt. Newcomb, Mt. Pickering and Joe
Devel Peak and returns via Miter Basin.

3rd and 4th Hiking Days: Retrace your steps, 13 miles.

Siberian Outpost   *Kurt Rademacher*

Cottonwood Creek Trailhead to Upper Rock Creek Lake 85

TRIP
From Cottonwood Creek Trailhead to Upper Rock Creek Lake via New Army Pass, return via Cottonwood Pass (shuttle trip). Topo maps *Olancha*, *Kern Peak*. Best mid or late season; 25 miles.

Grade	Trail/layover days	Total recommended days
Leisurely	4/3	7
Moderate	4/1	5
Strenuous	3/0	3

HILITES
One of the finest circuits in the Sierra, this route tours peaks of spectacle and grandeur, visits unforgettable lakes, traces streams that plummet, seep and meander, and blends them all together with a carpet of green forest and open meadows that will give all who come a sense of accomplishment and peace.

DESCRIPTION (Leisurely trip)

1st and 2nd Hiking Days: Follow trip 84 to **Upper Rock Creek Lake**, 13 miles.

3rd Hiking Day (**Upper Rock Creek Lake** to **Chicken Spring Lake**, 6½ miles): This hiking day begins by retracing your steps for 1 mile to the meadowed Siberian Pass Trail junction passed during the 2nd hiking day. From the junction this trail ascends southward moderately over a densely forested slope of foxtail and lodgepole pine. An old burn that swept over this hillside has left many darkened stumps that, with subsequent wind and rain weathering, have achieved beautiful sculptured forms. Overhead, the eastward-pointing treetops (prevailing wind) combine with the fire evidence on the ground to give an otherworldly feeling to the whole hillside—an impression that becomes even stronger as the trail crosses the eastern end of barren Siberian Outpost. Named for its bleak appearance in 1895 by Harvey Corbett, the entire area has the look of a sterile meadow. (Most of the surface is a coarse granite sand deposited as a result of mechanical and chemical erosion of nearby granite slabs.) Grassy strips follow seepage lines as they drain west from the trail, but otherwise the landscape seems lifeless. One mile south of the New Army Pass Trail junction we turn left on the Pacific Crest Trail and reverse the first part of the 2nd hiking day, trip 89, to Chicken Spring Lake.

4th Hiking Day (**Chicken Spring Lake** to **Horseshoe Meadow**, 5½ miles): Reverse the 1st hiking day, trip 89.

Mt. Whitney from Mt. Langley   *Kurt Rademacher*

Cottonwood Creek Trailhead to Mineral King 86

TRIP   From Cottonwood Creek Trailhead to Mineral King
via Army Pass, Rock Creek, Siberian Pass, Big
Whitney Meadow, Golden Trout Creek, Kern River,
Rattlesnake Creek, Franklin Pass (shuttle trip).
Topo maps *Olancha*, *Kern Peak*, *Mineral King*. Best
mid or late season; 59½ miles.

Grade	Trail/layover days	Total recom- mended days
Leisurely	....	....
Moderate	7/4	11
Strenuous	6/4	10

HILITIES This excellent trans-Sierra route visits the finest
fishing lakes and streams of the lower Kern River
drainage. The severe altitude changes inherent in
the route, however, recommend this trip for intermediate and experienced hikers only.

DESCRIPTION (Moderate trip)

1st and 2nd Hiking Days: Follow trip 84 to **Upper Rock Creek Lake**,
13 miles.

3rd Hiking Day (**Upper Rock Creek Lake** to **Big Whitney Meadow**, 7
miles): Follow the 3rd hiking day, trip 85, for the route to
Siberian Outpost. From where the Pacific Crest Trail turns east,
our route crosses the east end of Siberian Outpost and ascends
gently past a snowmarker site to the easy rise called Siberian
Pass (10,920') and a junction with the lower Rock Creek Trail,
where we leave Sequoia National Park.

The forest cover of foxtail pine, moderate near the pass, in-
creases in density, and later includes lodgepole. Our trail crosses

the headwaters of Golden Trout Creek midway down the descent, and then, climbing gently, crosses a ridge before descending a moderate slope to the western edge of Big Whitney Meadow. The underfooting of most of this descent has been dust and some rock, but as it nears the meadow it is mostly sand. Mats of yellow monkey flower color the forest floor, and as the trail emerges in the opener sections, one finds lupine, penstemon, cinquefoil and sagebrush. Keeping to the forest fringes on the west side of the very large grassland, our trail passes the Cottonwood Pass Trail, and a few hundred yards beyond arrives at the fair campsites at the Rocky Basin Lakes Trail junction. These campsites are just north of the Big Whitney Tourist Pasture (fenced). Anglers eager to practice their art may wish to sample the good-to-excellent fishing for golden and brook trout at Rocky Basin Lakes (see trip 87).

4th Hiking Day (**Big Whitney Meadow** to **Little Whitney Meadow**, 10 miles): Passing the fenced "Tourist Pasture," the winding meadow trail continues south over rolling terrain. Cattle-grazing permits are dispensed for this meadow and Little Whitney Meadow; hence the traveler may expect bovine company on these grassy sections. Many wildflowers line the route through the southern arm of the meadow and subsequent trail, including shooting star, monkey flower, lupine, wallflower, penstemon, mountain aster, cream cup, scarlet gilia, white cinquefoil, Bigelow sneezeweed and pussy paws. The sandy surface of the meadow trail continues into the moderate-to-dense forest cover of lodgepole and foxtail pine below. Shortly after re-entering forest cover, the trail fords Barigan Stringer and passes several nearby campsites. The polished granite canyon walls narrow, and the stream quickens for about ½ mile, and then as the canyon opens somewhat our trail passes the Barigan Stringer Trail (several campsites here). Anglers who wish to sample the good fishing on Golden Trout Creek will find plentiful golden (to 8"). This creek was the original source for fish used in subsequent plantings throughout the higher lakes and streams of the Sierra. The first recorded account of the discovery of the golden trout of this stream reflects the excitement of the writer, Dr. Barton Everman:

> This is the most beautiful of all the trouts: the brilliancy and richness of its coloration is not equaled in any other known species; the delicate golden olive of the head, back, and upper part of the side, the clear golden yellow along and below the lateral line, and the marvelously rich cadmium of the under parts fully entitle this species to be known above all others as *the* golden trout.*

The Golden Trout of the Southern High Sierras, Bulletin, Bureau of Fisheries, 1905, V. 25, p. 28.

With patriotic fervor the doctor named this trout *Salmo roosevelti*, after then-President Theodore Roosevelt—fortunately, this name, labeling an animal with a man's name, has not gained widespread use.

Beyond the Barigan Stringer Trail junction our trail continues a moderate sandy descent past several more campsites to the ford of Golden Trout Creek. Mounting a sandy shelf above the creek, the trail descends gently past the Tunnel Air Camp/Carroll Creek Trail to the multibuilding complex of Tunnel Guard Station (emergency services available). The final descent to the guard station affords views of the open reaches of the valley, and of the red-topped volcanic hills to the southwest. Just beyond the Tunnel Guard Station our route passes the Ramshaw Meadow Trail branching east, and then turns west to ford Golden Trout Creek. Fishing on Golden Trout Creek below Tunnel Guard Station is restricted to artificial lures.

Across sandy, moderately forested, level terrain, the faint trail (boggy and heavily trampled by cattle) stays well north of the creek, and passes the unmaintained trail to Groundhog Meadow. Rejoining the creek, the trail continues westerly, winding along the northernmost edge of a large late Pleistocene volcanic flow (post-glacial) known as Malpais Lava. The largest single concentration of volcanic action in the upper reaches of the Kern, this basalt flow shows itself near the trail in brilliant displays of colored rock. Predominant in the volcanic rock is a deep red, sometimes mixed with ochres and shades of tan. These colorful displays accompany the traveler all the way down this drainage, but the interested rockhound can see extensive fields of this rock by fording the creek and exploring the mile-wide strip of old lava flow to the south. Just east of Little Whitney Meadow, our trail drops steeply, and after passing the unmaintained trail to Salt Lick Meadow, fords Golden Trout Creek. On the west side of this meadowed ford are several good campsites (8420'). Fishing for golden in Golden Trout Creek (to 8") is good.

5th Hiking Day (**Little Whitney Meadow** to **Rattlesnake Creek/Kern River**, 11 miles): The trail skirts the southern end of beautiful Little Whitney Meadow, and passes another "Tourist Pasture." Descending steadily over a dusty, granite sand surface, the trail then refords Golden Trout Creek. Then, as the route continues its steady descent, the trail surface becomes pumice, and the forest cover of lodgepole gives way to Jeffrey and juniper. Large concentrations of wildflowers daub the opener stretches with yellows (monkey flower), whites (white Mariposa), mixed blues and purples (larkspur and penstemon), and reds (red dogwood). Leveling out to a moderate descent, the trail then recrosses a tributary of

Golden Trout Creek via a natural bridge of basalt. Easily eroded, this pink rock shows extensive water cutting and sculpting. After Natural Bridge, the grade of the trail steepens to a steady descent over pumice and sand through a forest cover of Jeffrey, white fir and some lodgepole. At the switchbacks dropping to the Kern Canyon floor, one can see the clearly delineated volcanic overlay with its subsurface of granite where the underlying rock has been laid bare by subsequent stream cutting that has knifed through the basalt layer and exposed a rainbow of blacks, reds, tans and whites. Some columnar basalt formations, usually associated with these lava flows, may also be seen to the north. Volcano Falls provides excellent views on the right as the trail twines steeply down over pumice and rock, and far to the north, above the west canyon wall, one has fleeting glimpses of Mt. Kaweah.

With the lower altitude come sugar pine and, on the canyon floor, quaking aspen, birch, black oak and incense-cedar. It is not until the canyon floor is reached that one has views of domelike Tower Rock to the south. Through a sparse forest cover and clumps of sage, manzanita, willows and chinquapin, the trail veers south to cross the Kern River (footbridge), and then pass the Kern Canyon Ranger Station (emergency services available). At the ranger station, our route meets and turns right onto the Kern Canyon Trail, and ascends the Kern Canyon by a series of moderate ups and downs. The forest cover is usually dense, with tiny wet sections that are made difficult of passage by dense concentrations of bracken fern. Their luxuriant growth is commonly associated with canyon bottoms, and they are frequently found in conjunction with riverside stands of alder, laurel, aspen and birch. The approach to Lower Funston Meadow is heralded by the lower drift fence, and then the trail begins a steady climb over the alluvial fan that results from Laurel Creek's contribution of silt and rock on the canyon floor. Fording Laurel Creek is accomplished via two crossings, each marked by a campsite; during high water, the second ford is sometimes hazardous.

Fishing in the Kern River, particularly near the confluences of the many tributary streams, is excellent. Angling is sometimes made difficult by the thickets of willows lining the river, but the rewards in rainbow trout (to 20″) more than make up for the casting problems. Fishermen, or those who simply enjoy the view from streamside, should keep a sharp eye out for beavers that work this section of the river. It is not surprising that one usually makes many wild animal sightings while traveling up this glacially carved trench. Animals, like men, are "channeled" down its steep-walled course, and within the canyon's relatively confined course, the hiker is apt to see bear, coyote, deer and the aforementioned beaver. From Laurel Creek the trail continues north through a moderate forest. Mostly duff, the trail surface makes pleasant walking, and the distance to the Rattlesnake Creek Trail junction is rapidly covered. At this junction, and just across the sometimes difficult ford of Rattlesnake Creek are excellent packer campsites (6600′). Fishing is as cited above. (Note: Yes, there are rattlesnakes in this area.)

6th Hiking Day (**Rattlesnake Creek/Kern River** to **Upper Rattlesnake Creek**, 8 miles): Reverse the 2nd hiking day, trip 100.

7th Hiking Day (**Upper Rattlesnake Creek** to **Mineral King,** 10½ miles): Reverse the 1st hiking day, trip 96.

Great Western Divide from Old Army Pass   *Kurt Rademacher*

87 Horseshoe Meadow to Rocky Basin Lakes

TRIP   From Horseshoe Meadow to Rocky Basin Lakes via Cottonwood Pass, Big Whitney Meadow (round trip). Topo maps *Olancha, Kern Peak*. Best mid or late season; 28 miles.

Grade	Trail/layover days	Total recommended days
Leisurely	6/2	8
Moderate	4/2	6
Strenuous	3/2	5

HILITES   The fine angling enjoyed at the culmination of this trip should make it a good selection for the intermediate hiker who wants good recreation as well as a challenging route.

DESCRIPTION (Moderate trip)

1st Hiking Day (**Horseshoe Meadow** to **Stokes Stringer Campsites**, 5 miles): The trail leaves the end of the Horseshoe Meadow Road on an upgrade that quickly flattens out after forking right at a junction with the Tunnel Meadow Trail. Breaks in the lodgepole and foxtail pine forest permit views to the south and west of Mulkey Pass, Trail Pass, Trail Peak, Cottonwood Pass and Cirque Peak. The rerouted trail along the forest margin is giving the overrutted meadows a chance to recover something like their pre-man condition—although ecological changes never exactly reverse themselves. On the long, gradual ascent west up the meadow, hikers who get an early start are sure to come upon a few late-grazing deer, and along with many other birds they may well see a long-eared owl, a resident of these grasslands. Usually this predatory bird is seen while swooping down on its prey—meadow mice, deer mice and other rodents, but in very early season it is sometimes seen in family groups among the willows near the stream.

The meadowy path passes a lateral trail to Cottonwood Creek, crosses an unmapped stream, and then boulderhops an unnamed stream near a 75-year-old cabin with fair campsites nearby. Eighteen gentle switchbacks bring one to a meadow heavy with willows, paintbrush, columbine and penstemon. Then a replay of 18 more switchbacks suffices to mount a rocky saddle, Cottonwood Pass. Views eastward include the Inyo and Panamint ranges, and to the west are the more Sierralike Great Western Divide and Kaweah Peaks Ridge. A few feet west of the pass, the Pacific Crest Trail veers right toward Chicken Spring Lake, and from this junction our route descends alpine slopes for ½ mile to the several fair campsites on Stokes Stringer.

2nd Hiking Day (**Stokes Stringer Campsites** to **Rocky Basin Lakes**, 9 miles): An easy downhill stroll looking west at a feast of peaks precedes a steeper slope, where 26 switchbacks are required to get down to a ford of Stokes Stringer, with good campsites nearby. The trail then zigzags down the last hill to the eastern precincts of Big Whitney Meadow. Most of the tiny creeks meandering through this enormous graze-land are as unhealthy as they look, and need purifying pills. After fording Stokes Stringer again, the trail crosses a forested island in the middle of the overgrazed meadow. Then the sandy path passes a shortcut to the Siberian Pass Trail, followed in a long half mile by the Siberian Pass Trail itself. Here we veer left and stroll 300 yards southwest past a large, dusty campsite to a junction where the Rocky Basin Lakes Trail leads west.

Our trail leaves the campsites on a moderate southwest ascent through dense and sometimes moderate stands of lodgepole and foxtail. This ascent makes a long, dusty southwest traverse of the moraine just west of Big Whitney Meadow, and then descends to the banks of Barigan Stringer, where it meets and turns right onto the Barigan Stringer Trail. The ascent following this junction is gentle, then moderate over increasingly rocky underfooting. The foxtail and lodgepole pine forest cover lining either side of this ravine ascent is a favorite habitat for a great variety of birdlife, including the long-eared owl, Steller jay, robin, chickadee, junco, calliope hummingbird, Clark nutcracker and rosy finch. The latter is often one's only contact with birdlife at the higher elevations, and is a frequently seen companion on exploratory trips around the rocky, barren expanses of Funston Lake. The trail emerges at the east end of the westernmost lake of the group. The north and west walls of this high cirque basin are heavily fractured granite, and are a haven for marmots. Crossing to the northeast corner of the westernmost lake, our route finishes at the fair campsites situated in a sparse stand of foxtail pines. Fishing for golden (to 16″) is good to excellent in all the lakes of this basin. Farther away, the fish at Johnson Lake are generally smaller, but equally abundant. Large fish have also been taken from Funston Lake.

3rd and 4th Hiking Days: Retrace your steps, 14 miles.

88   Cottonwood Creek Trailhead to Whitney Portal

TRIP
From Cottonwood Creek Trailhead to Whitney Portal via New Army Pass, Rock Creek, Crabtree Meadow, John Muir Trail (shuttle trip). Topo maps *Olancha*, *Kern Peak*, *Mt. Whitney*, *Lone Pine*. Best mid or late season; 39 miles.

Grade	Trail/layover days	Total recommended days
Leisurely	6/2	8
Moderate	5/1	6
Strenuous	4/0	4

HILITES
This fine shuttle trip surveys the Sierra crest from New Army Pass to Whitney Portal. Dozens of lakes are within a half day's walk from the campsites at the ends of these hiking days, making this selection a choice one for anglers.

DESCRIPTION (Leisurely trip)

1st and 2nd Hiking Days: Follow trip 84 to **Upper Rock Creek Lake**, 13 miles.

3rd Hiking Day (**Upper Rock Creek Lake** to **Lower Rock Creek Ford**, 4 miles): This short hiking day is an easy tramp down Rock Creek. This tumbling rill slows to a murmuring brook in the meadow flats, and its fresh-from-the-source waters are crystal clear and icy cold. Leaving the shallow outlet of Upper Rock Creek Lake, the trail descends steadily alongside the now-cascading stream. The dense green panoply overhead of foxtail pine and occasional lodgepole allows only sparse, shade-loving clumps of gooseberry to grow along the trail, but the virile willow maintains its verdant stream-bank growth, shade or sun. Willow growth is synonymous with birdlife, and Rock Creek has its share of robins, white-crowned sparrows, chickadees, juncos, woodpeckers and olive-sided flycatchers. It is often the "oh-see view" call of this flycatcher that reminds the passerby of the beauty of his surroundings—surroundings that, on this canyon descent, include a chain of lovely meadows. Unfortunately, this native tour guide leaves these environs in August, and the late-season traveler is left to rely on his own initiative.

In the middle of the second large meadow, the trail fords Rock Creek (difficult in high water) and veers away from the stream. Interestingly enough, most anglers ignore the waters of this tiny creek and thereby miss some fine fishing for golden. The fish are not too large, but there are several in every hole. The trail makes a reunion with the creek in a large, rolling meadow just above the ford by the campsites, where it passes the Siberian Pass Trail. (The tiny fenced plots in the meadow are Park meadow research areas, and should not be tampered with.) At the west end of the meadow, the trail descends to the good campsites at the log ford of lower Rock Creek (9500'). Here, fishing is good for golden (to 8"). *4th Hiking Day* (**Lower Rock Creek Ford** to **Crabtree Ranger Station**, 7 miles): Fording the stream, the trail climbs steeply up the north wall of the canyon, then levels somewhat to the ford of Guyot Creek. The jumbled, symmetrical crest of Mt. Guyot takes up the skyline to the west, and highly fractured Joe Devel Peak looms to the east as the trail begins another moderate ascent through a dense forest cover of lodgepole pine. This bouldery climb culminates at a saddle from which there are good views north across the Kern Canyon to the Kern-Kaweah drainage, Red Spur, Kern Ridge and the Great Western Divide. From the saddle, the trail descends moderately to the large sandy basin of Guyot Flat. Like the Chagoopa Plateau across the canyon, this flat and the subsequent "shelf" traversed later in this hiking day were part of an immense valley floor in preglacial times. However, much of the granular sand deposits are a result of later weathering and erosion of the granite peaks to the east.

Beyond Guyot Flat the trail undulates through a moderate forest cover before dropping steeply into the Whitney Creek drainage. The descent into this drainage affords views eastward to Mt. Whitney—the long, flat-topped, avalanche-chuted mountain that towers over the nearer, granite-spired shoulder of Mt. Hitchcock. This descent concludes over a barren, rocky stretch to Lower Crabtree Meadow, where, just beyond a good campsite, our route fords Whitney Creek and turns right (east) along its north bank. A half mile of gentle ascent ends at Upper Crabtree Meadow, where the route passes the Crabtree Lakes Trail. (This unmaintained trail leads to the good fishing on Crabtree Lakes

for golden, to 14″.) Continuing northeast beside Whitney Creek the trail ascends gently to meet the John Muir Trail immediately west of a ford of Whitney Creek. Beyond this ford is the Crabtree Ranger Station (emergency services available) and good campsites, where fishing in Whitney Creek is fair for golden (to 7″).
5th and 6th Hiking Days: Reverse the 2nd and 1st hiking days, trip 73, 15 miles.

Mt. Langley from Cottonwood Basin   *Kurt Rademacher*

Horseshoe Meadow to Whitney Portal   **89**

TRIP From Horseshoe Meadow to Whitney Portal via Cottonwood Pass, Rock Creek, Crabtree Meadow, John Muir Trail (shuttle trip). Topo maps *Olancha, Kern Peak, Mt. Whitney, Lone Pine*. Best mid or late season; 38 miles.

Grade	Trail/layover days	Total recommended days
Leisurely	6/2	8
Moderate	5/1	6
Strenuous	4/0	4

HILITES Crossing three passes, this route tarries in four drainages, offering a multitude of chances for angling that ranges from good to excellent. The scenery that graces most of this trail is exceeded nowhere in the Sierra, having an abundance of peaks exceeding 13,000 feet, and dozens of high, granitic cirque basins.

DESCRIPTION (Moderate trip)

1st Hiking Day (**Horseshoe Meadow** to **Chicken Spring Lake**, 5½ miles): Follow the 1st hiking day, trip 87 to Cottonwood Pass. At the pass we meet the Pacific Crest Trail and turn right onto it for 1 easy mile on level, dynamited footing to the good campsites east of the outlet of Chicken Spring Lake.

2nd Hiking Day (**Chicken Spring Lake** to **Lower Rock Creek Ford**, 10½ miles): There is no water until Siberian Outpost, so fill your canteen. The Pacific Crest Trail switchbacks westward up the wall of the Chicken Spring Lake cirque and then levels off over sandy slopes at the headwaters of Golden Trout Creek. After contouring around an intermittent pond in another cirque, our route leaves Kern County at an unnamed point (11,350') on a ridge west of Cirque Peak. From here we traverse northwest, then double back sharply south to Siberian Pass. (When the Pacific Crest Trail segment west from the hairpin turn is completed, the hiker will have a shorter route to Lower Rock Creek.)

At the pass our route leads a few yards south before turning left (west) across the open, gravelly expanses of Siberian Outpost. Green-rimmed runoff streams wind through these barren reaches, but the feeling that usually attends these wide-open spaces is one of desolation. This impression is heightened by the presence of numerous golden foxtail snags that stand like lonely sentinels around the periphery. Along the stream the telltale network of wormlike dirt piles betrays the presence of pocket gophers. Consistently good views of Miter Basin to the north attend the gentle descent along Siberian Pass Creek until forest cover is reached 2 miles to the west. The pleasantly winding trail continues its gentle-to-moderate downgrade through meadowy sections in which the nearby forest cover is first foxtail only, but later includes lodgepole. Leaving the last large meadow, the trail swings north away from Siberian Pass Creek on a descent that steepens and finally resolves into steep, rocky switchbacks. The forest cover, now predominantly lodgepole, thins as the trail levels and then emerges into lower Rock Creek meadow. Midway across the meadow our route meets the Rock Creek Trail and turns left (west) onto it. This wild, grassy meadow is filled with wildflowers, and they make a colorful backdrop for the meandering stream that touches the eastern end. (The fenced plots of meadow are part of a Park meadow research project, and should not be tampered with.) From the meadow it is but a short distance to the good campsites at the ford of lower Rock Creek (9500'), where fishing for golden (to 8") is good.

3rd, 4th and 5th Hiking Days: Follow trip 88, the 4th through the 6th hiking days, 22 miles.

Mineral King to Upper Cliff Creek **90**

TRIP   From Mineral King to Upper Cliff Creek (round trip). Topo map *Mineral King*. Best midseason; 17 miles.

Grade	Trail/layover days	Total recom- mended days
Leisurely	....	....
Moderate	2/0	2
Strenuous	....	....

HILITES   This is one of the easiest hikes into National Park wilderness in the western High Sierra, but still tough enough that the hiker will feel he has earned the privacy that awaits on the banks of Cliff Creek.

DESCRIPTION

1st Hiking Day (**Mineral King** to **Upper Cliff Creek**, 8½ miles): From the Timber Gap/Sawtooth Pass trailhead one mile beyond the Guard station in Mineral King Valley, our route ascends the sagebrush-flanked Sawtooth Pass Trail for ½ mile, and then diverges left at a signed junction. Our fork climbs relentlessly up on a southwest-facing slope that is warm indeed in midsummer, but blessed by some shade from juniper and red-fir trees. After a steep series of switchbacks, we climb more gently across a meadow and then enter a cool stand of red fir, which comes to include lodgepole and foxtail pine. According to a Forest Service sign, the world's largest known foxtail pine tree is on this slope.

This ascent tops out at Timber Gap (9400'), where we enter Sequoia National Park and begin to drop steeply in more forest. During early summer in this forest, hikers may hear the thumping of blue grouse and the melodic flutings of hermit thrushes. As we descend above Timber Gap Creek, we find the streams on the slope sometimes disappearing into the loosely consolidated metamorphic rock. Then the trail rounds the nose of the ridge on the east and switchbacks down to Cliff Creek through dense coniferous forest.

Beyond a ford of Cliff Creek are fair campsites and a junction with the trail to Redwood Meadow. After turning right, uphill through the campsites, our route climbs steadily through alternating brush and trees. In early summer the fine wildflower display near the creek includes Mariposa lily, rein orchis, wild strawberry, monkey flower, wallflower, corn lily, delphinium, yellow-throated gilia, yarrow and buckwheat. Beyond a grove of tree-sized willows near the creek our route goes out onto what looks like an abandoned stream bed, and ducks lead us right up to the base of the prominent falls of Cliff Creek. Here we finally veer away from the stream and climb to the left through dense willow, sagebrush, whitethorn and bitter cherry. Then our trail crosses the outlet stream of Pinto Lake, tops a small rise, and arrives at a three-way junction. The left fork is the trail to Black Rock Pass, and the right fork leads to good campsites near Cliff Creek.

2nd Hiking Day: Retrace your steps, 8½ miles.

Mineral King Road

Les Avery

Mineral King to Little Five Lakes **91**

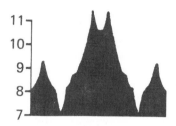

TRIP From Mineral King to Little Five Lakes via Cliff Creek, Black Rock Pass (round trip). Topo map *Mineral King*. Best mid or late season; 29 miles.

Grade	Trail/layover days	Total recommended days
Leisurely	5/2	7
Moderate	4/1	5
Strenuous	4/0	4

HILITES Next to the Sierra crest itself, the Great Western Divide is the most spectacular feature in Sequoia National Park. This trip crosses that sky-piercing divide at Black Rock Pass and leads to a large number of lakes to camp beside, all of them close under the colorful cliffs and peaks of the divide.

DESCRIPTION (Moderate trip)

1st Hiking Day (**Mineral King** to **Upper Cliff Creek,** 8½ miles): Follow the 1st hiking day, trip 90.

2nd Hiking Day (**Upper Cliff Creek** to **Little Five Lakes,** 6 miles): After crossing the meadows south of Pinto Lake, this day's route begins a 3000-foot ascent to Black Rock Pass. Given an early start, the hiker should be able to make it to the pass before the heat of the day reaches its maximum. Scattered foxtail pines dot the mostly open slopes, and in early summer wildflower gardens abound on the slopes above Cliff Creek, with their heather, paintbrush, phlox, wallflower, wild onion, groundsel and forget-me-nots. Pinto Lake comes into view below, a very small pond at the base of a talus slope. Past a series of meadows the trail begins the switchbacking slog to the pass, and views of the upper basin of Cliff Creek include the cascades below Spring Lake, Spring Lake itself, and then Cyclamen Lake, icebound in early summer. The solitary traveler, moving quietly, will see numerous deer on these subalpine slopes. Finally the rocky path attains Black Rock Pass, and a good rest stop affords moments for viewing the vast scene ahead. The companion basins of Little Five Lakes and Big Five Lakes drop off into Big Arroyo, and beyond this chasm rise the multicolored, cliffbound Kaweah Peaks. Farther east is the 14,000-foot Whitney Crest.

From the pass, the zigzagging downgrade trends southeast and then angles northeast to pass above the highest of the Little Five Lakes—actually over one dozen lakes. (When snow obscures the trail in early season, one should keep to the left so as not to get off-route too far to the right and come out onto some cliffs.) Little groves of lodgepole and foxtail pine at the second lake enhance the camping possibilities, and an evening meal here may be raised to four-star quality by the alpenglow on the Kaweah Peaks across Big Arroyo.

3rd and 4th Hiking Days: Retrace your steps, 14½ miles.

Northeast from Black Rock Pass   *Ron Felzer*

Mineral King to Nine Lake Basin   **92**

TRIP   From Mineral King to Nine Lake Basin via Timber
            Gap, Black Rock Pass and Big Arroyo (round trip).
            Topo maps *Mineral King, Triple Divide Peak*. Best
            mid or late season; 42 miles.

Grade	Trail/layover days	Total recommended days
Leisurely	8/3	11
Moderate	6/2	8
Strenuous	4/1	5

HILITES   Nine Lake Basin offers the seclusion that places not
            reached by maintained trail always possess. Located
            in a south-facing amphitheater between the tower-
            ing Great Western Divide and the blade-topped
            Kaweah Peaks Ridge, this lake basin is a perfect
            place to explore, fish, climb, photograph and recover
            your sense of marvel at nature's bounty.

DESCRIPTION (Moderate trip)

1st and 2nd Hiking Days: Follow trip 91 to **Little Five Lakes,** 14½
miles.

3rd Hiking Day (**Little Five Lakes** to **Nine Lake Basin,** 6½ miles):
Just below the second of the Little Five Lakes, our trail fords the
outlet and passes a trail to Big Five Lakes. We continue down
beside the tumbling stream past the next lake in the chain, then
ford the stream back to its north side. Soon the trail crosses the
outlet of the northern cluster of Little Five Lakes, and the trout in
this stream promise action to the angler who is willing to sweat
his way up to the lakes above.

After an easy rise out of the basin, the trail begins to descend
into Big Arroyo, a large right-bank tributary of the Kern River.
Diverging north of the topo-map trail, the actual trail reaches Big
Arroyo Creek about ½ mile upstream from the map ford. Beyond

the ford, an unsigned trail leads down Big Arroyo and our trail in a few yards meets the High Sierra Trail just east of a patrol cabin, also incorrectly located on the map. (Numerous extra paths in this trail-nexus area complicate the picture, and the hiker should take care that he leaves the area on the trail he wants.) We turn left (northwest) on this backcountry arterial and ascend gently up the broad glacial valley past numerous possible campsites with great views of granitic Lippincott Mountain and Eagle Scout Peak towering in the west, and metamorphic Black Kaweah and Red Kaweah piercing the eastern sky. The trail fords Big Arroyo Creek again and then climbs over grassy pockets and granite slabs toward Kaweah Gap, a distinctive low spot on the Great Western Divide in the northwest. Where this route swings west, an unmapped trail takes off north into Nine Lake Basin, and it soon arrives at the magnet-shaped first lake, with numerous fair-to-good campsites and good fishing for brook trout. A base camp here makes a springboard for excursions to the increasingly secluded and dramatic lakes north and east, and for climbing expeditions to the wealth of steep faces west and east of this fine base camp.

4th, 5th and 6th Hiking Days: Retrace your steps, 21 miles.

Blue flax

Thomas Winnett

Mineral King to Hamilton Lakes 93

TRIP From Mineral King to Hamilton Lakes via Timber Gap, Black Rock Pass, Big Arroyo, Kaweah Gap; return via Bearpaw Meadow, Redwood Meadow, Timber Gap (semiloop trip). Topo maps *Mineral King, Triple Divide Peak*. Best mid or late season; 43 miles.

Grade	Trail/layover days	Total recom- mended days
Leisurely	8/4	12
Moderate	7/3	10
Strenuous	5/2	7

HILITES Backpackers who want to sample the multifold attractions of Sequoia National Park will find in this one trip high passes and barren divides, subalpine stream valleys, inviting glacial lake basins, middle-altitude meadows, deep river canyons and giant sequoia groves.

DESCRIPTION (Moderate trip)

1st, 2nd and 3rd Hiking Days: Follow trip 92 to **Nine Lake Basin,** 21 miles.

4th Hiking Day (**Nine Lake Basin** to **Hamilton Lakes,** 4 miles): After retracing the steps to the High Sierra Trail, this route turns right (west) and quickly climbs the few hundred feet to Kaweah Gap (10,640'). This pass on the Great Western Divide lies between the waters of the Kern River and the Kaweah River, and it affords views of many of the peaks whose snow-clad slopes give birth to these rivers. From the pass, our route drops moderately and then

more steeply in granite sand. Early-season hikers are likely to see
some gray-crowned rosy finches feeding on aphids and other in-
sects that were blown onto the late-melting snow from lower elevations. The near-vertical faces of Mt. Stewart and Eagle Scout
Peak "cradle" the trail as it passes aptly named Precipice Lake.
This vertical world will delight photographers, especially early in
the day, and few of them will resist the spectacle of a channel for
the trail that was blasted out of the canyon wall to create a "tunnel" open on one side—the cliff side. On these cliffs, white-
throated swifts twinkle by, giving their mocking, laughlike cry as
the trail drops and drops, 2000 feet in about 2 miles. A long
switchback leg delivers the weary-kneed hiker to the west shore
of Upper Hamilton Lake (8235'), where there are several good
campsites around the glacially polished granite near the outlet.
Views from the campsites, including the silver waterfall ribbon
across the lake, are superb, and fishing is good for golden, rainbow and brook trout (to 16").

5th Hiking Day (**Hamilton Lakes** to **Little Bearpaw Meadow**, 5½
miles): From the campsites, the trail crosses Hamilton Creek just
below the outlet and descends in or near the riparian vegetation
along the stream. Below Lower Hamilton Lake the descending
trail refords the creek and then contours along an increasingly
steep rock face that gives a second and equally apt meaning to the
name of this trail, the *High* Sierra Trail.

Now off the cliff face, our route swings north to a culvert crossing of Lone Pine Creek above its gorge. From this creek to Bearpaw Meadow, the trail climbs more than it drops, as we traverse
the steep walls high above River Valley. Views back toward the
Great Western Divide and the glacier-carved canyons of Eagle
Scout, Hamilton and Granite creeks emanating from it are awesome. The trail has lost much elevation since leaving Kaweah
Gap, and it now enters mid-elevation vegetation of mountain
chaparral, Jeffrey pine, red and white fir, and black oak.

As we enter the Bearpaw Meadow area, the ranger station appears north of the trail, and south of it the tents of Bearpaw
Meadow Camp, where meals, lodging and candy bars can be
bought during the summer. We take the first trail to the left
through the campground, toward Redwood Meadow. This
campground gets heavy use, and it is dirty. More secluded campsites may be found at Little Bearpaw Meadow, about a mile south
on a gently descending trail that winds down under white fir,
incense-cedar and sugar pine.

6th Hiking Day (**Little Bearpaw Meadow** to **Cliff Creek**, 6½ miles):
Below Little Bearpaw Meadow we pass an unmarked trail to the
right and continue our descent in mid-elevation mixed forest. The

spicy scent of mountain misery is heavy in the air. At the bottom of this descent the trail crosses the Middle Fork of the Kaweah downstream on logs. Then our trail climbs slightly past a junction with a little-used trail down the Middle Fork, and we continue ahead, soon reaching cascading Eagle Scout Creek.

Rounding the next ridge, we come to Granite Creek, which is a roaring torrent in early season. An easy crossing by bridge and another short climb over a ridge in timber lead us to our last descent before Redwood Meadow. Even before we reach the meadow, we encounter red columnar giants standing tall among the lesser firs and pines in this forest. These are the giant sequoias, Sierra redwoods or big trees, earth's largest living things. However, as in most sequoia stands, there is not much reproduction of the giants here, because to reproduce they need disturbances like fires or landslides—ecological events which have not occurred here for some time—to clear the soil.

Our trail skirts the fenced meadow, where grazing is limited, and arrives at the Redwood Meadow Ranger Station. Camping is limited in this very peaceful place, as water is scarce. The trail climbs steadily, gradually leaving the big trees for mixed pine and fir, with patches of manzanita. Coralroot, a root parasite, grows here along the trail, commonly under firs and pines, where it feeds on living tree roots. Our route undulates through heavy forest for several miles, toward Cliff Creek and then away from it, and finally arrives at the fair campsites near the junction by Cliff Creek that we passed on the 1st hiking day.

7th Hiking Day (**Cliff Creek** to **Mineral King**, 6 miles): Retrace the steps of part of the 1st hiking day.

In a field of mule ears *Jeff Schaffer*

94 Mineral King to Spring Lake

TRIP From Mineral King to Spring Lake via Glacier Pass (round trip). Topo map *Mineral King.* Best mid-season; 10 miles.

Grade	Trail/layover days	Total recom- mended days
Leisurely	....	....
Moderate	....	....
Strenuous	2/0	2

HILITES This "weekender" makes a fine exercise for the experienced backpacker in good condition. This route sidesteps the main Great Western Divide crest, and crosses the Empire Mountain ridge by a little-used pass to beautiful Spring Lake. Rugged peaks, mirror-like tarns, possibilities for exploring old "prospects" and cascading streams are the rewards for a difficult climb. This trip is recommended for the hardier breed of hiker with experience in the hazards of cross-country travel.

DESCRIPTION (Strenuous trip)

1st Hiking Day (**Mineral King** to **Spring Lake,** 5 miles, part cross country): Beginning from the dirt parking lot on the north side of the road, at the point where the road bends south ("Harry's Bend") our trail jogs north and then turns east on ascending switchbacks. This dusty, oft-eroded trail winds up a dry slope of manzanita and chinquapin, offering some views, from the south ends of the switchbacks, up the Mineral King valley to Farewell Gap. Keeping to the right, our trail passes the Timber Gap Trail branching north, and continues east up the Monarch Creek drainage. Few trees screen this trail from the sun, but the rank manzanita thickets along the trail are, as one oldtimer put it, "shoulder high to a growed elephant." Sometimes but not always visible from the trail, Monarch Creek splashes down to the valley in a series of granite-bottomed falls from the "false cirque" just above. This bowl does, at first glance, appear to be a true cirque—the womb of a glacial *mer de glace*—but as the traveler continues, he will see that it is merely where the river of ice mid-way down the slope discovered a schistic weakness in the under-lying rock, and ground down on its heel, carving, scraping and sculpting the resulting amphitheater. Early local residents (the human sort) brought their eastern terminology to this country and, in honor of the many marmots that inhabit the rocky fringe of the grassy-bottomed bowl, named it Groundhog Meadow.

At Groundhog Meadow we take the right trail fork across Monarch Creek. The left fork climbs directly up the canyon to-ward Sawtooth Pass and Glacier Pass. However, this trail is on unstable talus and it is no longer maintained.

We pass a fair campsite and begin a series of long switchbacks which take us through open stands of red fir, silver pine and fox-tail pine with an understory of chinquapin, currant, gooseberry and lupine. The trail crosses a ridge in timber, and just beyond the next bend is a nice lunch stop, where there are seats cut from logs, and piped water. A short way up the trail from this lunch spot, a trail takes off to Crystal Lake.

Our trail, the new Monarch Lakes Trail, rounds a shoulder, and we can see the old trail across the canyon below, as well as Timber Gap, the Great Western Divide and Sawtooth Pass. We cross two forks of Monarch Creek and arrive at Lower Monarch Lake (10,380'), where camping is good. A well-defined trail goes around the north side of the lake and climbs through willows to Upper Monarch Lake (10,640'), which is dammed and lacks campsites.

The trail to Sawtooth Pass continues northward and drops a little through willows and corn lilies to an unsigned junction. Here we turn right and begin climbing steeply north up the ridge through paintbrush, wild buckwheat and various yellow flowers related to daisies. One is well advised to stay to the left and not to get onto the steep, loose, granite sand that leads directly up to-ward the pass. Instead, we follow ducks toward the ridge to the north. At the crest numerous tracks head for Glacier Pass, which lies a few hundred yards farther north.

Glacier Pass (11,100') is not named on the topo map, but is the next saddle west on the Sequoia National Park boundary. Views of the Cliff Creek drainage and barren Mt. Eisen are impressive, and they attend the hiker as he scrambles down the north side of the pass. Those with an exploratory bent may wish to detour across the barren granite slopes to the west, northeast of the summit of Empire Mountain, to the cairn-marked gold prospects and mines that dot the upper slopes.

This side of the pass is frequently covered with late-melting snow, and care should be taken to keep to the tundra-topped granite ledges east of and above the tarn beginnings of the west tributary of Spring Lake. Here a faint trail (sometimes ducked, sometimes worn into the grass) descends steeply to ford the tributary just above its final plunge into Spring Lake. The trail then traverses the sparsely timbered west slope of the Spring Lake cirque to the good campsites (somewhat exposed) at the northwest end and at the outlet of the lake (10,050'). Fishing for brook (to 8″) is good. Views from the campsites of the sheer, smoothed granite headwall at the south end of the lake fill the viewer with a sense of awe and respect for the glacier's power.
2nd Hiking Day: Retrace your steps, 5 miles.

Kaweah Peaks Ridge

Thomas Winnett

Mineral King to Lost Canyon   **95**

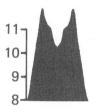

TRIP From Mineral King to Lost Canyon via Sawtooth Pass, Columbine Lake (round trip). Topo map *Mineral King*. Best midseason; 13 miles.

Grade	Trail/layover days	Total recom-mended days
Leisurely	....	....
Moderate	....	....
Strenuous	2/1	3

HILITES Strictly a knapsacker's route, this trail traces the Monarch Creek drainage to cross the Great Western Divide at Sawtooth Pass. High alpine scenery climaxed by the cold, often ice-filled waters of Columbine Lake make this a fine route for all who love the High Sierra. The excellent fishing in the upper Lost Canyon drainage will reward the angler who is willing to "walk for his supper."

DESCRIPTION (Strenuous trip)

1st Hiking Day (**Mineral King** to **Upper Lost Canyon,** 6½ miles): Follow the 1st hiking day, trip 94, to the crest where tracks lead north toward Glacier Pass. From here we climb to our right and finally top Sawtooth Pass (11,600′). From the summit of this high-ridged pass there are vistas of the surrounding country exceeded only by those from the tops of nearby Sawtooth Peak and Needham Mountain. One can see the length of the Monarch Creek drainage to the west, and on down into the wooded drainage of the East Fork Kaweah River. Empire Mountain and the ridge to its southeast dominate the view to the north, Sawtooth Peak and Mineral Peak divide the skyline to the south, and to the east one looks across the barren reaches of Columbine Lake, Lost Canyon and Big Arroyo to the timbered reaches of the Chagoopa Plateau. Far on the eastern horizon, one can see the Mt. Whitney complex of peaks, and a part of the backbone of the Sierra.

The descent on the east side of Sawtooth Pass, like the western ascent, is a steep, rocky, zigzagging affair that will give the knapsacker little chance to look at the spectacular scenery. This trail continues down, dropping steeply as it makes a long traverse on the north side of Columbine Lake. Here glacially scoured granite slabs tilt into the lake's usually mirrorlike surface. The reflections of the nearby mineralized, rust-colored rocks blend with the chalkier whites of the lakeside granites to leave an indelible impression of mellowness in the passerby's mind—this despite the basin's look of harsh, treeless sterility.

After rounding the north side of the lake, our route drops steeply down to the headwaters of Lost Canyon on a rocky surface that does not give way to grass and trees until one is almost due north of the westernmost spire of Needham Mountain. Here good campsites will be found in an open, grassy setting (10,200') amid a sparse forest cover of stunted lodgepole pine. Fishing for brook trout farther downstream is excellent.

2nd Hiking Day: Retrace your steps, 6½ miles.

The Palisades from Mather Pass   *Jason Winnett*

Mineral King to Upper Rattlesnake Creek **96**

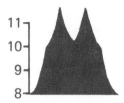

TRIP From Mineral King to Campsites, Upper Rattlesnake Creek via Franklin Pass (round trip). Topo map *Mineral King*. Best mid or late season; 21 miles.

Grade	Trail/layover days	Total recommended days
Leisurely	....	....
Moderate	....	....
Strenuous	2/1	3

HILITES To call this trip a colorful one is an understatement. The peaks cupping the Franklin Lakes cirque are an artist's canvas of grays, shades of red, and various tones of green. Across Franklin Pass the fine fishing and beautifully intimate scenery of Rattlesnake Creek beckon to anglers and appreciative naturalists.

DESCRIPTION (Strenuous trip)

1st Hiking Day (**Mineral King** to **Upper Rattlesnake Creek,** 10½ miles): For this trip you may be able to park at the Sawtooth Pass/Timber Gap trailhead or you may have to park at the lot about halfway from the ranger station to that lot. You then walk up the road past the Mineral King Pack Station and go by a locked gate. A rough jeep road continues from this gate for about 1 mile, to an unimproved campground near the junction of Crystal Creek and the East Fork Kaweah River. Looking up-canyon from this point, one can readily make out Farewell Gap at the top of V-shaped upper Farewell Canyon. Just west of the trail the hurrying waters of the Kaweah River are hidden by a screen of willows, and the early-morning hiker is very apt to see a late garbage-can-breakfasting bear wandering a parallel course south through the sagebrush of the valley floor. Scattered clumps of juniper and red fir contrast with the ghostly white of aspen trunks just below the point where the trail fords Crystal Creek and, keeping left at a fork, begins a gentle-to-moderate ascent. Along the shaley trail the fetid smell of corn lily assails the nostrils, and between the snowbrush and manzanita of these lower slopes, spots of wildflower color provided by Indian paintbrush, fleabane, cow parsnip and blue gentian dot the way. The trail then fords Franklin Creek, and begins a steep ascent above a section of the Kaweah River that flows down a deep wash.

About ½ mile north of Farewell Gap our route doubles back north, passing a junction with a trail to Farewell Gap, and begins a stuttering, long traverse around the northwest side of Tulare Peak. This turn provides excellent views back down the Kaweah River watershed to Mineral King and beyond to Timber Gap. The long traverse enters a sparse forest cover of mature foxtail pine and crosses rocky stretches as it turns northeast into the Franklin Creek drainage. Descending briefly to ford Franklin Creek, the trail then rises steeply to the rock- and concrete-dammed outlet of lower Franklin Lake. The colors in this dramatically walled cirque basin are a bizarre conglomeration. To the northeast Rainbow Mountain is a study of gray-white marble whorls set in a sea of pink, red and black metamorphic rock. To the south the slate ridge joining Tulare Peak and Florence Peak is a hue of vermilion red that sends color photographers scrambling for viewpoints from which to foreground the contrasting blue of Franklin Lake against this colorful headwall. Anglers will find the fishing for brook (to 10″) good on the lower lake, and even better at the upper lake. There are a few poor, overused campsites along the northeast shore of lower Franklin Lake.

From this lake the trail rises steadily, and then steeply on switchbacks. Views of the Franklin Lakes cirque improve with altitude, and it isn't long before both the upper and lower lakes are in view. This ascent leaves the forest cover behind, as it crosses and recrosses a field of coarse granite granules. Despite the sievelike drainage of this slope, shooting star and wallflower are frequently seen—even at the pass. At windy Franklin Pass the views are panoramic. Landmarks to the northwest include Castle Rocks and Paradise Peak; to the north the jumbled crests of Rainbow and Needham mountains; to the east the immediate unglaciated plateau about the headwaters of Rattlesnake Creek, and Forester Lake (on the wooded bench just north of Rattlesnake Creek). East of the Kern trench and plateaus, one can make out Mt. Whitney on the Sierra crest.

The initial descent from the pass is over the ancient (pre-Pleistocene uplift) bench seen from the pass. Mostly covered with a layer of disintegrated quartz sand, it is oddly dotted with miniature granite domes. After crossing this bench, the trail drops steeply over rocky, rough switchbacks that twine back and forth over the headwaters runoff of Rattlesnake Creek. This steep descent levels out on the north side of the creek, and enters a friendly forest of young lodgepole pine broken by pleasant meadow patches. Several excellent campsites (10,300') line the creek here. Fishing for brook trout (to 8") is good to excellent, and the stream is ideal for fly fishermen. These streamside campsites are fine base camps for angling side trips to the several nearby lakes situated on the benches on either side of the Rattlesnake Creek drainage.

2nd Hiking Day: Retrace your steps, 10½ miles.

Mineral King Valley from the south   *Ron Felzer*

97 Mineral King to Little Claire Lake

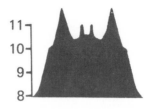

TRIP   From Mineral King to Little Claire Lake via Frank-
                  lin Pass, Rattlesnake Creek, Forester Lake (round
                  trip). Topo map *Mineral King*. Best mid-to-late sea-
                  son; 24 miles.

Grade	Trail/layover days	Total recom- mended days
Leisurely	....	....
Moderate	....	....
Strenuous	3/1	4

HILITES   For fine fishing, superlative scenery and a whole
                  range of side-trip possibilities, this trip is hard to
                  beat. As the opportunities for recreation are varied,
                  so are the watersheds that this trip visits. Crossing
                  into Sequoia National Park via Franklin Pass, this
                  route hooks around to visit the headwaters of two
                  alpine headwaters of tributaries of the Kern River.

DESCRIPTION (Strenuous trip)

1st Hiking Day (**Mineral King** to **Franklin Lakes,** 5½ miles): Follow
the 1st hiking day, trip 96, as far as Franklin Lakes.

2nd Hiking Day (**Franklin Lakes** to **Little Claire Lake,** 6½ miles):
Follow the 1st hiking day, trip 96, to the campsites on **Upper Rattlesnake Creek.** From the streamside campsites the trail descends
moderately through an increasingly dense forest cover of
lodgepole pine. At the first ford of Rattlesnake Creek, in the large
meadowed area where the Rattlesnake Creek Trail jogs south,
our route branches left (east) away from the creek. A short distance beyond the junction, the trail fords the outlet stream from
Forester Lake and ascends gently over a rocky slope. Then the
trail arrives at the charmingly meadowed west side of Forester
Lake, where fine campsites look across the azure blue waters to a
dense forest fringe, and an occasional dimpling on the surface
indicates the presence of brook trout. Turning northwestward,

the trail ascends stepladder fashion through a moderate forest cover and a meadowed bench, and then makes another ascent to the sandy crown of the ridge dividing the Rattlesnake and Soda Creek drainages. From this rounded summit the crests of Sawtooth Peak and Needham Mountain are easily visible to the north, and they continue to be seen as the trail descends moderately to the south end of Little Claire Lake. The effervescent, burbling call of the Brewer blackbird and the raucous call of the Clark nutcracker frequently are heard as the traveler circles the east side of Little Claire Lake (10,450') to the excellent campsites at the north end of the lake, around the outlet. Fishing for brook trout is excellent (to 11″). Views to the east from the outlet-situated campsites should be ample reason for planning a stay here. If the views do not provide sufficient incentive, this camp is a fine starting point for discovery and fishing trips to the nearby lakes at the headwaters of Soda Creek.

3rd Hiking Day: Retrace your steps, 12 miles.

Upper Gardiner Basin   *Thomas Winnett*

98 Mineral King to Big Five Lakes

TRIP
From Mineral King to Big Five Lakes via Franklin Pass, Rattlesnake Creek, Little Claire Lake, Soda Creek, Lost Canyon, return via Little Five Lakes, Black Rock Pass, Spring Lake, Glacier Pass (loop trip). Topo maps *Mineral King, Kern Peak*. Best mid or late season, 30½ miles.

Grade	Trail/layover days	Total recom- mended days
Leisurely	....	....
Moderate	....	....
Strenuous	5/2	7

HILITES
This is perhaps the best knapsacker's route for looping the fine fishing country east of Mineral King. Challenging cross-country routes and remote lakes are the attractions to the hiker. For the angler, the chance to wet a line in excellent golden-trout waters should be sufficient inducement. This trip is only for experienced cross-country hikers.

DESCRIPTION (Strenuous trip)

1st 2 Hiking Days: Follow trip 97 to **Little Claire Lake,** 12 miles.

3rd Hiking Day(**Little Claire Lake** to **Lower Big Five Lake,** 8 miles): The trail west of the outlet stream from Little Claire Lake is a steep, scrambling climb down a faint trail marked by ducks. At the foot of this precipitous duff-and-rock slope, the route fords Soda Creek and our route first descends gently over duff and sand through a moderate forest cover, then becomes steeper. Marmots on the rocky slopes south of the creek whistle excitedly as unexpected visitors to their domain pass by, but they do not usually stir from their watching posts unless the traveler shows more than passing interest.

As the trail follows the steadily descending stream bed, the creek's banks become willow-infested, and are separated from the trail by dells of cottonwood and quaking aspen. Among the evergreens one now finds an occasional silver pine, and then red fir appears. Clumps of sagebrush space the stands of timber, and nestled next to their aromatic branches are much Douglas phlox and Indian paintbrush. The steadily descending trail crosses two jump-across tributaries before encountering the first Jeffrey pine and juniper of the trip. The appearance of these trees heralds the junction where the trail down into Big Arroyo branches right and our route, after a steep, rocky, exposed ascent to the waterfalls marking the foot of Lost Canyon, doubles back to the northwest. Just above these falls, our route fords Lost Canyon Creek and begins a steady ascent on a duff-and-sand trail. About 1 mile after the ford, the trail passes a series of streamside campsites located in the wooded sections between tiny meadows.

At the second ford of Lost Canyon Creek, the obscurely marked trail to Big Five Lakes branches right (north), and, leaving Lost Canyon, climbs the steep north wall. This ascent, after its initial, faint, ducked beginnings, makes a clear series of short, steep switchbacks. These switchbacks afford fine views west to the barren headwaters of Lost Canyon Creek and the cirque holding Columbine Lake. Mostly lodgepole and foxtail pine, the timber cover thickens as the trail passes a tiny, unnamed lake (due east of the granite spur, in the *Kern Peak* topo map), and the hiker can enjoy the luxuriant growth of the wildflowers around its meadow fringes. Fields of shooting star, bunches of ground-hugging primrose, and a sprinkling of cheerful western mountain aster brighten the meadow and the adjoining trail. After circling the east side of this tiny lake, the trail fords the sometimes dry outlet stream, and then crosses a long, steady ridge that is heavily laid with fallen snags. The ground trail is sometimes faint, but it is well ducked. Above Big Five Lakes, the trail tops the ridge to fine views of Empire Mountain and Black Rock Pass to the west, and the lowest of the Big Five Lakes (9840′) immediately below to the west. The descent to the excellent campsites near the outlet and along the north side of this lake is a rocky, steep downgrade. Fishing for golden trout is excellent (to 14″).

4th Hiking Day (**Lower Big Five Lake** to **Spring Lake**, 5½ miles, part cross country): After passing west around the north side of the lake, the trail ascends along the north side of the lake's inlet through rank growths of ferns and moderate stands of foxtail. This moderately ascending trail fords the stream ¼ mile below the outlet of the largest lake in the Big Five chain, and climbs over glacially smoothed granite to the lake's east shore. Our route fords the outlet and passes a packer campsite and several primitive campsites before crossing the swampy area around the north inlet of the lake. Just west of this inlet, the trail passes the Little Five Lakes Trail branching right (north), and continues west up the Big Five Lakes basin. Fishermen will find the angling for golden trout good to excellent in all the lakes of the upper basin except the highest.

The ascent to the third lake we pass is gentle over grass and swampy areas, and, near the outlet of this lake, the trail passes two primitive, exposed campsites. The grassy trail continues around the lake, but our cross-country route turns right (northwest) and ascends the steep granite ridge separating the Big Five Lakes and Little Five Lakes drainages. This ascent climbs by grass-topped ledges to the cairned saddle just south of the uppermost lake of the Little Five Lakes chain.

From this ridge one can see across Big Arroyo to the Kaweah Peaks and Red Spur. To the west, aptly named Black Rock Pass stands out in startling relief from the surrounding white granite. The steep, difficult, rocky descent on the north side of the ridge is clearly ducked, but some scrambling is required to bring one to the edge of the uppermost lake. (Fishing for golden in the two lower lakes of this chain is good.) Crossing the outlet stream from this lake, our ducked route meets and turns left onto the Black Rock Pass Trail. First ascending across alpine meadows, the trail veers north and then climbs a steep, very rocky series of switchbacks to the summit of Black Rock Pass (11,630'). This pass provides one of the finer viewpoints on this trip. Looking east one can see the Kaweah Peaks Ridge, the wooded flats of Chagoopa Plateau, a considerable length of Big Arroyo, and both the Little and the Big Five Lakes basins. On the south side of the pass, there are heart-stopping panoramas of the deep Cliff Creek drainage and towering Empire Mountain, seeming to be almost at fingertip distance.

Descending on the west side of the pass, the rocky trail makes one long traverse and then drops by steady and steep zigzags to the grass-bottomed basin just north of Spring Lake. Here our route leaves the Black Rock Pass Trail and contours around the head of this basin. After fording the tributary stream northeast of Spring Lake, our route ascends the waterfall outlet of Spring Lake itself, and arrives at the good campsites (somewhat exposed) on the east side of the outlet and in the sparse timber cover of the northwest shore (10,050'). Views from these campsites of the massive cirque headwall and the ribboned waterfall inlets are satisfying, and fishing for brook trout (to 8″) is good. (Less experienced backpackers should not go via Spring Lake but should stay on the trail from Black Rock Pass down Cliff Creek to the Timber Gap Trail and return via it; 1st hiking day, trip 90.)

5th Hiking Day (**Spring Lake** to **Mineral King,** 5 miles, part cross country): Reverse the 1st hiking day, trip 94. Note that Glacier Pass is the third saddle to the right of Empire Mountain.

Mineral King to Big Five Lakes   **99**

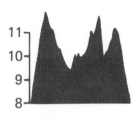

TRIP From Mineral King to Big Five Lakes via Sawtooth Pass, Columbine Lake, Lost Canyon, return via Little Five Lakes, Black Rock Pass, Spring Lake, Glacier Pass (semiloop trip). Topo maps *Mineral King, Kern Peak*. Best mid or late season, 21½ miles.

Grade	Trail/layover days	Total recommended days
Leisurely	....	....
Moderate	....	....
Strenuous	4/2	6

HILITES This fine, short, looping trip is an angler's delight. In this route's short mileage 5 creeks and 15 lakes are touched, providing a variety of fishing water—and trout—that the fisherman will certainly want to try.

DESCRIPTION (Strenuous trip)

1st Hiking Day: Follow trip 95 to **Upper Lost Canyon,** 6½ miles.

2nd Hiking Day (**Upper Lost Canyon** to **Lower Big Five Lake,** 4½ miles): From the alpine-meadowed bench below Columbine Lake, the trail enters forest cover (sparse lodgepole and foxtail), and then drops steeply over broken granite and meadowy sections. This stepladdering descent keeps to the north side of Lost Canyon Creek for about 1 mile, and then fords the creek twice in the space of the next mile. The second ford returns to the north side of the creek, where our route branches north, away from Lost Canyon, on the poorly signed Big Five Lakes Trail. From this junction, proceed as described in the second half of the 3rd hiking day, trip 98.

3rd and 4th Hiking Days: Follow 4th and 5th hiking days, trip 98, to **Mineral King,** 10½ miles.

00   Mineral King to Crescent Meadow

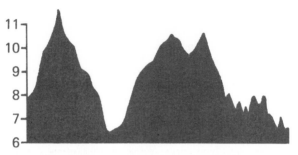

TRIP   From Mineral King to Crescent Meadow via Frank-
lin Pass, Rattlesnake Creek, Kern River, Hamilton
Lakes (shuttle trip). Topo maps *Mineral King, Kern
Peak, Mt. Whitney, Triple Divide Peak, Giant Forest.*
Best mid or late season; 56 miles.

Grade	Trail/layover days	Total recom- mended days
Leisurely	....	....
Moderate	8/2	10
Strenuous	7/1	8

HILITES   This loop trip is one that should be taken by all who
would say, "I know the Great Western Divide coun-
try," or "I know the Kern trench and its wooded
plateaus." This route surveys a 5000-foot range of
Sierran biota, and the scope of the glaciated terrain
one travels over reads like the synopsis of a geology
textbook.

DESCRIPTION (Strenuous trip)

1st Hiking Day: Follow trip 96 to the campsites on **Upper Rattlesnake Creek,** 10½ miles.

2nd Hiking Day (**Upper Rattlesnake Creek** to **Rattlesnake Creek/Kern
River,** 8 miles): Traveling down through the upper reaches of Rattlesnake Creek is a delightful study in intimate meadows, dense
stands of lodgepole pine and a classic, murmuring mountain
creek. Within a mile from the timberline campsites, our trail passes the signed turnoff to Forester and Little Claire lakes, and
then jogs across the winding meadow stream, only to return to
the north side a few hundred yards downstream. Below this ford
the creek picks up speed as its meandering course is constricted

by narrowing canyon walls, and the trail climbs briefly on the north wall. In the narrow canyon the trail stays high above the swiftly tumbling creek waters as it descends on a long, steady, rocky traverse of the canyon wall. Rounding the fractured granite nose of a ridge, the trail descends steeply to ford an unnamed tributary cascading down from the north wall, and then rejoins Rattlesnake Creek in the level stretches at Cow Camp Meadows.

This green grassland, once a way-camp for stockmen, is now given over to the many mule deer in the vicinity and an occasional bear. Reflecting the lower altitude, the meadow's fringes show a forest cover of lodgepole, fir and some juniper, and as the trail continues to descend steadily, Jeffrey pine, aspen and birch begin to make their predictable appearance.

Just above the final steep descent into the Kern trench, our trail passes a trail to the Big Arroyo, branching north, and then switchbacks down abruptly to the good packer campsites just south of the junction with the Kern River Trail. (Those wishing to take in the geologically instructive views from Rattlesnake Point should follow the fire trail leaving the Rattlesnake Creek Trail at the Big Arroyo Trail junction. From this point, one has unobstructed views of the canyon's distinctive, glacially formed U shape, and the wooded plateaus that were part of a pre-uplift valley floor.) Fishing for rainbow in the Kern is excellent (to 20″).

3rd Hiking Day (**Rattlesnake Creek/Kern River** to **Moraine Lake,** 7½ miles): Reverse the steps of the last part of the 4th hiking day, trip 70 to the junction of Kern River Trail and High Sierra Trail. Then proceed west on High Sierra Trail, reversing the steps of the first part of the 5th hiking day, trip 81.

4th, 5th, 6th and 7th Hiking Days: Reverse the first 4 hiking days, trip 81, 30 miles.

Trip Cross-reference Table

Trip No.	No. Hiking Days	Season			Pace			Trip Type			
		Early	Mid	Late	Leis.	Mod.	Stren.	Round	Shuttle	Loop	Semiloop
1	2	X		X	X			X			
2	4		X	X	X			X			
3	3	X		X		X			X		
4	6		X	X	X			X			
5	7		X	X	X						X
6	4		X	X		X		X			
7	6		X	X		X					X
8	4		X	X		X			X		
9	7		X	X		X					X
10	7			X		X					X
11	6		X	X	X			X			
12	2		X		X			X			
13	4		X		X			X			
14	5		X	X	X				X		
15	7		X	X		X				X	
16	2		X	X	X			X			
17	3		X	X		X		X			
18	4		X	X	X				X		
19	2		X	X	X			X			
20	2		X	X	X			X			
21	2	X	X		X			X			
22	2	X	X		X				X		
23	2	X	X		X			X			
24	4	X	X		X			X			
25	4		X	X	X			X			
26	6		X	X	X						X
27	6		X	X	X			X			
28	7		X	X	X						X
29	6		X	X	X			X			
30	5		X	X		X			X		
31	6		X	X			X		X		
32	4	X	X		X			X			

Trip No.	No. Hiking Days	Season			Pace			Trip Type			
		Early	Mid	Late	Leis.	Mod.	Stren.	Round	Shuttle	Loop	Semiloop
33	6		x		x			x			
34	4	x	x		x						x
35	8		x	x	x			x			
36	10		x	x	x			x			
37	9		x	x		x			x		
38	2		x	x	x			x			
39	2		x	x	x						x
40	2		x	x		x		x			
41	4		x	x		x			x		
42	2		x		x			x			
43	3		x	x	x						x
44	6		x	x		x					x
45	9		x	x		x			x		
46	10		x	x		x			x		
47	4		x	x			x	x			
48	6		x	x			x	x			
49	2	x					x	x			
50	4		x	x			x	x			
51	4		x				x		x		
52	4		x	x			x	x			
53	4		x	x			x		x		
54	2	x		x			x	x			
55	4	x		x			x	x			
56	6		x	x			x		x		
57	3	x	x			x		x			
58	5		x	x	x			x			
59	7		x	x	x			x			
60	5			x		x		x			
61	6			x		x				x	
62	5			x		x			x		
63	4		x	x		x		x			
64	6			x			x				x
65	9		x	x		x					x
66	2	x	x		x			x			

Trip No.	No. Hiking Days	Season			Pace			Trip Type			
		Early	Mid	Late	Leis.	Mod.	Stren.	Round	Shuttle	Loop	Semiloop
67	6		x	x	x				x		
68	3		x	x			x	x			
69	4		x	x			x	x			
70	6		x	x			x		x		
71	8		x	x			x		x		
72	2		x	x	x			x			
73	4		x	x			x	x			
74	6			x			x	x			
75	8		x	x			x				x
76	8		x	x			x	x			
77	5		x	x			x		x		
78	2		x	x		x		x			
79	6		x	x	x			x			
80	6			x		x			x		
81	9		x	x		x			x		
82	16		x	x		x					x
83	2		x	x	x					x	
84	4		x	x	x			x			
85	4		x	x	x				x		
86	7		x	x		x			x		
87	4		x	x		x		x			
88	6		x	x	x				x		
89	5		x	x		x			x		
90	2		x			x		x			
91	4		x	x		x		x			
92	6		x	x		x		x			
93	7		x	x		x					x
94	2		x				x	x			
95	2		x				x	x			
96	2		x	x			x	x			
97	3		x	x			x	x			
98	5		x	x			x			x	
99	4		x	x			x				x
100	7		x	x			x		x		

Index